PSYCHOANALYTIC AESTHETICS

PSYCHOANALYTIC AESTHETICS

An Introduction to the British School

Nicky Glover

Published for the
Harris Meltzer Trust
by

KARNAC

Published in 2009 by
Karnac Books Ltd
118 Finchley Road, London NW3 5HT

Copyright © 2009 Nicky Glover
Copyright © 2009 Neil Maizels for the Preface

The right of Nicky Glover to be identified as the author of this work has been asserted with §§77 and 78 of the Copyright Design and Patents Act 1988.

All rights reserved. No part of this publication may be reproduced, stored in a retrieval system, or transmitted, in any form or by any means, electronic, mechanical, photocopying, recording, or otherwise, without the prior written permission of the publisher.

British Library Cataloguing in Publication Data

A C.I.P. for this book is available from the British Library

ISBN 978 1 85575 686 1

Edited, designed, and produced by The Studio Publishing Services Ltd
www.publishingservicesuk.co.uk
e-mail: studio@publishingservicesuk.co.uk

www.karnacbooks.com
www.harris-meltzer-trust.org.uk

CONTENTS

ABOUT THE AUTHOR	vii
FOREWORD by Neil Maizels	ix
INTRODUCTION	xiii
PART I: THE LEGACY OF FREUD	1
CHAPTER ONE Freud's theory of art and creativity	3
PART II: KLEIN'S CONTRIBUTION TO THE AESTHETICS OF THE BRITISH SCHOOL	27
CHAPTER TWO Essentials of Kleinian theory	29
CHAPTER THREE The development of Kleinian aesthetics	65
PART III: DEVELOPMENTS IN THE BRITISH SCHOOL	101

CHAPTER FOUR
The legacy of Wilfred Bion   103

CHAPTER FIVE
Ehrenzweig and the hidden order of art   137

CHAPTER SIX
Art, creativity, and the potential space   159

CHAPTER SEVEN
Painting as the body: the aesthetics of Fuller   187
and Wollheim

CONCLUSION   219

REFERENCES   233

INDEX   247

ABOUT THE AUTHOR

Nicola Glover has a long-standing interest in psychoanalysis, culture, and social issues. She took her MPhil in Psychoanalysis and Art History at the University of Kent, and gained her MSc in Social Work from Southampton University. Nicola emigrated to Australia in 1999 and currently works as a psychotherapist in private practice in Adelaide, South Australia.

FOREWORD

Neil Maizels

In many ways, this book does not need any welcoming soul at the doorway to outline what lies within. The book itself is introductory—and each of its chapters are welcoming enough to give the reader a good signpost as to what lies within. So, the deftest introduction to the book, as a whole, would be to stand back from the rich detail of the canvas, in order to note a few striking features of the tone of Nicky Glover's stance, which lies subtly embedded within the dense constellation of content.

Although the author's own theoretical favourites can be inferred, like a fair-minded mother she gives each a considered, clear, but unsimplified platform for the reader to consider both the charms and limitations of each particular slant on the aesthetic sensibility of the growing child-mind. Throughout this book, each planet of thinking, with its particular spin, gravity, and atmospheric conditions, is not just gazed at from a distant, high-powered telescope; Glover actually takes us down on to the planet's ground, and then offers a perspective of the other planets, from that place. Thereby, each view presented in the book can itself be a "filter" through which to look at the other views. It is this issue of *perspective* that shines through the whole book, chapter by chapter.

The theories become diaphanous through Glover's knack for finding the crucial elements, and then illuminating their fine filaments to produce the perfect "mood lighting" for rich, but relaxed, fireside contemplation.

The quiet, meditative tone of the book invokes far more than the intellectual sum of its theoretical parts. Even in these "postmodern" days, the "territorial imperative" almost totally precludes the possibility of any adherent to a Kleinian, Winnicottian, Bionic, or Freudian "creed" ever writing such a book. And if they could, it is unlikely that they could include an Ehrenzweig, a Stokes, or a Wollheim to weigh in on equal terms with the usual stalwarts (Freud, Klein, Segal, Meltzer, Winnicott, and Bion) of the psychoanalytic bibliographies. Glover deftly finds the words for more than just a compare-and-contrast schoolroom fly-by of the views of each of the theorists presented. Through simplicity, and with a poetic method of economy and distillation, she enables the reader to hold similar-but-different perspectives at once. So, rather than championing any one writer–theorist, she sets out to cast more light on the phenomenon itself—of creativity, and therefore the life of the mind.

In doing so, Glover builds a new scaffolding, to reveal enormous complexity, cross-angulation and cross-fertilization among British theory-building about how the mind builds upon itself.

This theory-building is always—must be—a shared human enterprise, in order to grasp and understand our own condition. Yet, there are beacons, shiny stars from the sceptred isle, that sparkle and grab at Glover's receptive imagination. Here, for example, on Milner, Glover writes:

> This heightened awareness could be reached only through an "inner gesture" of letting go of the "narrow" focus (that is, everyday discursive thinking) and a deeper order would be revealed to her that sometimes had a very frightening quality, almost like a death itself, but when she submitted herself to it, it felt more like a liberation. This "deeper order" (cf. Ehrenzweig's "hidden order") was characterized by a sense of more fluid boundaries between self and the world—even to the point of subject–object union. This is a theme that was to play an important part in her writings, as in Winnicott's thinking, especially with regard to understanding

aesthetic experience and the way in which creative perception is fostered by a negotiation of the "gap" between self and other, involving the active surrendering of conscious ego control.

Later, spurred by the freedom enlarged by Glover, by the aforementioned fireside, the reader might ponder a co-mingling of Milner's "inner gesture" with Bion's "catastrophic change" in relation to "O".

Just as Freud shocked the establishment with news of unconscious infantile sexuality, and Klein shocked the Freudians with news of infantile unconscious sadism, depression, and reparation, Meltzer and Harris Williams shocked the Kleinians—even the Bionians—with news of a crucial aesthetic sensibility and conflict in the mental life of the infant, arching back into pre-natal curiosity, and ready to bolt out of the gate at the caesura of birth. Glover pans back from this chain of psychoanalytic development to give it a much wider context and history, sometimes within the realms of aesthetic theory, sometimes through art criticism, and sometimes back through the work of some lesser-known psychoanalytic contributors, such as Rank. Although much is underpinned by Klein's astonishing and brave conception of the depressive position, Glover does not see Klein as having the first or the final word. Rather, Klein's momentous work is yet another—albeit major—twist in the kaleidoscope.

Glover's comprehensive perspective modulates these twists for the reader, chapter by chapter, so that by the conclusion, we do not just have an erudite, well-written, for-the-record textbook, with an assemblage of prominent British aesthetic theories. We have, as well, a new aesthetic object in its own write (to slightly misquote John Lennon) capable of continuing its thought-provoking re-combinations long after it finds its home on the bookshelves at the junction of psychoanalysis and aesthetics—with their combined mutual preoccupation with the child and its vision of Beauty in the inner and outer worlds. For it is this unique emphasis on the aesthetic struggle within the *infant* mind that places these British psychoanalytic thinkers in a class of their own, where the theoretical cannot develop meaningfully unless it is anchored in the "sagacity of the body"—the partnership of body and mind, when "the head and the heart are working together"--whose crucible is the new mother, with her new child, developing and being developed by each other through interplay.

It may be that Glover, originally from the UK and now living in Australia, with one cultural foot outside of the British tradition, may be well placed to observe and muse about this quietly-tilled, but growing field.

Introduction

Although it will be argued that the theoreticians examined in this study are united by a number of important and fundamental assumptions and values (ostensibly those of the "British School" of psychoanalysis), their approach to art is by no means homogenous. For, as we shall see, each theorist construes the nature of, and the relationship between, aesthetic value, aesthetic experience, and creativity somewhat differently. Thus, although this study is concerned with identifying a specifically "British School" aesthetic, it should be remembered that the theorists discussed here are, first and foremost, *individuals*. Each of the protagonists examined here approaches art from the perspective of his or her own clinical and theoretical background, together with their own particular projects, preoccupations, and life experiences, and I shall endeavour to give due acknowledgement to these in this study. (For my understanding of the historical and theoretical context of the "British School" of Psychoanalysis, I have been influenced by the work of Rayner [1990], Kohon [1986], and Hughes [1990].)

However, before we examine the respective approaches of these thinkers, it would be helpful to consider how to define the "terms of the dialogue" between aesthetics and psychoanalysis, and to demarcate what are the main areas of concern to the aesthetician and the analyst looking at the visual arts .We should ask what kind of dialogue is possible, and how does psychoanalysis add value to this dialogue? (I am indebted to E. H. Spitz for her insightful mapping of the "terms of the dialogue" [1985, pp. 1–24] between psychoanalysis and aesthetics.)

Broadly speaking, the discipline of aesthetics is concerned with exploring three overlapping aspects: the nature of the creative process and the experience of the artist; the *interpretation* of art; and also the nature of the aesthetic encounter. The theorists considered here approach these three areas in interestingly different ways, in terms of how they construe the links between them, or in perhaps emphasizing one of the aspects over another. But what they all clearly demonstrate is that these areas are not entirely separate, but are mutually interdependent modes. For instance, we can appreciate that the artist is both the creator and also the spectator of his own work—a point that is central to Wollheim's account of art (1987). In this role he must therefore continually step back to assess it critically: he engages in a dialogue with the medium, so to speak. Regarding the role of the critic, not only does he draw upon his general knowledge and experience, but also upon the rich reservoir of his own unconscious phantasy life (Klein). The sensitive critic and the audience enter into the "potential space" between the art object and the private world of fantasy (Winnicott) and engage in aesthetic reciprocity with the object—thinking "with" the object rather than merely "about" it (Meltzer & Williams, 1988). And, as far as the audience is concerned, they, in turn, imaginatively re-create aspects of the work encountered; they employ the same kind of creative perception as that which produced the work (Ehrenzweig, 1967).

Before examining the general scope of the British Psychoanalytic contribution, let us briefly explore some of the ways in which this dialogue between art and psychoanalysis has evolved: how psychoanalytic ideas have been taken up by a number of eminent theorists, such as Gombrich, Kris, Ehrenzweig, and Wollheim. Their contributions are an index of some of the issues and challenges arising from the interchange between art and psychoanalysis.

Ever since Freud gave an account of the dynamic unconscious and the psychic mechanisms which ground mental life (1900a), the study of art and the nature of creativity has been of great interest to psychoanalysts. The practice of dream interpretation was regarded as a potentially rich source of understanding when applied to the domain of art. The early attempts at psychoanalytic criticism meant that the artwork was subjected to a piecemeal analysis of individual symbols, involving the accumulation of a considerable amount of biographical material and analysis along the lines of detective work on the part of the interpreter. Indeed, Freud made significant attempts at this method of artistic interpretation (1907a, 1910c , 1914b). Yet, as Freud himself recognized, this kind of "pathographic" approach was ill-equipped to analyse the formal qualities of the art object and the nature of aesthetic value, and this limitation was recognized by thinkers in both fields. Thus, the art historian Herbert Read (1951) was highly sceptical of the capacity of psychoanalysis to address the questions of aesthetic value and the formal nature of the artwork. He argued that the aesthetician's concern is essentially with *products*, and the psychologist's with the *processes* of mental activity, of which art is seen as perhaps "merely" one expression. Read claimed that the psychologist "analyses the product only to arrive at the process" and is generally "indifferent to literary values" (*ibid.*, p. 73). This is view was echoed by others, such as the American psychoanalyst Lawrence Friedman (1958), who also distinguished sharply between the concerns of the philosopher–aesthetician and the psychologist–psychoanalyst. In his view, the former is concerned with structure, while the latter is concerned with the origins of aesthetic response. And, despite significant developments in psychoanalytic theory, this scepticism regarding the fitness of psychoanalysis to address the formal aspects of art and the nature of aesthetic value has continued. (For further reading on the background to Freud's aesthetics, see Spector [1972], Kofman [1988], Adams [1994], Sayers [2007].) For example, in her survey of psychoanalytic approaches to critical theory and practice, Elizabeth Wright, in her post-structuralist critique, maintains that although psychoanalysis "contributes to an understanding of the creative process", like most other approaches "it has not been able to provide a satisfactory account of aesthetic value" (1984, p. 5). Even though Wright devotes a section to "Object relations" aesthetics, it would seem that she has perhaps not engaged fully with the rich possibilities of British School thinking regarding the arts. As we shall see in Chapter Two, the Kleinian approach to art is very much concerned with the formal, aesthetic qualities of the artwork, and there have also been aestheticians very interested in analysing the phenomenology of the processes in art and the origins of aesthetic feeling: for example, Langer (1953) and Dewey (1934).

First, however, there are certain aspects of Freudian theory that, according to the art historian Ernst Gombrich, may be considered highly illuminating for the study of art. One of the ways he develops the dialogue between art theory and psychoanalysis is to give a psychoanalytic perspective on connoisseurship in the visual arts. In "Psychoanalysis and the history of art" (1954), he examines the stages of psychosexual development formulated by Freud (1905d) and Karl Abraham (1927), arguing that oral gratification can be viewed as a genetic model for aesthetic pleasure. For instance, he draws an analogy between our response to easily readable, too immediately obvious or gratifying art, and the stage of passive, oral instinctual development. He speculates that a repugnance to such art may serve as a defence against its regressive pull. By linking the "idea of the soft and yielding with passivity, of the hard and crunchy with activity" (1954, p. 196), Gombrich accounts for the preference of sophisticated critics for art that is "difficult", that demands action on their part, that offers an opportunity to act on what is presented, to experience a challenge in the process of re-creation. Thus, the critic's preference for demanding art may correspond to the second, aggressive, stage of oral development. However, Gombrich warns us about the dangers of pursuing this analogy too far. Although he has ingeniously applied an aspect of psychoanalytic theory of erotogenic zones to aesthetic enjoyment and preference, he counters this by saying that there are many ways of appreciating the "soft" and the "crunchy" aspects of aesthetic experience. These differing responses, he argues, are dependent on "the social context of the aesthetic attitude". For example, he argues that after Impressionism, literary allusions no longer constituted a "crunchy" challenge for the critic (*ibid.*, p. 198). Gombrich thus wisely cautions the psychoanalytic critic that, at least as far as the visual arts are concerned, tradition and convention far outweigh personal elements. Even if we could disclose the unconscious meanings of an artwork, this would not be relevant unless the most important aspect of a work of art were, in fact, its quality of being a "shared dream"—an idea that he doubts. Further, he shows that if we take seriously the fact that art has a history (unlike perceptions and dreams), and recognize that this history is built through a "constant extension and modification of symbols" (*ibid.*, p. 187), we must acknowledge that all art is derivative, and that without recourse to the development of style, modes of representation, and so forth, we cannot play Pygmalion to any Galatea. Without a thorough knowledge of the history of art, we are unable to re-create any work of art in terms of its personal meaning. Without the social factors (the attitudes of the audience, the style, or the trend), the private needs could not be transmuted into art. In this transmutation "the private meaning is all but swallowed up" (*ibid.*, p. 200).

One of the most comprehensive statements of the potentialities inherent in the dialogue between psychoanalysis and aesthetics has been offered by Ernst Kris (1952). He argued that most attempts to apply psychoanalytic theory to aesthetics suffered from a tendency to equate psychoanalysis with one or two isolated remarks from Freud's early work, that is, to equate art with neurosis. Kris believes that it is Freud's structural account of the joke which has the most scope for understanding the relationship between psychic mechanisms, economy of mental energy, and the formal, aesthetic qualities of art. The art teacher and theorist Anton Ehrenzweig agreed with Kris that Freud's account of art had much to offer the analysis of artistic structure and aesthetic experience (Ehrenzweig, 1962, 1967). However, as we shall see in Chapter One, the trajectory of their respective views differs in some important respects. Where Kris drove a wedge between "higher" and "lower" levels of the mind (between primary and secondary process functioning) and took artistic activity to be an *adaptive* function of the ego, autonomous from instinctual conflict, Ehrenzweig stressed that the id (primary process) was only "chaotic" and "primitive" from the perspective of the conscious, rational mind. As we shall explore in Chapter Five, Ehrenzweig's theory of "undifferentiated imagemaking" stresses the vital, constructive role played by the primary processes in art, and their partnership with the secondary processes.

It is important to note that Ehrenzweig's aesthetic theory was partly developed from a critique of Gestalt psychology. This branch of psychology was pioneered in the 1920s by Michael Wertheimer, Wolfgang Köhler, & Kurt Koffka out of a dissatisfaction with atomistic explanations in science, social science, and art. As a theory of perception, it seeks to investigate the principles that govern the selection and formation of one particular figure in preference to others. From a number of possible constellations into which the visual stimuli can be grouped, Gestalt psychologists suggest that we will tend to select the most compact, simple and coherent pattern which is said to have the characteristics of a 'good' gestalt. The Gestalt principle not only governs that selection of the best pattern from within the visual field, it will also improve on it by smoothing away little gaps and imperfections. These insights were applied particularly rigorously by the psychologist Rudolph Arnheim in his studies of artistic expression and style in the visual arts (1943, 1949, 1954). Generally speaking however, this Gestalt approach to art has perhaps not been as productive as was hoped. For example, although Gombrich found Arnheim's (1954) account of child art and perceptual development very "instructive", he felt that "for the historian and his problems of style ... the book yields less" (Gombrich, 1960, p. 22). Kris also was sceptical of attempts to use Gestalt psychology to explain problems in aesthetics, arguing that the search (by those such as Arnheim) for a "good" Gestalt that was valid under all historical circumstances has not been successful. Nor has it led to new insight into the psychology of style or expression (Kris, 1952, pp. 21–22).

A thorough critique of the Gestalt view was delivered by Ehrenzweig (1953, 1967). He was specifically concerned with elucidating the nature of perception, and a major aspect of his work concerns the issue of how objects come to be selected for perception in the first place. He argued that this account of perception does not do justice to the facts of art and actual artistic practice. He regards it as crucial for the artist, and for the creative individual in general, to be able to return to a state of child-like "syncretistic" vision or "undifferentiated" perception. The Gestalt account is criticized for its postulation of a firm and stable structure in perception—such a structure has to be learnt first, says Ehrenzweig, for, at the start of life, perception is uncertain in its ranging over a wide field of view. However reliable our mature perception might be, early sensing is fluid and unstable: vestiges of it are accessible in dreams, mental imagery, and in the hypnagogic visions that occur between sleep and waking (1971 (1967], p. 87). He maintains that Gestalt psychology makes too ready an assumption that simple organization, the so-called "good gestalts", are inevitably selected from the beginning, and, by a fortunate coincidence, just happen to correspond to the external objects of perception. Moreover, the so-called "goodness" of a gestalt depends upon the aesthetic preferences at a particular historical moment, which implies that the Gestalt approach itself depends upon an implicit aesthetic view, and this is surely not a very firm ground for any theory seeking to address the nature of art. Ehrenzweig's main point is that the objects selected by perception are by no means immune from libidinal interest (*ibid.*, p. 18). To substantiate his view, he deploys both by Freud's theories of libidinal development and the Kleinian account of unconscious phantasy. His theory of "undifferentiated image-making", emphasizes that what is selected for perception is closely geared to the needs of the developing id; as these become more precisely aimed, so do those of the ego. As he argues, the "ego's perception is at the disposal of unconscious symbolic needs" and "unconscious phantasy life during our whole lifetime is supplied with new imagery which feeds into the matrix of image-making" (*ibid.*, p. 263). Ehrenzweig's account of artistic form and creative perception is discussed more fully in Chapter Five.

Major contributions to the interdisciplinary study of psychoanalysis and art have also been made by the philosopher and aesthetician Richard Wollheim. Like Kris, he too laments the tendency to reduce the significance of Freud's contribution to aesthetics. Wollheim argues that, contrary to the general view, Freud's account of the artwork is by no means a simple equation with joke, dream, or neurotic symptom, with a "sudden vehicle of buried desires" that requires a lapse of consciousness and attention (1987, p. 218). He sees Freud as recognizing the work of art as being "a piece of *work*"—that is, essentially "constructive" rather than purely expressive. According to Wollehim, Freud believed that a work of art affects us through a sense of confusion or ambiguity (*ibid.*, p. 217). Freud shows us that an engaging work of art necessarily involves us in complex mental activities, which include sophisticated as well as regressive aspects. Wollheim credits Freud's aesthetics with an awareness of mental functions that have subsequently been identified as synthetic, integrative, and adaptive. Wollheim thinks it is unfortunate that Freud never developed this "constructive" side of his aesthetic in theoretical terms, a side that Wollheim believes is shown as early as Freud's *Moses* study (1914b). Wollehim suggests that this omission can be explained by observing that during the early years, when the first studies on art were being written, Freud had sufficient leisure to pursue non-clinical interests. By the time he had become interested in ego-functioning, he was no longer free to pursue his enquiries into the aesthetic and develop them in accordance with his later theory (*ibid.*, p. 219).

It would seem that both Kris and Wollheim are on the right track in their emphasis that Freud's aesthetic gains considerable enrichment by developing the implications of his account of the joke-mechanism (a theme explored further in Chapter One). But Wollheim's remark about Freud's "lack of time" to pursue art surely needs qualification. It must be acknowledged that, after his structural revisions of 1923, Freud *did* go on to write such non-clinical works as *The Future of An Illusion* (1927c), "Dostoevsky and parricide" (1928b), and *Civilization and its Discontents* (1930a). It would seem reasonable to assume (as Wollheim does) that if Freud had had any desire to review his previous, pathographical account of art to bring it more into line with his later, structural theory of the joke and with developments in ego psychology, he would have done so. Perhaps it would be better to gain a clearer understanding of what he *did* say (as Kris and Ehrenzweig have attempted to) rather than apologize for what he did *not* say. However, as we shall see in Chapter Seven, Wollheim did not only elucidate the aesthetic theory implicit in Freudian thinking, but was also very much influenced by Kleinian theory, particularly through the writings of the art historian, poet, painter, and critic, Adrian Stokes.

Taking the above pathways into account, it becomes clear that a number of general issues arise concerning the applicability of psychoanalysis to the arts. First, as Gombrich makes clear, precisely how psychoanalysis (or indeed any psychological approach) tackles the problem of "art history" needs exploration. In other words, how far can *intra*psychic experience provide a model for what is essentially *inter*subjective and public? The art historian is no doubt right to emphasize that psychoanalytic approaches to art tend to ignore the fact that art is not like a "shared dream" but has its own unique tradition and public frame of reference: it has a history and a social context. On this subject Kris writes:

> Historical and social forces . . . shape the function of art in general and more specifically that of any given medium in any given historical setting, determining the frame of reference in which creation is enacted. We have long come to realize that art is not produced in an empty space, that no artist is independent of predecessors and models, that he no less than the scientist and the philosopher is part of a specific tradition and works in a structured area of problems. [1952, p. 21]

It is somewhat of a problem that classical criticism focused on the artwork as a "carrier" for buried desires, conflicts, and anxieties; that it concentrated on specific symbols and imagery and ignored the far more interesting and important question of *why a painting itself is precious to us*. For, as art historian Michael Podro suggests, "the skills and traditions of painting must have been acquired. And not only acquired but acquired in such a way that enables us to make them into an *art*" (1990, p. 401, my italics).

However, particularly with the developments in the British School pioneered by clinicians such as Klein, Winnicott, Bion, Milner, and Meltzer on the one hand, and writers on art such as Wollheim, Peter Fuller, Meg Harris Williams, and Margot Waddell on the other, psychoanalysis has evolved a set of conceptual tools which *can* look beyond the pattern of the art symbol and to analyse (as it were) the very fabric upon which it is printed, and, most significantly, using these tools they can explore what the meaning of creating that fabric itself means both to the artist and engaged viewer: the symbolic importance of the actual physical encounter with the medium and our corporeal response to the art work (a theme explored in Chapter Seven). Podro emphasizes that it was the work of those in the British School such as Marion Milner who

> questioned within the language of psychoanalysis the relation between representing the perceived world and the feeling with which painting could be imbued and with which it must be imbued in order to be an art at all. [Podro, 1990, p. 401]

As we shall see in Chapter Six, Milner is one of the first analysts to raise this question of what it is that gives painting its vitality—what distinguishes it from being just the deployment of mechanical skills, or merely the rendering of a mundane copy of the world. In the non-clinical domain, Wollheim (1987) also explores under what conditions painting becomes an "art", and he draws heavily on Kleinian theory to do so.

What I hope will become increasingly apparent here is the extent to which a British School aesthetic is grounded in a corporeal account of art and aesthetic experience; that it offers a corporeal theory of meaning. This point about "meaning" may be clarified further by the British psychoanalyst, Charles Rycroft:

> The statement that psychoanalysis is a theory of meaning is incomplete and misleading unless one qualifies it by saying that it is a *biological* theory of meaning. By this I mean that psychoanalysis interprets human behaviour in terms of the self that experiences it and not in terms of entities external to it, such as other-worldly deities or political parties and leaders, and that it regards the self as a psychobiological entity which is always striving for *self-realization and self-fulfilment*. [1966 p. 20]

Indeed, I shall argue that it is this broadly humanistic view that is one of the distinguishing hallmarks of the British School approach to both human behaviour and artistic activity. What Rycroft is saying is that psychoanalysis is not merely interested in physical causes but, more importantly, the *meaning* of those causes to individuals who have their own projects and desires, their own psychohistory. Rycroft's qualification is thus of great significance, for it indicates how far removed such an approach is from the linguistically orientated model of European post-structuralist thinking championed by Althusser, Derrida, and Lacan. Their account is radically sceptical of humanism, and questions the very concept of a unified self as a locus of "meaning" and "value" (see Sarup [1988] for an expansion on this theme.)

In the light of the above, we may ask what psychoanalysis can offer the study of aesthetics. To respond, we can say that, broadly speaking, psychoanalysis offers both a highly refined map of the mind and a method for investigating its functioning—thus, it offers both a metapsychological as well as a clinical theory. The model it provides has a number of aspects: dynamic, economic, structural, adaptive, and developmental. Its method involves an approach that is highly sensitive to the way in which meanings are metaphorized through the play of language, as well as via the actual materials of the visual arts. It addresses the artwork with an evenly suspended, "free-floating attention", based on the model of "free-association". Psychoanalysis is thus a rich, many-faceted conglomerate that, when applied to the three areas of aesthetic functioning identified earlier, has the capacity to yield insights unobtainable in any other way. And as this study intends to show, it is British psychoanalysis which seems to yield the most possibilities in tackling both the intra-psychic processes involved in creativity and the way these are implicated in the formal structure of art. Because British psychoanalysis is primarily concerned with the relationships between human beings and their objects, it would seem particularly well suited to addressing the *visual* arts, for these are concerned (among other things) with the impact of outward objects upon inner experience—the artist's physical engagement with his medium, and the spectator's response to the art object *qua* object.

Of course, as well as the British School, a number of other psychoanalytic Schools have developed since psychoanalysis was first discovered by Freud at the turn of the century. Before looking at the general contribution of the British School to aesthetics, I shall give a brief overview of the main trajectories taken by psychoanalytic theory since Freud, so we can see more precisely where the British School is located on the map.

The evolution of psychoanalysis may be considered to fall into three main stages, beginning with Freud and Breuer's *Studies in Hysteria* (1895d) and Freud's *Interpretation of Dreams* (1900a). Here was set out his discovery of the dynamic unconscious, the account of repression, and the nature of the primary and secondary processes—the opposing set of dynamic mechanisms that ground our psychic life. In this first stage (referred to as "orthodox" or "classical" psychoanalysis) artistic form is regarded as essentially a neurotic and wish-fulfilling activity for both artist and viewer, and it shares the same structure as that of dreams, symptoms, and parapraxes. The perspective changed with the development of ego psychology pioneered by Anna Freud, Hans Hartmann, and Ernst Kris, a tradition that has largely flourished in America. The production of art and its enjoyment is deemed to represent the relatively autonomous functioning of the ego: i.e., artistic form can develop more or less independently of drives and instinctual energy. Kris (1952) has been the leading exponent of this view.

However, psychoanalysis in Europe, particularly France, has evolved with a distinctive stance of its own, one that has a particularly strong link to French intellectual life; for example, the influence of intellectuals such as Roland Barthes, Jacques Derrida, and Michel Foucault has been very significant. This interchange is perhaps also to be seen as an index of the privileged role philosophy plays in French intellectual life, where it is integral to the school curriculum. French psychoanalysis, by comparison with either the ego psychologists or the British School, does not represent a unified and homogenous body of thought, although it has loosely grouped itself around the teachings of the psychoanalyst Jacques Lacan. In contrast, there is only one Institute of Psychoanalysis in London, which provides a professional and ordered training, but this has had not quite the same impact on cultural life as its French counterpart. The British Society is also much more clinically orientated, discussing concepts mainly in a therapeutic context. Indeed, the contrast between French and British psychoanalysis is made clear by Benvenuto and Kennedy, who remark that, in France, "the organisation of analytic practice seems as ordered as a heated conversation in a French café'!" (1986, p. 14). The main distinction between the French psychoanalysts and their British and American counterparts lies in the former's emphasis on the role of language and, more specifically, the play of desire through language (Kristeva, 1980) and how the human subject is constructed through the linguistic register (Lacan). Compared to the British School, this takes a radically *anti-humanistic* stance, in which the human subject is regarded as being fundamentally fragmented, thus calling into question the whole notion of the unitary self as a locus of "meaning" and "value".

As this study of aesthetics primarily concerns itself with exploring the contributions of the British School of Psychoanalysis, it lies outside of the scope of this study to do justice to the relevance of Jung's ideas to this domain. (For an exploration of Carl Jung's own thoughts on aesthetics, see Jung [1971]. More recently, there have been a number of fruitful studies exploring Jungian aesthetics, for example: Philipson [1994]; Adams and Duncan [2003]; Bishop [2007].) However, it should be noted that there have been some important connections made between Kleinian, post-Kleinian, and Jungian ideas, by Wilfred Bion himself and by a number of Jungians. When asked whether his notion of a "primorial mind" was related to Jung's archetypes, Bion replied "I think he [Jung] was probably talking about the same thing. There exists some fundamental mind, something that seems to remain unaltered in us all" (Bion, 1978, p. 4). (For an exploration of resonances between Jungian and Psychoanalytic concepts, see Fordham [1998]; Plaut [1974]; Astor [2002].)

It is to the British School of psychoanalysis, the main focus of this book, that we now turn. As we shall see, this School construes the nature of the human subject very differently. The focus is on the importance of the *pre-verbal* realm of experience and the interchange (reverie) between mother and baby and its role in subsequent psychic development. Analyst Adam Phillips remarks that "in British Psychoanalysis . . . there was not so much a return to Freud, as there had been in France with the work of Lacan, as a return to *Mother*" (1988, p. 10, my italic). (For an account of the development of French psychoanalysis and its vicissitudes, see Turkle [1986].) However, it would be simplistic and inaccurate to say that "British School" refers to only one approach. It is, rather, a broad tradition which combines a variety of different approaches that stand on common ground and enjoy shared values. According to analyst Eric Rayner, it is "a humanistic, decent-minded, democratic, kindly philosophy, and it is strong enough to inspire a way of life" (1990, p. 10). Like the French School, the British Psychoanalytic Society has encountered the storms of great upheaval and dissent, but has weathered them more successfully. In 1926, Anna Freud and Melanie Klein came into conflict, one that resurfaced as the bitter "Controversial Discussions" of 1941–1945; and then in 1951 Winnicott and Klein came to blows, resulting in a parting of the ways. However, it was the "Controversial Discussions" which most powerfully threatened to fragment the British Society. Yet, despite the huge theoretical gulf between the rival groups, the Society managed to contain its differences, and a "gentlemen's agreement" was forged between the rival factions (much of this was due to the tact and diplomacy of Winnicott). Out of this, two separate groups emerged specifically for training purposes: the "A Group" (led by Klein), and the "B Group" (led by Anna Freud). A third group also emerged (although more informally) and this became known as the "Independent" or "Middle Group", comprising those who had no desire to align themselves with either side, such as Ronald Fairbairn, John Rickman, Marion Milner, Winnicott, Charles Rycroft, and, more recently, Christopher Bollas, Eric Rayner, and Adam Phillips. (For an account of the history of the British School, see Hughes [1990]. For an account of the "Controversial Discussions", see King and Steiner [1992]. The history of "Independent" tradition and its main theoretical approaches have been explored by both Kohon [1986], and by Rayner [1990].)

Those clinicians who identify as working within the British School emphasize the relationship between individuals, the reciprocity between self and other—hence the term "object-relations", a term also used to describe the orientation of these clinicians. Because their theory is concerned with the structural dynamics (not just the content) of psychic experience, it is well equipped to tackle the structural, formal nature of artwork and the way that specific psychic mechanisms are implicated. Their theories can help us to make sense of the aesthetic encounter and the artist's interchange with his medium. For both the artist and the spectator are concerned with the negotiation between the private inner world and that of the outer, and since this school of psychoanalysis is very much concerned with the specific ways in which the structure of inner experience shapes the perception of reality, then it would seem well able to help us explore the dynamics of aesthetic experience. It is important to emphasize that, for the purposes of this study, my understanding of the "British School" encompasses the Kleinians together with a number of clinicians who identify as working within the "Independent" territory.

An outline of how this book is structured

Although we are not concerned specifically with an analysis of Freud's aesthetics, his account of art will be the starting point from which to evaluate subsequent developments in psychoanalytic aesthetics pioneered by the British School.

Part One, "The Legacy of Freud": Chapter One examines two distinctive approaches to art discernible in Freud's writings. The first section explores Freud's "neurotic model" and the nature of "pathography". The second section looks at Freud's theory of the joke, which a number of theorists have developed into a possible model for understanding the formal qualities of art, aspects that the first model left unaddressed. However, although this approach has yielded new insights (Kris, 1952; Ehrenzweig, 1967), I concur with John Spector's view that "Freud's choice of subjects had less to do with central aesthetic questions than with his own personal needs and obsessions" (1972, p. 34).

Part Two explores the work of Melanie Klein and her contribution to developments of the British School and its aesthetics. Chapter Two explores how Klein's account of (for example) infantile development, unconscious phantasy, and symbol formation significantly developed the Freudian paradigm and created new possibilities in psychoanalytic aesthetics. However, because Klein did not herself develop a systematic account of art, Chapter Three explores how Klein's ideas were taken up by Hanna Segal (Klein's main standard bearer), and also through the work of the art critic and historian, Adrian Stokes (an analysand of Klein). I examine how their work lays the foundation of what can be identified as a "traditional" Kleinian aesthetic.

Since Klein and Segal's contributions, however, there have been significant developments in British School thinking that have had consequence for aesthetics. Part Three of this study: "Developments in the British School", will explore how Kleinian ideas have progressed since Klein's death in 1960, primarily through the clinical contributions of "post-Kleinians" such as Bion, Meltzer, Milner, and Winnicott. (In this study, the term "post-Kleinian" is sometimes used, and a distinction must be made between its clinical, theoretical reference and my own use of the term, which is largely historical. *Clinically* speaking, the term "post-Kleinian" refers to a group of analysts who have taken up Bion's ideas and who believe that he has essentially moved *beyond* Klein and pioneered a new paradigm or School of his own. My use is somewhat different. I include with Bion and Meltzer the "Independent" analysts, Milner and Winnicott. For they [like Bion] were pupils of Klein and also went on to develop new insights after her death, and in this historical sense they deserve to be called "post-Kleinian". However, most clinicians would take issue with my inclusion of Milner and Winnicott in the "post-Kleinian" tradition, because the two analysts disagreed with the fundamental Kleinian view that the child is born with an innate sense of an ego boundary and that unconscious phantasy operates from the very start of life. But it is for ease of reference and grouping that I have included them with Bion in the category "post-Kleinian". Indeed, I would disagree with those who see a stark division between the ideas of (say) Bion and Winnicott, for even Winnicott himself saw a number of resonances between his thinking and that of Bion [(see Winnicott, 1987)]. Milner (1987b) also noted resonances between her work and that of Bion, especially his regarding later ideas concerning reverie, aesthetic experience, and mystical states.)

Chapter Four explores Wilfred Bion's insights concerning thinking, creativity, and his re-mapping of the Kleinian account of mental space. Although his work does not deal specifically with the *visual* arts, it will become clear that he has played an essential role in the development of Kleinian aesthetics. For, as we will see, his insights have considerably enlarged the Kleinian paradigm with wider literary and philosophical dimensions. Indeed, his writings increasingly stress the importance of the veridicality of aesthetic experience and its necessity for our meaningful apprehension of the world. In many ways this represents a return to the traditional (Neo-Platonic) view that art concerns "the True, the Good and the Beautiful"—the belief that it is through art that we apprehend the order and harmony of the world, and our place within it. However, there is a debate as to how far Bion *has* established a new, "post-Kleinian" paradigm of his own, or whether he is part and parcel of a more general development of Kleinian thought that includes Segal's development of the Kleinian theory of symbolism and aesthetic experience and the work of others such as Bick and Rosenfeld on the schizoid personality and narcissistic disorders. Hinshelwood (1989) is inclined to view Bion in the latter category, while my own view (following Meltzer) is that Bion represents the coming-of-age of psychoanalysis, and has transformed the Kleinian model by aligning psychoanalytic insight with literature and philosophy. Milton, Shakespeare, Keats, Coleridge, the Old Testament, and the *Bhagavad Gita* are among the classical texts that inspired Bion's thinking and helped provide models for his psychoanalytic theories.

The implications of Bion's thinking for psychoanalytic aesthetics and criticism have been developed mainly through the work of analysts and writers such as Donald Meltzer, Meg Harris Williams, and Margot Waddell. The fourth section of Chapter Four ("The remapping of mental space") explores the contribution of these authors to what can be identified as a "Bionian" approach to literary and aesthetic criticism, which is combined with a deep appreciation of Stokes's critical writings. The fifth section ("Donald Meltzer and 'aesthetic conflict'") looks specifically at the "dialogue" between Meltzer and Stokes concerning the social basis of art, for it is an interesting example of the fruitful interchange possible between the clinical and non-clinical spheres directed specifically towards the understanding of art. The final section ("Psychoanalysis as an art") gives an overview of the trajectory and scope of Bion's thinking, and emphasizes the way in which post-Kleinian psychoanalysis seems to be increasingly identified as an *art form*, rather than a "mirror" of scientific objectivity as emphasized in classical psychoanalysis.

Turning to the non-clinical domain, in Chapter Five, I explore the work of art teacher and theorist, Anton Ehrenzweig. His concern is primarily with the unconscious, "hidden order of art" and the undifferentiated nature of creative perception. However, he can be regarded as somewhat of a "Flying Dutchman" figure here, for (as his Appendix to *The Hidden Order of Art* makes clear) he deploys psychoanalytic theory a little idiosyncratically, "mixing and matching" various concepts, combining insights from Freud, Kris, Klein, Bion, Milner, and Winnicott to suit his purposes—there is even a strong Jungian resonance in his account of "poemagogic imagery". Broadly speaking, his view that the essence of art is *not* reparative concurs with that of Milner and Winnicott. He regards the paradoxical, "in-between" phase of undifferentiation between inner and outer, the "manic–oceanic womb of rebirth", as the matrix of all artistic creativity and aesthetic perception.

Chapter Six turns once again to the clinical domain, exploring the respective contributions of Winnicott and Milner, two "Independent" analysts who have focused less on the formal structure of art and its reparative elements than on the nature of the interchange between viewer and object, the reciprocity between artist and medium, the "potential space" of illusion believed to characterize "authentic" artistic experience.

Chapter Seven returns to the non-clinical domain, examining the aesthetics and criticism of Fuller and Wollheim, and the overriding theme is the *corporeal* basis of painting and aesthetic appreciation: "painting as the body". As discussed above, this is a major element underlying the British School account of art, and thus I have chosen to look specifically at its development within the context of actual critical practice. However, where Fuller believes the "post-Kleinian" ideas of Bion, Milner, and Winnicott are the most fruitful, Wollheim's loyalty is primarily to the insights of Klein and Stokes. Yet, as I argue, the combined contributions of Fuller and Wollheim not only show how successfully a range of British School concepts have been deployed in the criticism of art, they reveal that the fundamental link between the thinkers in the British School is the emphasis on the *body*, the corporeal basis of what Stokes called the "image in form", that structure of art which is "container for the sum of meanings" (see Stokes [1978], *III*, p. 334). The work of Fuller and Wollheim reveals how British School theory can account for the material, corporeal basis of aesthetic appreciation, and can also address the question of why it is that the *activity* of painting is itself meaningful—a theme which most "ideological" and structural–linguistic theories of art seem unable to explain (Fuller, 1980, p. 183).

My Conclusion gives an overview of the main elements that comprise a British psychoanalytic aesthetic and some of the broader, philosophical ideas implicated in these. I also examine how British School theory invites us to rethink the classical account of the relation between art and madness, creativity and psychoneurosis, and the distinction between the primary and secondary processes.

The overriding goal of this study is to demonstrate that the work of the British School presents a significant contribution to psychoanalytic aesthetics and criticism. Given the various different approaches within this School (Kleinian, Bionian, Winnicottian, for example) it will become clear that there are a number of fundamental, shared assumptions that characterize what is an essentially a *humanistic* and *material* (corporeal) aesthetic. In this account, aesthetic and cultural experience are regarded as being central to both our psychic health and the continuation of our "going-on-being" (Winnicott). Through an exploration of the respective contributions of both the practitioners and the non-practitioners who have furthered the debate between aesthetics and psychoanalysis, my intention is to identify and argue for the existence of a uniquely British psychoanalytic aesthetic.

PART I
THE LEGACY OF FREUD

CHAPTER ONE

Freud's theory of art and creativity

This chapter explores the general direction of Freud's writings on art and its relationship to his metapsychology. I hope to show that Freud's contribution to aesthetics, although criticized for being ambivalent and incomplete, is significant largely because it made subsequent developments possible within the British School of Psychoanalysis.

First, I explore Freud's interest in "pathography"—the viewing of art as a privileged form of neurosis where the analyst–critic explores the artwork in order to understand and unearth the creator's psychological motivations. We will see the limitations of focusing solely on the content of the artwork and the inner world of the artist. This view is enriched and expanded, however, by Freud's later (1905c) theory of the joke mechanism and its relationship to his account of the primary and secondary processes. Although Freud did not fully pursue his investigation into the relationship between the joke mechanism and aesthetic experience, we will see that this aspect of Freud's theory seems better equipped than the pathographic approach to address the formal structure of art and the nature of aesthetic experience. Rather than just an object to be investigated on the analytic dissecting table, the artwork can be viewed as the outcome of a *process*.

Pathography and the neurotic model

Freud first introduces the term "pathography" in his essay on Leonardo (1910c) where it is described negatively, focusing on what it does not (yet) do. Pathography, according to Freud, does not aim, for instance, at making Leonardo's achievements intelligible; and surely (he argues) no one should be blamed for not carrying out something he has never promised to do. With this disclaimer in mind, Freud continues by comparing the practice of biography with that of pathography. The essential difference is that "biographers are fixated upon their heroes" and it is implied that the pathographer (in this case, Freud) has outgrown the omnipotent, infantile wish to idealize his subject and can get on with the real business of unearthing the truth. Freud's approach centres on the experience of the individual artist, and, like a detective, reconstructs his subject's past, discovering possible complexes, repressions, and neuroses. The artist is treated as a patient and his products are analysed in terms of these psychological considerations. The artwork is seen as a means of giving expression to, and/or dealing with, various psychic pressures. The pathographer manifests the same qualities as the so-called "objective" analyst who is able to look at the artist and his work as if he were conducting an analysis, but with the significant absence of a patient who can speak for himself. It is assumed that the artwork will shed light on the artist's inner conflicts and repressed anxieties, usually of an infantile nature.

However, one of the main problems with this approach is that little or no account of the *origin* of the creative impulse is given, nor does Freud give an explanation of the *value* of specific art works; i.e., why we may value one work more than another. What is crucial for the pathographical model is the way in which the analyst–critic is able to use biographical data to reveal psychological insights about the creator and the meaning of his creations. This is a two-way process: the artwork can help explain the artist's psyche in the same way that the artist's own experiences can illuminate his oeuvre. However, just as Freud neglected the significance and value of the countertransference (the analyst's emotional response to his patient) in his own clinical work and even saw it as a hindrance to analytic work (see the "Dora" case history [1905e] as an example), he also tended to de-emphasize the role of his own emotional reactions as significant critical tools in his analysis of art. But, despite a supposedly detached critical stance, Freud was undoubtedly drawn to certain artists and artworks that resonated with his own concerns, and, thus, Freud's identification with his subjects, however well disguised, significantly shapes his interpretations.

The Moses of Michelangelo (1914b) is especially notable for its disclaimers *vis-à-vis* Freud's own artistic preferences and critical abilities. He tells us somewhat modestly that he is "no connoisseur in art but simply a layman", and that the "subject-matter of works of art" attract him more than their formal and technical qualities. Because of this, he says he is "unable rightly to appreciate many of the methods used and the effects obtained in art". Yet Freud's interpretation is very much based on his own identification with the sculptor and with the subject, Moses. Freud first identifies himself with Michelangelo to see what his particular motivation might have been, and then assumes that the sculptor, in order to arrive at the form of his artwork, also identified himself with his subject, Moses. This subjective interpretation is based not on formal qualities of the work of art, but on an identification of the critic with its subject matter. We might ask why Freud should have felt such an attraction to this particular subject and we can find an answer in Freud's last work, *Moses and Monotheism* (1939a). "It was one man", Freud wrote in that book, "the man Moses, who created the Jews. To him the people owes its tenacity in supporting life; to him, however, also much of the hostility which it has met and is meeting still". As a Jew himself, Freud was forcibly aware of the psychological significance of the historical Moses and the statue exerted an extreme fascination for the psychoanalyst. He describes

> ... how often have I mounted the steep steps from the unlovely Corso Cavour to the lonely piazza where the deserted church stands, and have essayed to support the angry scorn of the hero's glance! Sometimes I have crept cautiously out of the half-gloom of the interior as though I myself belonged to the mob upon whom his eye is turned—the mob which can hold fast no conviction, which

has neither faith nor patience and which rejoices when it has regained its illusory idols. [1939a, p. 130]

It could be argued that Freud's interpretation of the statue is more closely linked with his own feelings of kinship with Moses than he would like to admit. Just as Moses struggled to retain authority over his people, so Freud, as the founding father of psychoanalysis, also had to struggle with his "disloyal" followers to retain what he believed was his rightful position of authority within his psychoanalytic circle. For two contrasting readings of Freud's identification with Moses, see Fuller (1980) and Wollheim (1974).

Pathography can also be approached within the terms of the critical tradition of Romanticism. (For an understanding of this tradition, see Abrams [1971].) What is at stake for both Romantic and pathographic models is how, and to what extent, a particular work yields insights into the psyche of its creator, and whether his work is genuine, spontaneous, and sincere. The external world, as depicted in visual art, or described in poetry, is seen first as a *projection of the artist's state of mind*—an assumption that the artwork is essentially an externalization of the artist's inner state. The relevant question asked by the pathographer is, what underlying feelings, psychic states, conflicts, or desires (possibly disguised) are being expressed? The Romantic critic assumes (but does not explain exactly why and how) the artist's inner life of feeling finds concrete expression in his work. This approach was one that informed the general climate that received both Freud's clinical writings and his aesthetic theories.

We must bear in mind that this Romantic view not only shaped Freud's ideas (particularly the case histories, which are works of literature in their own right as much as clinical texts), but also aided their favourable reception. Within the Romantic approach to artistic practice there is a focus on a certain kind of conception of the artistic personality—that the artist is fragile, particularly sensitive, even "possessed"—reviving the Platonic belief in the artist's (dangerous) madness. It is not unusual, even today, to encounter the view that artists are persons with particularly intense and deep conflicts—and this is further connoted by the term "pathography". Those who adopt this model assume that the psychoanalytically motivated enquirer will be able to uncover repressions, complexes, and anxieties through studying the artist's oeuvre, and that interpretations of such works can be made in the light of biographical knowledge. But this is a rather limited model because it assumes that works of art are by nature the outcome of conflict. It has little contribution to make to the notion of *aesthetic value* or the origin of the creative impulse itself, and it does not give a full account of the nature of aesthetic experience, either. Its significance mainly lies in what it may tell us about the psycho-history of the artist and its reflection in his work. As a model for an aesthetic theory, however, it is inadequate.

Freud was ambivalent about the capacity of psychoanalysis to illuminate artistic and aesthetic experience and its capacity to address the value of art. (For further analysis of this aspect of Freud, see Storr [1972], Chapter One.) On the one hand Freud is optimistic that psychoanalysis could

> take inter-relations between the impressions of the artist's life, his chance experiences, and his works and from them construct his [mental] constitution and the instinctual impulses at work in it—that is to say, that part of him he shared with all men. [1925d, p. 65]

Indeed, his Leonardo study was certainly done with this in mind, based on a single childhood memory. On the other hand, Freud admits only a few lines later that psychoanalytic study can do nothing towards elucidating the "two problems which probably interest . . . [the layman] most": the "nature of the artistic gift . . . and the means by which the artist works—artistic technique". This ambivalence towards a psychoanalytic understanding of art was not new, and it recurs throughout his scattered writings on the subject. Although he regarded the connections between the impressions of the artist's childhood and his life history on the one hand, and his works as reactions to these impressions on the other, as "one of the most attractive subjects of analytic examination", he remarks that the "problems of artistic creation and appreciation await further study". Still, he remains confident that psychoanalysis will be equipped to address them eventually. Until then, precisely "whence it is that the artist derives his creative capacity is not a question for psychology" (as he had written some twelve years before "Leonardo") (1913j, p. 187).

We might object that it is this very capacity that allows the artist to *create and not become ill*, and thus is vitally important. But what Freud and those who followed his approach were predominantly concerned with was the eliciting of unconscious conflicts and phantasies embodied in a work of art (for example, Jones, 1916; Rank, 1932; Sachs, 1940, 1942). Some of his papers aim at psychobiography of the artist, using the works of art as revealing of his inner conflicts and psychological history. Thus, in "Leonardo", he uses scant biographical data—a screen memory and two of his paintings, *The Mona Lisa* and *St Anne, St Mary and Jesus*—to attempt a reconstruction of the artist's psycho-sexual development, relating Leonardo's childhood experiences to his later conflicts between his scientific and artistic creativity. In his essay "Dostoevsky and parricide" (1928b), through an analysis of *The Brothers Karamazov* in the light of Dostoevsky's early experience, Freud attempts to analyse the writer's personality, trying to account for his epilepsy, gambling, and morality.

Although this psychobiographical approach has been criticized on many counts (for an inclusive summary example see Spitz, 1985, pp. 50–53), its value lies not in the restructuring of the artist's inner life, but in the uncovering of the phantasies expressed by the artwork itself. His study of Leonardo, for instance, introduced for the first time the clinical description of a certain form of narcissism and narcissistic object-choice, and illustrates many other aspects of infantile psycho-sexuality. In the essay on Dostoevsky, Freud illustrates the clinical insights he had already gained into the universal theme of the Oedipus complex, yet is also able to derive new insights from his analysis of this writer. For example, he describes the splitting of the personality into many characters in the book, maybe more clearly than he does in his more clinically orientated writings.

The paper most frequently cited as a general statement of the Freudian view of art and creativity is "Creative writers and daydreaming" (1908e). Here, Freud gives an account of creativity that casts the artist as a neurotic day-dreamer who allows us to enjoy our own dreams without shame. He is portrayed as an egotist, whose creations are only valuable to the extent that they provide a kind of narcotic effect, offering both the artist and audience a substitute for, and an escape from, reality. The day-dreamer ignores reality in his dream and gives full rein to the pleasure principle in evolving wishful phantasies. Similarly, the artist creates a world of phantasy in which he can fulfil his unconscious wishes. But he differs from the dreamer in one significant respect: he is able to find a way back to reality in his creation, and in that way his achievement resembles children's play, where the external world is moulded to certain desires. Freud, however, contrasts play with what is *real*, a view that has been challenged by the British school. Later, we shall see that for Klein and Winnicott play is inextricably linked to the development of a reality sense and is viewed as an activity that is essential to our psychological well-being as well as our creative development.

In "Formulations regarding the two principles in mental functioning", Freud writes that art

> brings about a reconciliation of the two principles [pleasure and reality] in a peculiar way. An artist is originally a man who turns away from reality because he cannot come to terms with the renunciation of instinctual satisfaction which it at first demands, and who allows his erotic and ambitious wishes full play in the life of phantasy. He finds the way back to reality, however, from this world of phantasy by making use of his special gifts to mould his phantasies into truths of a new kind, which are valued by men as precious reflections of reality. Thus in a certain fashion he actually becomes the hero, the king, the creator, or the favourite he desired to be, without following the long, roundabout path of making real alterations in the external world. But he can only achieve this because other men feel the same dissatisfaction as he does with the renunciation demanded by reality, and because that dissatisfaction, which results from the replacement of the pleasure-principle by the reality principle, is itself part of reality. [1911b, p. 224]

This is virtually the same formulation that Freud was to make in his *Introductory Lectures* of 1915–1917. Once again, it concerns the dynamics of the creative process in the artist, and we are given little clue as to the problem of the formal aspects of art and aesthetic value. But, in drawing a contrast between the authentic artist and "those who are not artists", Freud suggests that the "true artist" is exceptional in that he can find his way back to reality again, knowing how to elaborate his day-dreams so that they lose what is too personal about them and repels strangers, and make it possible for others to share in the enjoyment of them. He understands, too, how to tone them down so that they do not easily betray their origin from proscribed sources. Furthermore, he possesses the mysterious power of shaping some particular material until it has become a particular image of his phantasy; and he knows, moreover, how to link so large a yield of pleasure to this representation of his unconscious phantasy that, for the time being at least, repressions are outweighed and lifted by it. If he is able to accomplish all this, he makes it possible for other people once more to derive consolation and alleviation from their own sources of pleasure in their unconscious which have become inaccessible to them. [Freud, 1915–1917, p. 376]

But all this mysterious ability, according to Freud, has only one object: "to win honour, power and the love of women". Nevertheless, Freud is aware that there is more to art than pure neurotic wish-fulfilment, something that concerns the way the artist transforms his egotistic phantasies into a structure that renders them acceptable for public appreciation. In "Creative writers and day-dreaming" (1908e) he admits that the relation of the phantasies of a "man of literary talent" gives pleasure, whereas the phantasies of an ordinary day-dreamer merely bore us, or even repel us. But exactly how it is that the writer accomplishes his effect of pleasure remains his

> innermost secret; the essential *ars poetica* lies in the technique of overcoming the feeling of repulsion in us which is undoubtedly connected with the barriers that rise between each single ego and the others. We can guess two of methods used by this technique. The writer softens the character of his egotistic day-dreams by altering and disguising it, and he bribes us by the *purely formal*—that is, aesthetic—yield of pleasure which he offers us in the presentation of his phantasies. [1908e, p. 153, my italics]

This passage is one of the few times where Freud admits that the purely formal values in a work of art give pleasure. But the implications of this are not taken further; the artwork remains merely a bait to catch the fish, an "incentive bonus or fore pleasure". Freud concludes that *all* the aesthetic pleasure we gain from the works of imaginative writers is of the same type as this "fore pleasure", and that the true enjoyment of literature proceeds from the "release of tensions in our minds". So, despite an awareness of the significance of purely formal attributes or aesthetic considerations, Freud always returns to the dynamics of the artistic event, where art is viewed as essentially a therapy for those instinctual renunciations demanded by civilization.

Is there any kind of justification or value in an approach that centres on the subject matter, the content of the artwork, and interprets this as if it were the artist's psyche laid bare, with the critic's own identifications possibly implicated in the proceedings? The pathographer must grapple with the issues of the relation between an artist's life and work, the nature of artistic creativity, and the problems of intention and expression. Although psychoanalysis is more concerned with inner realities than with external events, and though the purpose of reconstruction is to gain a clearer picture of the artist's psyche, not to find out what "really happened", one of the paradoxes in applied psychoanalysis is that, in the absence of clinical data, the pathographer must use the *external* as a pathway to the *internal*. Such a method is fraught with dangers, the most common of which are incomplete or inaccurate external data and an intrusive countertransference; in this context, the unconscious affects and fantasies that the subject evokes in the interpreter. However, in cases where the critic has succumbed to these dangers, the resulting interpretation might still have value. This might be partly due to the appeal of "narrative truth" in the interpretation, and to the unconscious resonances of the artwork with the critic. One might also want to say that there is a need to find meaning through sympathetic identification, to trace patterns that cohere with one's own inner world and that of the artist and the artwork. (Indeed, this is the spirit that informs the aesthetic criticism of Adrian Stokes, which will be examined in Chapter Three, Sections ?? and ?? below.) Granted that there is an unconscious phantasy world that we are able to share, even an interpretation of this type might sometimes ring true. There are, however, various styles of pathographic approach that place varying emphases on the relationship between the artist and his work, and conceive the need to interpret these somewhat differently. (See Spector, 1972, and Wright, 1984 for an overview of the various approaches to pathography.)

Perhaps the main value of the pathographic approach is the way it helps us to discover the distinct and personal meanings to the artist of his imagery, and to explore the genesis and quality of affect evoked by this. The pathographer also restricts his or her enquiry by tying works to their creators in a way that assumes there is a direct link between the artist's inner world and his artwork, and it is implied that the value of the artwork is directly linked to the nature of the artist's psyche. With this pathographic approach, there is the danger that the viewer of the artwork will be ignored. As we shall see in Part II, this dimension of the aesthetic, peripheral to pathography, is absolutely central to the aesthetics of the British School of psychoanalysis.

The joke mechanism

In his analysis of the structure of the joke mechanism, Freud elaborates an embryonic aesthetic, an alternative to his pathographic account. Although it was left undeveloped in relation to the understanding of art, Freud recognized its scope for the study of aesthetics. Thus, he writes in "On the history of the psychoanalytic movement" (1914d) that the "first example of an application of the analytic mode of thought to the problems of aesthetics was contained in my book on jokes" (p. 37). And, although Freud's theory of the joke mechanism has received less attention than that of his "neurotic model", there have been a number of commentators who agree that this is Freud's most promising approach to a psychoanalytic aesthetic, mainly because it gives a much fuller account than that of the neurotic model of the way psychic processes are brought to bear on the *formal* aspects of art, and how this relates to the experience of aesthetic pleasure (e.g., Ehrenzweig, 1967; Gombrich, 1966; Kris, 1952; Wollheim, 1974).

Freud distinguishes three stages in the evolution of the joke, arising from a basis of primitive play. The first is at the level of the child's delight in games of recognition, which often manifests itself in verbal play, for "children, who, as we know, are in the habit of treating words as things, tend to expect words that are the same or similar to have the same meaning behind them" (1905c, p. 120). The pleasure of such recognition, Freud maintains, does not come from a sense of power but from a saving of psychic energy. This saving is in itself enjoyable, and so, according to Freud, "the games founded on this pleasure make use of the mechanism of damming up only in order to increase the amount of pleasure" (*ibid.*, p. 122). The second stage of the joke's development moves it from the level of play to that of the "jest". It entails making a concession to the growing demands of the intellect, which is not content to rest on mere pleasure in the rhyming of words. There is a meaning, but it is of no consequence: "the meaning of the joke is merely intended to protect that pleasure from being done away with by criticism" (*ibid.*, p. 131). What distinguishes the jest from the joke proper is that it is "non-tendentious"; it has no axe to grind—its sole purpose is to give pleasure. The third stage is the joke proper, the "tendentious" joke, in which there is a distinct purpose, taking the form of challenging either a person or social inhibitions of all kinds. There are two forms, the hostile and the obscene, the first giving the opportunity to express "aggressiveness, satire, or defence", the second "serving the purpose of an exposure" (*ibid.*, p. 133). At this level, the verbal play is now working in conjunction with this tendentious purpose.

Freud envisages this type of joke as a three-person relationship. The teller requires a listener as an "ally": the first and third person are thus in an alliance against the second person or object, the butt of the joke. As a prototype of the tendentious joke, Freud cites the example of "smut", the dirty joke, where the first and third person are enabled to share mastery over the forbidden and inaccessible sexual object, the woman, allowing a discharge of frustration in a seduction whose imaginary nature partakes of a fancied reality through being publicly shared. The alliance is confirmed by the spontaneous laughter in which the complicity of a third person in this mutual release of tension (the "saving" of psychic energy) is made obvious to both. This "economy of psychical expenditure" involves a double pleasure, the verbal play itself, which is the core, and the pleasure of lifting the inhibition, which is the "casing".

The ego psychologist Ernst Kris (1952) regards the pleasure of the joke as being due to its bringing about the play of energies in the psyche, for the ultimate benefit of the rational ego, which emerges fresh and fortified. This assumes, however, that the *conscious ego* is the locus of aesthetic experience; a model presupposing an ordered, rational structure: the ego as a stabilizing and synthesizing force. The art historian, Ernst Gombrich, who collaborated with Kris (1952), was similarly encouraged by Freud's work on the joke mechanism, hailing it as "the germinal model for any account of artistic creation along Freudian lines" (Gombrich, 1966, p. 35). He remarks that Freud made a step forward for psychoanalytic aesthetics when he described the joke as a preconscious idea that has been exposed briefly to the workings of the unconscious. This means that it is not the content so much as the form—the dream-like condensation of meaning that is characteristic of the primary process—that is important. Gombrich stresses that the two supreme virtues that recommend it to the historian and the critic of art are the ways in which it explains the "relevance of both the medium and its mastery", these being elements that have often been neglected in many psychoanalytic approaches to art. Gombrich also emphasizes the importance of the role of the child's pleasure in *playing* with language, which Freud sees as part of the functional pleasure connected with achieving control and mastery. Despite his recognition of the relation between the primary processes and aesthetic pleasure, Freud did not see any intrinsic value in the primary process. In his *New Introductory Lectures* (1933a), he regarded the id as being

> the dark inaccessible part of our personality; what little we know of it we have learned from our study of the dream-work and of the construction of neurotic symptoms, and most of that is of a negative character and can be described only as a contrast to the ego. We approach the id with analogies: we call it a chaos, a cauldron full of seething excitations. [*ibid.*, p. 73]

However, there have been a number of analysts within the British School, such as Rycroft, Milner, and Winnicott, who saw the primary process and its relationship to the secondary process as having important consequences for the understanding of creative and artistic activity. The tendency in contemporary British psychoanalysis is to see the two modes as interlocking elements grounding all mental life: the creative force of the primary process as inextricably part of "sophisticated" secondary process thinking. This is an important theme which runs throughout this study; it is through the filter of a growing body of research contributed by those working within the domain of aesthetics and psychoanalysis that aspects of clinical theory have themselves been reviewed. This has led to an ongoing respectful dialogue between aesthetics and clinical theory that has been mutually influential.

As we have explored above, Gombrich and Kris have focused on the adaptive, stabilizing aspect of aesthetic experience, which relies on the model of an integrated ego and a clear demarcation between its *conscious* and *unconscious* workings. The value of art, according to this model, lies in the degree of adjustment to reality it yields—the belief that the dream-work (primary process) is somehow able to translate what is unconscious, repressed, and unacceptable into an artistic construction that is itself analogous to the stabile, integrated ego. In the light of this approach, only those unconscious ideas that can be adjusted to the reality of formal structures become communicable, and their shared value lies as much in their formal elements as in the idea. As Gombrich says, "the code generates the message" (1966, p. 36). Here, Gombrich is also drawing attention to the limitations of a naïve form of Expressionism, which construes artistic work to be the outpouring of the artist's inner world into his work. According to this model, it is this inner life that determines the form of the work. The account of Kris and Gombrich rests on the firm conviction that the goal of art is to attain control and stability in the external world. In the light of this account, art is essentially an *adaptive* phenomenon allowing communion between what is unacceptable and repressed (unconscious) and what is capable of being expressed to a wider, social realm. Art is thus a form of problem-solving, a testing-out of the medium, within a given tradition.

Kris's approach emphasizes the ego's control of the instinctual drives: for instance, the rhythmic shaking of the body in laughter, an activity where an "archaic pleasure in movement is reactivated and is socially permissible" (1952, p. 225). He argues that the adult's enjoyment of wit can be "justified before the superego" and this arises from the child's delight in word-playing (*ibid.*, p. 207). Similarly, Gombrich (1966) calls on Freud's theory of the joke for a view of play as innocent experimentation, arguing that the artist's "social game", his playing with given historical forms and conventions, involves a combination of preconscious and unconscious activity. However, in the arguments of both Kris and Gombrich, we may question whether sufficient place has been given to laughter and play as *corrective* of social convention. (In Part Two, we will see that Kleinians do not regard play as an innocent activity, but one that is fraught with painful unconscious phantasies, usually of a sadistic kind. Winnicott, however, took a more benign view of play, regarding it as a safe space in which the growing child is initiated into culture and learns to endow the outside world with enriching symbolic experience.)

The art teacher and theoretician, Anton Ehrenzweig, also looks at the implications of the joke-mechanism and its relation to primary process functioning. In "A new psychoanalytical approach to aesthetics", Ehrenzweig challenges those essentially Romantic, nineteenth-century accounts of art that "turned away from the analysis of objective structure to the analysis of subjective experience" (1962, p. 304). Such theories had been popular with psychologists such as Fechner and Lipps, who had in turn influenced the development of Freud's aesthetics. Like Kris and Gombrich, Ehrenzweig sees Freud's analysis of the joke (and the primary process functioning it represents) as particularly valuable for a better understanding of the formal aspects of art, and their relationship to what Ehrenzweig calls the "hidden order of art". They make an effort to de-emphasize pathographical interpretations of art and to highlight its *autonomous nature*. However, where Kris regards the primary process as an essentially archaic form of thinking (hence his term, "regression at the service of the ego"), Ehrenzweig sees it as primitive, chaotic, and uncontrolled only from the point of view of our rational, conscious modes of perception. Indeed, he argues (as do Milner and Rycroft) that there is probably less distinction than is usually accepted between primary and secondary process functioning. Ehrenzweig believed that a substantial revision of traditional Freudian theory was needed to fit in with the facts of artistic experience. The major task of his *The Hidden Order of Art* (1967) is an attempt to refine and modify a number of key traditional psychoanalytic concepts in the light of his own research, as well as that of British School practitioners. It is this aspect of Ehrenzweig's work that makes him particularly relevant to this study.

As is well-known, Freud viewed the primary process mode of thinking as one that displays the psychic mechanisms of condensation and displacement characteristic of the dream-work. (Freud's first theoretical expression of this discovery is to be found in his *Project for a Scientific Psychology* [1895]; it was developed further in Chapter VII of *The Interpretation of Dreams* [1900a] and it remained an unchanging element in his thought.) These activities refer not only to dreams, but also point to the tendency of images to fuse and readily come to symbolize one another. According to Freud, these are processes characteristic of id functioning: they ignore the categories of space and time, use mobile energy, and are governed by the pleasure principle. The secondary process, on the other hand, is ego-orientated. It obeys the laws of grammar and formal logic, uses bound energy, and is governed by the reality principle—i.e., it reduces the unpleasure of instinctual tension by adaptive behaviour. Freud believed the primary processes to be ontologically and phylogenetically earlier than the secondary processes—hence the terminology—and regarded the development of the ego as following on from their repression. The secondary processes, in Freud's view, developed alongside the ego, adapting to the external world, inextricably linked with verbal thinking. The primary processes are exemplified by dreams and the joke structure, the secondary processes by thought (see Freud, 1900a, 1917e). The two processes closely resemble the "non-discursive" and "discursive" symbolism described by the American philosopher and aesthetician, Susanne Langer (1953), whose work will be discussed in relation to the aesthetics of the British School (Chapter Two, below).

How exactly does the primary process relate to the joke mechanism? Ehrenzweig emphasized that in his study of the joke, Freud was able to describe how "[. . .] the joke condenses, displaces and twists the rational structure of everyday language in the manner of the dream's primary process" (1971 [1967], p. 265). He also found that the structure of jokes expressed a suppressed aggressive, or obscene, meaning through the same primary process forms by which a dream would symbolize its hidden phantasy content. Freud gives examples of the analogy between the joke mechanism and the primary process. In one joke recorded by Heine, a poor man boasts about the familiar way in which he is treated by a very rich relative. But, instead of speaking about his relative's gratifying familiarity, he twists the word and speaks of the "famillionaire" treatment he had met. The neologism "famillionaire" is condensed from the words "familiar" and "millionaire" and expresses a suppressed meaning: the money-proud man had not really shown a real friendship, but only that superficial politeness that emphasized his social superiority. The apparent gratification suddenly reveals the poor man's resentment. Words that have been telescoped together like this are also apparent in dreams; but Ehrenzweig stresses that usually it is *visual images* that are condensed, for in dreams we often combine features belonging to a number of figures that our conscious minds could not possibly make sense of. He points out that there are other characteristics shared by the joke and the dream: displacement is such an example. A dream image might give undue prominence to an unimportant feature and neglect the really significant detail. The dream's significance, says Ehrenzweig, will then have to give an inconspicuous detail an unsuspected significance and so shift the emphasis back to where it belongs. The joke employs the same technique of displacement.

Both the dream and the joke may also express a meaning by the use of the exact opposite. Our unconscious mind is able to understand the hidden meaning because, Ehrenzweig says, "the technique of unconscious perception and image-making is *less differentiated* than our conscious language and imagery" (1962, p. 303). Freud compared the undifferentiated language of the dream to old languages such as Latin, which did not distinguish between opposite meanings. The reason why our unconscious mind understands so readily a nonsensical conflation like "famillionaire", fusing friendship and hostility, is its failure to differentiate between opposites. According to Ehrenzweig's theory, this gradual dissolution of separateness is preceded by a necessary schizoid "scattering" of conscious faculties, and ultimately reaches an "oceanic limit" where all distinctions are fused into a single image.

Ehrenzweig also believes that Freud's analysis of the joke conquers "an old problem of aesthetics ... by firmly relating the joke's witty effect to objectively defined structures" (*ibid.*, p. 303), which are the workings of the primary process. However, he thinks that there has been little progress made in psychoanalytic aesthetics because Freudian interpretations were over-concerned with content analysis. The failure of classical theory to "discover the unconscious roots of art" lies in its denial that one exists—a conclusion that Ehrenzweig wholeheartedly rejects (*ibid.* p. 304). In his view there is a "hidden order" in the deceptive chaos of the primary process that could be perceived if we could make ourselves sensitive to it, and artists are the ones who can do this most easily. This dual aspect of undifferentiation (conscious chaos on the one hand, and unconscious discipline on the other) leads back to what Ehrenzweig identifies as the central question of psychoanalytic aesthetics: how can those primary process functions that are implicated in the chaos and disintegration characteristic of mental illness, become highly structured and result in the production of creative work? Ehrenzweig believes that it is the "structural undifferentiation of low-level imagery" that is the common denominator to both, and this is a theme that continued to preoccupy him. In a paper that can be regarded as an *envoi* to *The Hidden Order of Art*, he observes that

> psychoanalytic theory will have to accept that the imagery of the primary process can possess an invisible order of its own at least as far as creative work is concerned. The great psychoanalyst and art historian, E. Kris, prepared the way for recasting our concept of the primary process by suggesting that the creative mind can allow conscious functions to lapse in a controlled regression towards the primary process. But this does not yet mean that the primary process is itself accessible to control and order. [*ibid.*, p. 317]

Because this unconscious substructure, the "hidden order", "rises from deeper levels than those that shape the manifest dream and the joke", psychoanalytic aesthetics has been largely unsuccessful in probing it. To a much greater extent than Kris, Ehrenzweig explores from a variety of perspectives the way id processes are implicated in the creation and our perception of artistic form, and this is the main thesis of *The Hidden Order of Art*.

Although Enhrenzweig praises Freud's "brilliant analysis of the joke", he thinks it strange that it could not "act as a pacemaker for the analysis of art" when "the stage seemed set for Freud's triumphant entry into the core of aesthetics" (1967, p. 266). This failure to develop into a coherent psychoanalytic aesthetic "should have warned us that something was amiss, or even wrong, in the current concepts". The "missing concept", says Ehrenzweig, was the

> undifferentiated matrix below the more superficial condensations, displacements and other so-called primary process forms. These

more superficial forms may be irrational in content, but are not so in their formal gestalt structure. I have suggested that their structure is a secondary revision imposed on the truly unconscious undifferentiated matrix below them. [*ibid.*, p. 269]

Ehrenzweig develops his argument by criticizing the ego psychological approach, which disposes of the problem of unconscious form by attributing the entire aesthetic structure of art to the work of the conscious and preconscious mind—the secondary process—and this reduces the primary process of the unconscious to the "role of a purveyor of unstructured raw material, wild and destructive phantasies, that have first to be tamed and moulded by the secondary process in order to be aesthetically appreciated" (*ibid.*, p. 305). Although this interpretation may cohere with the facts of mental illness, where the intrusion of unconscious phantasy threatens the patient's sanity, Ehrenzweig believes that it "does not fit the facts of art", and he puts forward an alternative to Kris's ego psychological account of the value and role of the primary process. Where Kris regards creativity as a "regression at the service of the ego", Ehrenzweig's formula of creative activity involves a three-phased rhythm that may or may not result in the creation of a specific art object. His notion of the creative process was largely informed by Freud's dual instinct theory, one that was developed more fully in the work of Melanie Klein. This model views the dynamic interplay between the life and death instincts, and the structural role of Kleinian unconscious phantasy, as the basis of all human endeavour. In Chapter Five, we shall explore how Ehrenzweig's idea of creative rhythm was significantly shaped by this Kleinian model of the mind, as well as the developments in British School pioneered by post-Kleinian analysts such as Milner, Winnicott, and Bion. (Ehrenzweig [1967] describes this three-phased creative process thus: first, there is an initial *fragmentation* of reality, followed by the "manic-oceanic" de-differentiation of these fragments into a *receiving womb* within the unconscious, and then an eventual *re-integration* of fragmented reality into the new structure, which may or may not result in the creation of a physical object *per se*. See Chapter Five, below.)

We have seen that the aesthetics of classical psychoanalysis are essentially grounded in the belief that the artwork is the manifestation of the creator's unconscious desires. Classical criticism relates the work back to the author's psyche, which is explored via the analysis of his earliest childhood experiences, and the analysis of "typical" symbols that recur in the work. Despite its neglect of the formal structure of the artwork, such an approach can be useful in illuminating the artist's unconscious phantasies and preoccupations. The ego psychologists, such as Kris, oppose this classical view of art as a neurotic, infantile wish that becomes embedded in the artwork. They believe that the pleasure of art derives from a controlled play with infantile material that is thereby transformed into something *publicly shareable*. This approach differs from Freud's theory of creativity as neurosis, in that what is pleasurable is not infantile wish-fulfilment, but the fact of bringing the primary process into action for the ego's needs.

The models of Kris and Ehrenzweig are supported by Freud's second topography of the psyche. In the first model, Freud thought of the ego as entirely equivalent to the conscious and preconscious; the instinctual energies were confined to the unconscious. The second model, elaborated in *The Ego and the Id* (1923b), suggests that the ego developed from the instinctual energies derived from bodily sensations, there being, therefore, no logical boundary between the ego and the unconscious. Similarly, the superego also has an unconscious component. With the second model, a deciphering of the unconscious does not involve a strict interpretation, but must take into account the interplay between unconscious and conscious systems. Forces operative in the id are also operative in the ego and superego. Thus, the simplistic conscious–unconscious, id–ego boundaries cannot be maintained; it is the ego that performs a mediating role between both. Where id psychology privileges the instinctual drives and related phantasies, ego psychology looks at the way the fantasies are manipulated by the psyche. Ego psychology largely concerns itself with psychic mechanisms that mediate the relationship between the ego and the id and the consequences this has for the artwork and audience. Although ego psychology has initiated developments in traditional Freudian aesthetics, it has not been able to address fully the intersubjectivity of aesthetic experience, nor does it look closely enough at the interplay between the instinctual forces in the psyche (the theory of the life and the death instincts) that Freud put forward in later speculative writings and that ground the Kleinian account of the mind. In *Beyond the Pleasure Principle* (1920g), Freud realizes that "the original opposition between the ego-instincts and the sexual instincts proved to be inadequate". He recasts it in the form of a new dichotomy, between the life and death instincts: the former including both sexual and survival instincts, the latter being the drive to return to the inanimate state—entropy. In the early 1930s, Klein developed Freud's theory of the silent death instinct and emphasized that, far from being silent, it is a significant clinical phenomenon, visible in the harsh, persecuting superego itself. (See Chapter Two, below.) The Kleinian (British School) view focuses on the psychic processes that mediate the relationship between the *self and the world*, and how these influence the formal aspects of art and aesthetic experience. Emphasis is put on what happens *between one psyche and another*, and on the interplay between artist and his medium, audience and the artwork.

Some of the important divergences between the ego-psychological approach and an aesthetic grounded in object relations theory are shown by the different emphases in the work of Kris and Ehrenzweig. Unlike the ego psychologists, Ehrenzweig took into account the interplay between the instincts, and did not reduce creativity to a notion of a "controlled regression". He held that the creative process involves a necessary psychic disintegration—both of the self and the image of what is loved in the external world— under the direct influence of Thanatos (the death instinct). The desire to rebuild the destroyed self and object through the forces of Eros (the life instinct) is the next stage in the process. In fact, Ehrenzweig did not discount ego psychology entirely. Like Kris, he believed that any psychoanalytic account of art should not be an analysis of the contents of id phantasy, but should engage with dynamic, economic, and structural influences, which lie in the domain of ego functioning. He also held that ego and id both evolve from the same undifferentiated matrix: infantile bodily sensations. The crucial difference between Ehrenzweig and Kris lies in the different roles they attribute to perception, and its relationship to the primary processes. Where Kris views perceptual mechanisms as being a part of the "conflict-free area of the ego", Ehrenzweig firmly believes that, far from being an autonomous ego function, perception is strongly implicated in the workings of the id. This view has important consequences for his account of creative perception, one that emphasizes the *libidinal* component involved.

However, Kris and Ehrenzweig do reach similar conclusions about the specific capacity of the artist. They agree that the primary process involves the deliberate reversion to a different, more childlike (syncretistic) way of functioning, where there is a special kind of interplay between the two levels of experience. Ehrenzweig sees this as part of a natural rhythm between various psychic layers, involving disruption and reintegration; Kris constructs a rather more rigid theoretical framework, construing all artistic activity in terms of a "controlled regression of the ego to the primary process". (For further analysis of the dialogue between Freud, Kris, and Ehrenzweig, see Chapter Five, below.) Ehrenzweig further links the role of the primary process with the death instinct—the destructive force that will allow the "eventual death and rebirth of constructive, ordered reality through Eros". He emphasizes the influence of instinctual life on perceptual experience and the way that unconscious phantasies structure our perception of reality. However, this raises questions of how objects come to be selected for perception in the first place. One way Ehrenzweig tackles this is to regard the disintegration of the ego as not a wholly regressive experience, taking an opposing view to that of Kris, who does not give the unconscious a sufficiently constructive role in the creative process. Where Kris thinks of the primary process as a regression to primitive phantasies, Ehrenzweig postulates a developing unconscious that turns disruption and chaos into constructive, ordered experience. It is called "unconscious scanning", an activity where both the ego and id sort from an undifferentiated matrix of experience, a process where rational preconceptions are temporarily suspended. This phenomenon (to be explored more fully in Chapter Six) has also been identified by Marion Milner in her analysis of the "wide focus" and "diffuse stare" characteristic of artistic perception.

In this chapter, we have explored the extent to which the development of a "British School psychoanalytic aesthetic" has helped to redress the balance between the pathographical approach of classical id psychoanalysis and the limitations of ego psychology. The developments by Klein and her School have led to an approach to art that is well equipped to explore the interplay between unconscious, instinctual energies and both the creation and appreciation of art. It does not rely on psychobiographical interpretation and (like the ego psychologists) regards the artwork as the outcome of a *process*. However, as we have seen, Kris's aesthetics do not fully address the relationship between the artist and his medium, or the *intersubjectivity* of aesthetic experience. This is largely because such theorists regard the ego and the strengthening of its defences to be the *raison d'être* informing the psychoanalytic encounter, and the interplay between the life and death forces (the lifeblood of the Kleinian model) is not given a constructive role in creativity. Ehrenzweig's work builds upon the insights of ego psychology, together with a critique of Gestalt theory, to incorporate the insights of Freud's later writings, which were developed by Klein. His approach gives due significance to the interplay between instinctual energies and the structuring role of unconscious phantasy in art.

Overview

Freud's account of art is certainly stimulating, although incomplete and somewhat limited. He was a cultured man, well-read in philosophy and the classics, and an avid collector of antiquities. However, as his biographer Ernest Jones points out, he was not really concerned with what *makes* a work of art. Lionel Trilling, who had great respect for Freud, wrote that "he is always, I think, outside the process of literature. Much as he responds to the product, he does not really imagine the process. He does not have what we call the *feel* of the thing" (Trilling, 1955, p. 92).

Freud's approach to the understanding of art was limited by a number of factors. First, he over-emphasized the neurotic aspects of artistic experience, and his analysis of individual artists was fuelled largely by his need to develop and demonstrate the psychoanalytic theory he was working with at the time. He admitted that he was less able to deal with the formal and technical aspects of art, and that psychoanalysis was not yet able to delve into the "innermost secret" of the artist's "mysterious ability". Although he did not elaborate his joke theory fully for the understanding of art and aesthetic value, he did realize its significance and potential.

However, Freud's theory of the primary process and his analysis of the related structure of the joke have laid the foundations for a psychoanalytic approach to art and creativity which can address the formal aspects of art, as well as the way they shape the reception of its content. This has had important consequences for psychoanalytic aesthetics, particularly through the work of Kris and Ehrenzweig. Their contributions demonstrate how Freud's theory of the primary process and the joke structure have offset the pathographical model with which Freud (and classical psychoanalytic criticism) is associated. As I shall show in more depth in Chapter Five, both Kris and Ehrenzweig—with differing emphasis—demonstrate that psychoanalysis can address the nature of creative work without recourse to "wild analysis" and delving too deeply into the psychopathology of the artist.

Chapters Two and Three will explore the valuable contributions that Kleinian theory makes to psychoanalytic aesthetics—largely through forging a link between the formal, specifically *aesthetic* elements of art (aspects which orthodox psychoanalysis largely ignored) and specific psychic mechanisms. With its focus on the formal, structuring role of our unconscious phantasy life as well as its content, Kleinian theory is well equipped to explore the artist's relationship to his medium and also the viewer's encounter with the aesthetic object.

For orthodox psychoanalysis, art interpretation was modelled on the paradigm of dream interpretation as the piecemeal analysis of individual symbols. Naturally, this was impractical, for it demanded access to biographical information, so that art interpretation became a form of detective work. As we will see, Klein and her co-workers re-evaluated not only the significance of symbols, but also the process of symbol formation itself (the mechanism responsible for all art, dream, and phantasy) and its developmental role. With this new account, it is not so much the meaning of individual symbols or phantasies that are paramount, but how psychic mechanisms are themselves implicated in symbolic activity. So, rather than analysing what is "in" the dream or "in" the artwork, Kleinian theory explores what *the activity of making and experiencing art means to both artist and spectator*. One could say that the concern is not so much with the pattern, but more with the structure of the fabric itself upon which the pattern is printed.

PART II

KLEIN'S CONTRIBUTION TO THE AESTHETICS OF THE BRITISH SCHOOL

CHAPTER TWO

Essentials of Kleinian theory

Klein significantly contributed to the refinement of psychoanalytic aesthetics, although she did not actually develop a fully articulated theory of her own as such. She was interested in art and literature and, like Freud, drew on them for the exegesis of her clinical theory, and three of her earlier papers were specifically devoted to the analysis of artistic and creative themes.

At the same time, these foreshadowed what were to be some of her most important concepts: the depressive position (1930) and her account of the inner world and unconscious phantasy. However, as will be shown in the next chapter, it was her pupil Hanna Segal (Klein's main expositor) who first developed a systematic theory of creativity and aesthetics based on Klein's insights. Another important exponent of Kleinian aesthetics was the art critic and historian Adrian Stokes. He was also an analysand of Klein, and successfully integrated Klein's account of infantile experience into his aesthetic criticism. It was largely through the work of Segal and Stokes that Kleinian aesthetics became fully established as a coherent approach to the visual arts and, as we shall explore further in this study, has continued to influence a number of philosophers, writers, and academics.

Segal divides Klein's work into three main phases. The first phase, spanning the years from 1921 to 1932, laid the foundations of child analysis, tracing the Oedipus complex and superego to early developmental roots. The second phase led to the formulation of the concept of the "depressive position" and the manic defences, described in Klein's papers "A contribution to the psychogenesis of the manic depressive states" (1935) and "Mourning and its relation to manic-depressive states" (1940). The third phase was concerned with the earliest stage, which she called the "paranoid–schizoid position", mainly formulated in her paper "Notes on some schizoid mechanisms" (1946) and in her book, *Envy and Gratitude* (1988b). In this chapter I shall explore how Klein's model evolved from Freudian theory, in order to see in what way it laid the foundations for a fuller theory of aesthetics. After a summary of some of the political disruptions and upheavals that formed the background to her achievements in the British School, I shall focus on the ideas formulated since 1930 that have been significant for the understanding of art and creativity. These are the related concepts of symbol formation; unconscious phantasy and the inner world, her theory of the paranoid–schizoid and depressive positions, and the theory of innate envy. Although I have separated these elements, they are, of course, closely interlinked and it is inevitable that any discussion of them will involve some repetition.

The Kleinian development

In September 1926, Melanie Klein moved from Berlin to settle in London at the behest of Ernest Jones, who was the president of the British Psychoanalytical Society at the time. In the year preceding her journey to Britain, Klein had suffered the death of her analyst, Karl Abraham, who had provided her with much of the emotional and intellectual support that she needed. The loss of her analyst, combined with the failure of her marriage, were no doubt precipitating factors in Klein's decision to move to Britain.[1] Freud had left the area of child analysis largely unexplored; even his analysis of "Little Hans" had largely been conducted via the boy's father rather than through any real contact with the child. Klein's work, which concentrated on child analysis, had been introduced to the Society by Alex Strachey a year before and had caused much interest, particularly since this subject was becoming much more active. The analysts Sylvia Payne, Susan Isaacs, and Nina Searle, who were all professionally trained in child education and psychology, had already presented papers to the British Society on the theoretical and technical problems in child analysis, so the time was certainly ripe for Klein's arrival in London.

Klein's first point of departure from classical analysis was her treatment of children's play as the equivalent of adult free association. Through her close study of children's play, usually with little wooden toys, she revealed the presence in very young children of complex systems of phantasy that had not been conceived of before (see the section headed "Unconscious phantasy and the inner world", below). These were sometimes consciously reported but were usually inferred by Klein from the child's play. Naturally, no data were received directly from the children under two years old, but Klein saw good reason to infer systems of unconscious phantasy in the early weeks and months of life. (Here we should distinguish between "phantasy" as distinct from "fantasy". The latter suggests day-dreaming, whim, or caprice, where the former connotes something thought of as deeper, such as imagination or a visionary experience [see Rycroft, 1968b].) Then, in the late 1920s and the early 1930s, Klein began to be more definite about the dating of the origin of neuroses. She took this back in time much earlier than Freud, placing the origins of the Oedipus complex in the earliest months of life (Klein, 1929). If this triadic set of relationships comes so early, it could not have been developed over time in a family setting, as in Freud's account. For Klein, it was much more deeply rooted in infantile psychic functioning and structure.

Klein was very interested in the individual's relation to objects, and it is for this reason that she is called an "object-relations theorist". But she was more interested in early instinctual impulses and their influence on *inner* objects than in the details of how real external objects might contribute to phantasies and to psychopathology in general. Indeed, this came to be one of the focuses of contention with the Independents, and in particular Klein's pupil, the paediatrician, Donald Winnicott, whose "debate" with Klein in 1952 over the status of his concept of the "transitional object" polarized their respective views on early infantile experience and had profound consequences for their respective accounts of art and creativity. It also led to their parting company.

In 1927, Anna Freud and Klein came to blows over a number of issues, relating particularly to the technique of child analysis. The main difference between the two women concerned their respective views on the feasibility of the psychoanalytic method for treating children and the nature of the therapeutic relationship. Anna Freud believed that the play technique was not the equivalent of adult free association; neither did she regard it as a compulsion to repeat anxiety situations. Because Klein's interpretations of the play could not be confirmed, Anna Freud argued that the early analysis of children was neither appropriate nor possible. Indeed, she thought that probing into a child's unconscious might even aggravate his condition and make him psychologically unstable. Klein, however, was interested in probing these deeper recesses of the mind, and wanted to expose the roots of anxiety rather than just alleviating the symptoms, which she saw as only superficial indicators of the turmoil beneath. Klein fiercely rebutted Anna Freud's criticisms and claimed that the latter's technique was not truly analytic. She also asserted that Anna's method did not expose the Oedipal conflict— surely a devastating attack to make on Freud's daughter! Klein produced a large amount of clinical support for her technique and claimed that interpreting the child's anxiety often cleared it up completely. She felt that her technique was more truly analytical in its stress on the importance of interpreting the transference. Klein was accused by the Anna Freudian camp of making "wild interpretations" of the child's play. This she strongly denied, and insisted that she always had evidence of the link between the figure in the play and the primary object (usually the mother's body) before interpreting. Maybe the criticisms were somewhat justified, however, for, as Kleinian analyst Hinshelwood has noted, in her papers Klein frequently omits to give the actual links that came out in the sessions with patients (Hinshelwood, 1989, pp. 26–27).

The result of these hostile exchanges was a polarization of opinions between the Viennese analysts and those who followed Klein in London. They were a foretaste of the bitter feuds that were to disrupt the British Society in the early 1940s, during what became known as the "Controversial Discussions" (King & Steiner, 1992).

By the mid-1930s, Klein was turning her investigations to the part played by destructiveness—derived from the death instinct—and to the importance of remorse and concern about this in both normal and pathological development. Klein made a great theoretical leap when she introduced the concept of the "depressive position" (Klein, 1935, 1940). This has become a significant part of British psychoanalytic thinking and also in the elaboration of Kleinian aesthetics and the account of creativity. For the first time, Klein distinguished between two kinds of anxiety: paranoiac (later called persecutory) and depressive. This is a fundamental distinction and the beginning of her true metapsychological break from Freud, whose physiological and economic models did not accord with her own ways of seeing development. The Darwinian language of Freud was couched in mechanistic, linear terms. Klein's reformulation of psychoanalytic models, describing the processes of development in terms of *positions*, rather than in the classical terms of psycho-sexual stages (oral, anal, phallic, genital), was of enormous impact. It implies that the notion of development is a fluid, dynamic, and an ongoing process, oscillating between two ways of relating to objects—the paranoid or the depressive mode. In addition, Klein introduced a new opposition into psychoanalysis: the difference between the relation to a *part-object* and the relation to a *whole-object*.

According to Klein, the depressive position is reached when the infant realizes that his or her love and hate are directed to the same object: the mother and her body. The child begins to experience ambivalence (e.g., the same object can be both loved and hated) and also his own effects upon another object. Klein was the first to point to the importance of the unconscious impulse to repair objects felt to have been damaged by destructive attacks of hate. This is inherent in depressive feeling. Klein believed that anxiety originated in aggression, and she regarded this as fundamentally innate and grounded in the projection of the death instinct outwards from the self. This emphasis on anxiety, internal danger threats, and the workings of the death instinct were to have important consequences for her formulation of the concept of phantasy and also the nature of creativity. Indeed, Klein was to suggest that true artistic and creative activity were both rooted in anxiety and the urge to make good the destructive and sadistic phantasies set in motion by the death instinct. It was not until just over ten years later that Klein was to turn her interest fully towards schizoid phenomena and developed her account of the "paranoid–schizoid" position (Klein, 1946).

In the meantime, between Klein's formulation of the depressive position in 1935 and the account of the paranoid–schizoid position in 1946, events in both Klein's personal life and in Europe were becoming more unstable. When Hitler invaded Austria in 1938 it became unsafe for Jewish analysts to stay in Vienna. So, Jones and the other members of the British Society arranged for thirty-eight Viennese analysts, including Freud and his daughter, to come to London. At this time, the relationship between Klein and her daughter, Melitta, also a member of the British Society, was becoming increasingly hostile. Another trauma Klein faced was the death of her son, Hans, in April 1934; he had apparently fallen from a precipice while out walking. Melitta's immediate reaction was that it had been suicide, although their brother Eric strongly repudiated this and maintained that Hans's death was a source of grief to Klein throughout her life. Once again, death and grief had shattered Klein's world and must have acted as a contributory factor in her preoccupation with the nature of grief, loneliness, mourning, loss, and despair—experiences that formed a gloomy coda to her own private life. For all that, it must be said that she would eventually come to emphasize the power of love over hate, the processes of reparation and the triumph of gratitude over envy.

We get an inkling of the personal experience that underlies her theories expressed in her paper "Mourning and its relation to manic-depressive states" (1940). Here she describes how a "Mrs A", who had suffered the loss of her son, had gone for a walk in the town in the attempt to re-establish old social bonds. Klein describes vividly and poignantly the anxiety and chaos felt by the woman who, feeling overwhelmed by the streets and experiencing them as alien and removed from the flux of life, had retreated into a quiet restaurant. But there she had felt "as if the ceiling were coming down" (Klein 1988a, p. 361) and the only place of security "seemed to be her own house" (*ibid.*). The "frightening indifference" of the external world was "reflected in her internal objects" (*ibid.*), which had turned persecutory. It is truly a moving piece of writing, one that speaks of lived experience, most poignantly expressed by the feeling that "trust in real goodness had gone" (*ibid.*, p. 00).

Disagreements with the Kleinians and the need for a revision in the constitution in favour of limiting tenure of offices and the possibility of holding multiple offices in the Society precipitated the "Controversial Discussions" in the early 1940s. It was also felt by the analyst John Rickman that the Society was not sufficiently attuned to the public and failed to respond to its needs. A series of meetings was held over eighteen months, and four papers were discussed on the controversial aspects of Klein's theories, including one very important contribution from Isaacs (1948) on the nature of phantasy. Unfortunately, no theoretical agreements were worked out in the Scientific Meetings, and the hoped-for clarification did not materialize. In fact, divergences became even more polarized as a result. Jones resigned in 1944 as president, and Sylvia Payne took over. During the war, the paediatrician and psychoanalyst Donald Winnicott became the representative spokesman for the Society. Although he had aligned himself with the Kleinian Group and supported Klein's position throughout the Discussions, he did his best to remain impartial. In an amusing anecdote which reveals much about Winnicott's personality, the analyst Margaret Little recalls that in the first Scientific Meeting of the "Controversial Discussions" that she attended, there were

> bombs dropping every few minutes and people ducking as each crash came. In the middle of the discussion someone I later came to know as D.W. stood up and said, "I should like to point out that there is an air raid going on," and sat down. No notice was taken, and the meeting went on as before!. [Little, 1985, p. 24]

This is certainly an interesting remark from the analyst who was to emphasize in his work the need to acknowledge the realities and pressures of the external world—a position which eventually distanced him from Klein, as we shall explore later in this chapter.

In 1946, the Society agreed to the introduction of two distinct courses to be referred to as "Course A", whose teachers were drawn from both groups (it later became known as the "Middle" or "Independent" Group), and "Course B", which would teach along the lines of Anna Freud, although both courses would be under one training committee that would be responsible for the selection and training of students. Thus, the Society became semi-officially split into three groups, which still exist today: those loyal to Klein; those loyal to the Classical approach of Anna Freud; and the Independents, who took issue with aspects of both Kleinian and Classical theory and have developed an alternative body of thinking within the British School. (See Rayner, 1990 for a detailed exposition of their differences and similarities.) As stated earlier, my understanding of the "British School" encompasses the Kleinians and a number of those working in Independent territory.

Symbols and symbol formation

Klein's work has contributed to developments in the theory of symbolism both directly, through her work on symbols, and indirectly, through the conceptual implications of her contribution to the theory of early mental states. The papers that establish a new trend in the analysis of symbols were written between 1923 and 1930, when she formulated the main aspects of her technique and metapsychology. Of particular significance are "Early analysis" (1923) and "The importance of symbol-formation in the development of the ego" (1930). Since then, her ideas have been developed by clinicians such as Segal (1952), Milner (1952), Bion (1962), and Rycroft (1962). Klein's work with children on a pre-verbal level was a great step forward in the development of psychoanalysis. She regarded children's play as highly symbolic, expressive of the inner world of phantasy that tinges every aspect of intellectual and emotional life, and equivalent to adult free association, dreams, and symptoms. Klein believed that in their play

> children represent symbolically phantasies, wishes and their experiences. Here they are employing the same language, the same archaic, phylogenetically acquired mode of expression as we are familiar with in dreams. We can only fully understand it if we approach it by the method Freud has evolved for unravelling dreams. Symbolism is only a part of it; if we want rightly to comprehend children's play . . . we must take into account not only the symbolism which often appears so clearly in their games, but also the means of representation and the mechanisms employed in dream-work. [Klein, 1988a, p. 134]

Dreams were allowed by Freud as a symbolic alternative to words for the discharge of mental energy—allowed because both words and dreams avoid recourse to muscular action. Klein, however, showed that play was as symbolic as words, even though it involved muscular discharge. Phantasy was not necessarily an alternative method of discharge to bodily action, as Freud had been content to leave it; it was a profoundly important concomitant, if not the mainspring, of the physical discharge of energy. This point is important because it suggests how the muscular activity—the actual physical business involved in much artistic work—can be itself symbolic. Unconscious phantasy has its roots in bodily processes and is inextricable from our corporeality—our physical sensations, bodily processes out of which the ego is formed. This in fact goes back to Freud, who himself suggested that the ego was "first and foremost a body-ego" (1923b).

Klein's focus on the importance of unconscious phantasy as constituting both the content and mechanism (form) of psychological processes had a profound influence on the developmental study of symbolic processes and the nature of art and creativity. The notion of phantasy as an inherent tendency of the mind, and the idea that symbol formation is a uniquely human achievement, brings Kleinian theory in line with the semiotics and aesthetics of the American pragmatic philosophers, Susanne Langer (1942, 1953, 1967) and Charles S. Peirce. (For a discussion of the relationship between the semiotics of Peirce and the study of creativity in general, see Anderson [1987]. For a specific application of Peirce to the work of the Kleinian analyst, Bion, see Silver [1981].) In the early part of her career, Klein charted the vicissitudes of symbol formation and the causes and effects of defective symbolization, and she showed that from the earliest stages the infant begins to search for symbols in order to relieve himself of painful experiences. The conflicts and persecution in phantasy from primal objects (i.e., the mother's body) promote a search for new, conflict-free relationships with substitute objects (symbols). Nevertheless, these conflicts tend to follow and often affect the relationship with the substitute symbol, which eventually promotes further search for yet another substitute. Klein described a substitution similar to displacement, which Freud also believed to be one of the underlying factors in dream symbolization. Substitution of one object for another becomes symbol formation in the narrower sense, when a non-material object of satisfaction is substituted for a physical object of direct bodily gratification.

Klein draws on a number of analytic theories to support her theory of symbolization: Ferenczi's idea that identification is the precursor of symbolism, arising out of the baby's endeavour to rediscover in every object his own organs and their functioning; Jones' (1916) view that the pleasure principle allows two very different things to be equated due to a similarity marked by pleasure or interest; and on her own conclusion, reached in 1923, that "symbolism is the foundation of all sublimation and of every talent since it is by way of symbolic equation that things, activities, and interest become the subject of 'libidinal phantasies'" (Klein, 1988a, p. 220). The earliest forms of symbol formation are symbolic equations and identifications. Alongside the libidinal interest, it is the anxiety arising in the early stages of sadism that activates the mechanism of identification. This is because the child wishes to destroy the organs (penis, vagina) standing for the objects (felt to be contained in the mother's body) that later cause him dread. This anxiety spurs him on to equate these organs with other things, and, in turn, these become objects of anxiety. He is impelled to make new and other equations that "form the basis of his interest in the new objects and of symbolism". Klein concludes that not only does symbolism come to be the foundation of all phantasy and sublimation, but, more than that, it is the basis of the subject's relation to the outside world and to reality. So, although in her earlier papers Klein viewed anxiety as an inhibitor of development, during the 1920s she gradually came to believe that development was dependent on the resolution of anxiety, and by the time she published her paper "Infantile anxiety situations" (1929), she saw anxiety as the spur to creative achievement. As the ego develops, a true relation to reality is gradually established. Both ego development and perception of reality depend upon the ego's capacity to withstand the pressure of the earliest anxiety situations; and a certain amount of anxiety is needed for an abundance of symbolic activity and phantasy life (Klein, 1988a, pp. 220–221).

In the paper on symbol development, published just after this, Klein argued that the working-through of anxiety is the precondition of all development. "The importance of symbol-formation in the development of the ego" (1930) elaborates her embryonic theory of symbol formation (Klein, 1998a, pp. 219–233: this paper articulates core concepts that became the basis of her theory of the paranoid–schizoid position and formed the precursor to her fuller articulation of the concept of projective identification in 1946). Its clinical material begins a new phase, for it is the first published report of the analysis of a psychotic child, and shows that it is possible to make analytic contact and set development in train, even where a child has no speech or manifest emotion and displays only a very primitive kind of symbolism. Klein's paper examines the nature of childhood psychosis, and is an attempt to identify the origins of schizophrenia. She suggests that the ego defends itself from intense anxiety by an excessive expulsion of its sadism, so that there remains no experience of anxiety and no exploration of the world through symbol formation: thus, normal development is halted.

In this paper she describes four-year-old Dick, in whom there was an unusually inhibited ego development. His emotional and intellectual level was comparable to that of a fifteen- to eighteen-month-old child. Dick manifested signs of what we would now call autistic behaviour: adaptation to reality and emotional relations were almost absent, he was devoid of affects, indifferent to the presence or absence of his mother or nurse, and he did not play. Despite criticisms that Klein often overlooked the role of the environment at the expense of the inner world, she took into careful account Dick's environmental situation and family history. This revealed that he had experienced difficulty in accepting the breast very early on, and had almost died of starvation. Apparently, no real love had been shown by his parents or his first nurse. However, his grandmother and the second nurse were caring towards the child, and their influence contributed to his development. He attained better control of his bodily functions, showing a certain amount of ambition and apprehension. But Dick had still failed to make emotional contact with anyone. Klein says that his inhibitions derived from the earliest period of his life, and together with a "constitutional incapacity to tolerate anxiety" (*ibid.*, p. 224), his ego had ceased to develop a phantasy life. He had no interests except "trains, stations and also in door-handles, doors, and the opening and shutting of them" (*ibid.*). Klein interpreted this as relating to the "penetration of the penis into the mother's body": what had halted symbol formation was the "dread of what would be done to him ... after he had penetrated into the mother's body" (*ibid.*). His defences against aggression had put a stop to his development as he was rendered incapable of feeling anxiety or aggression at all—this was shown in his eating difficulty and in his inability to grasp sharp implements, like knives and scissors.

The fundamental problem facing Klein was the lack of symbolic material in the start of the analysis—unlike her other patients, Dick was completely indifferent to the toys she provided. Her usual procedure was to refrain from interpreting material until it had found expression in various representations, but with Dick she had to modify her technique. In order to make contact with his unconscious, she set out immediately to activate his repressed anxiety. Klein put two trains side by side, and told him that the larger one was the "Daddy-train" and the smaller one the "Dick-train". He rolled the latter to the window and said "Station". Klein interpreted to him that the station was "mummy", and "Dick is going into mummy". At this point, Dick left the train and shut himself into the space between the outer and inner doors of the room, saying "dark", and ran out again. He repeated this a few more times. Klein was thus able to create a symbolic setting for Dick, so that he could represent his anxieties and aggression. Out of this came a capacity to show interest in his surroundings and also a sense of dependence. Klein had managed to gain access to his unconscious by getting in touch with the very rudimentary symbolic activity he displayed. This resulted in a lowering of latent anxiety, which allowed a certain amount of it to become manifest. As he turned away from his objects of anxiety, he turned his aggressive and epistemophilic impulses towards new ones. His vocabulary enlarged and he made efforts to communicate with others. This case illustrated that even an undeveloped ego, such as Dick's, was adequate for establishing contact with the unconscious, and this established Klein's belief in the possibility of a psychoanalytic treatment of the psychoses.

Although the role of symbol development remained implicit in her work, Klein's interest in it waned as she became more interested in "defining the contents of phantasies, rather than in the nature of the process of their expression" (see Hinshelwood, 1989, p. 430).

Hanna Segal greatly refined Klein's account of symbols. She drew attention to two different kinds of symbolization, the "symbolic equation" and the "symbolic representation", which she came to associate with the paranoid–schizoid and the depressive position, respectively (Segal, 1952, 1957). A very elegant clinical example is given to illustrate the difference between the two kinds of symbol:

> Patient A was a schizophrenic in a mental hospital. He was once asked why he had stopped playing the violin since his illness. He replied with some violence, "Why? do you expect me to masturbate in public?" Another patient, B, dreamed one night that he and a young girl were playing a violin duet. He had associations to fiddling, masturbating, etc., from which it emerged clearly that the violin represented a masturbation phantasy of a relation with the girl. [Segal, 1986, p. 49]

Segal points out that, although these two patients seem to use the same symbols in the same situation (the violin representing the male genital and playing with it representing masturbation), the symbols are actually functioning very differently. For A, playing the violin was felt to be the *same* as masturbating, and the anxiety aroused by this halted his playing. For B, playing the violin was an important *sublimation*, and it was only through free-associating to his dream that the meaning of the symbol became clear. In the first case, the violin was felt to *be* the genital (symbolic equation), and in the second, to *represent* it (symbolic representation). It is interesting to note that Ehrenzweig feels that Segal's term "symbolic equation" is "not a very happy choice". With Patient A, "what happens is neither symbolic nor an equation", it is rather that "one thing has pushed itself into the place of another because it refused to be equated with it" (Ehrenzweig, 1967, p. 194). Ehrenzweig believes that the term "symbolic equation" fits better his notion of the "unconscious substructure of creative work where symbol and symbolised object freely interpenetrate without doing each other violence" (*ibid.*).

Segal argues that Jones' (1916) belief that symbols are formed when there is no sublimation is inaccurate; the classical distinction between symbolization and sublimation becomes untenable in the light of Klein's work. This has confirmed that when a desire is given up because of a conflict and is repressed, it may express itself in a symbolic way, and the object of desire can be replaced by a symbol. Klein's analysis of children's play—a sublimation—showed that this activity expresses unconscious wishes, anxiety, and is developmentally very important. For Freud and Jones, symbolization was an archaic, primitive, essentially regressive phenomenon that led away from reality towards wish fulfilment, under the domination of the pleasure principle. Klein's approach placed a whole new perspective on the matter; now symbolization was regarded as essential to the development of a reality sense.

This has repercussions for their respective approaches to art and creativity. The classical view of symbols led to the view that art—a symbolic activity *par excellence*—was a wish-fulfilment and had little to do with ego development and the establishment of a reality sense. For Freud, the artist is distinguished from the neurotic in that he somehow finds a way back to reality in spite of his creative activity, whereas for Klein and Segal, it is through his creative capacity that the artist is able to establish a harmony between the inner and outer world. While Freud regarded the source of the artist's creative capacity as somewhat of a mystery, the Kleinian view places it firmly within the context of fundamental developmental processes that establish a rich, communicative phantasy life and a realistic relationship to the external world. In "The function of dreams", Segal summarizes her account of the relationship between symbolization and development:

> When projective identification is in ascendance and the ego is identified and confused with the object, then the symbol, a creation of the ego, becomes identified and confused with the thing symbolised . . . giving rise to concrete thinking. Only when separation and separateness are accepted [in the working-through of the depressive position] does the symbol become a representation of the object rather than being equated with the object. [1986, p. 90]

To Jones' (1916) formulation that "only what is repressed needs to be symbolised" (p. 116), Segal's emphasis is that only what is *adequately mourned* can be adequately symbolised. The capacity for non-concrete symbol formation is thus seen as an achievement of the ego that underlies the formation of phantasy, dreams, play, art, and all varieties of intellectual and creative achievement. Segal makes the point that successful artists "have an acute reality sense" (1986, p. 197) and are able to combine their mastery of the materials with a capacity to express their internal world through the chosen medium. This point is further developed in the aesthetics of the art historian Stokes (see Chapter Three). Segal's account characterizes the relationship between the ego and the object (in this case, the artist and his material) as one of working-through the depressive position. In this view, the thing symbolized and the object representing the thing symbolized are clearly separate and there is an acknowledgement of the object's qualities and a respect for its independent existence.

Unconscious phantasy and the inner world

Hanna Segal points out that "Freud's discovery of unconscious thoughts underlying hysterical symptoms can be seen as the equivalent to the discovery of unconscious phantasy" (1991, p. 16). His view that hysterical symptoms are not attached to actual memories but to phantasies erected on the basis of memories illustrates the importance Freud attached to fantasy and its role in structuring past experiences. (See his analysis of the "Wolf Man", 1918b; and "Dora", 1905e.) When he abandoned the seduction hypothesis in the late 1890s, sexual fantasies replaced sexual experience in his revised account of hysteria. But it was not until his "Formulations on the two principles of mental functioning" (1911b) that he tried to find a place for fantasy in his mental apparatus:

> In the psychology which is founded on psycho-analysis we have become accustomed to taking as our starting point the unconscious mental processes [...] We consider these to be the older, primary processes, the residues of a phase of development in which they were the only kind of mental process. The governing purpose obeyed by these primary processes is easy to recognise; it is described as the pleasure–unpleasure principle or more shortly, the pleasure principle ... [*ibid.*, pp. 218–219, 222]

With the introduction of the reality principle, one species of thought activity was split off; it was kept free from reality testing and remained subordinated to the pleasure principle alone. This activity is phantasying, which begins already in children's play, and later, continued as daydreaming, abandons dependence on real objects.

Even though Freud affirmed that there could be a species of phantasy that never became conscious at all, it did not hold centre stage for him as it did for Klein. Klein believed that phantasy and instinctual life were inseparable, bound up with introjective and projective mechanisms, together with the love and hate impulses, which she saw as operating from the very start of life. Unconscious phantasies are not the same as daydreams (though they are related to them), but are an activity of the mind that occurs on deep unconscious levels and accompanies every impulse experienced by the infant. In "Our adult world and its roots in infancy" (1959), one of Klein's more accessible papers, written for a wider audience, she outlines her view of unconscious phantasy and how it is inextricable from the notion of an inner world. The phantasy of orally incorporating an object (introjection) and expelling an object (projection) are closely bound up with the infant's capacity to project emotions (love and hate) on to the mother, making her into a good, as well as a hostile, dangerous object. Klein gives the example of a hungry baby who temporarily deals with his hunger by hallucinating the satisfaction of being given the breast, and being held and loved by the mother. But she adds that the unconscious phantasy also takes the opposite form of being deprived and persecuted by the breast, which refuses to give this satisfaction. The mechanisms of introjection and projection (mental processes grounded in instinctual life) are part of the infant's phantasies, which "help to mould his impression of his surroundings; and by introjection this changed picture of the external world influences what goes on in his mind" (1988b, p. 250). In this way, an inner world is constructed that is also a reflection of the external one. Unconscious phantasy does not only refer to the *content* of psychic experience, it also refers to the actual *mechanism* (the interaction of projection and introjection) that structures our inner life. Although rooted in infancy, this is not only an infantile process. It continues throughout every stage of life, and though it is modified in the course of maturation, it never loses its importance for the individual's relation to the world around him. Phantasies—becoming more elaborate and referring to a wider variety of objects and situations—continue throughout development and accompany all activities. Indeed, Klein stresses that "the influence of unconscious phantasy on art, on scientific work, and on the activities of every-day life cannot be overrated" (*ibid.*, p. 251).

The concept of unconscious phantasy received its most rigorous conceptual and philosophical elaboration through the work of Susan Isaacs, a staunch supporter of Klein. In "The nature and function of phantasy" (1948), read to the British Society during the "Controversial Discussions", Isaacs succinctly expressed the kernel of the theory thus: "phantasy is the primary content of unconscious mental processes" (*ibid.*, p. 81: for an account of the profound impact of these heated discussions on the politics and structure of the British Society, see King and Steiner, 1992). Where Freud saw phantasy occupying the vague frontier between the mental and the somatic, Isaacs stressed the non-physicality of instinct. Phantasy could then be seen as

> the mental corollary, the psychical representative of instinct . . . there is no impulse, no instinctual urge or response that is not experienced as unconscious phantasy [. . .] A phantasy represents the particular content of the urges or feelings (for example, wishes, fears, anxieties, triumphs, love or sorrow) dominating the mind at the moment. [Isaacs, 1948, pp. 81–82]

Klein believed that the operation of an instinct is expressed and represented in mental life by the phantasy of the satisfaction of that instinct by an appropriate object. Since instincts are active from birth, some primitive phantasy life is assumed to operate from the very beginning. Phantasies derive from two main sources. Primary phantasies are innate and wholly unconscious; they include knowledge of the nipple and mouth, innately conceived by the newborn for sucking. Isaacs anticipates a common objection to this view of an innate phantasy activity:

> It has sometimes been suggested that unconscious phantasies such as that of "tearing to bits" would not arise in the child's mind before he had gained the conscious knowledge that tearing a person to bits would mean killing him or her. Such a view does not

meet the case. It overlooks the fact that such knowledge is inherent in bodily impulses as a vehicle of instinct, in the aim of instinct, in the excitation of the organ, i.e. in this case, the mouth. [*ibid.*, pp. 93–94]

Second, she tells us that phantasies are largely of somatic origin, and an unconscious phantasy is a belief (conscious or unconscious) in the activity of concretely felt "internal objects".

This is a difficult concept to grasp, and one that underpins all Kleinian thinking. According to the theory, a somatic sensation brings along with it a mental experience that is interpreted as a relationship with an object that wishes to cause that sensation, and is loved or hated by the subject according to whether the object is well-meaning or has evil intentions (i.e., pleasant or unpleasant sensations). Thus, the unpleasant sensation is mentally represented as a relationship with a "bad" object that intends to attack the subject. For example, a baby who is hungry will experience unpleasant hunger pangs in his stomach. This will become mentally represented by the baby feeling a persecuting object actually in his stomach that wants to hurt him. (This is reflected in our language: for example, in the colloquialisms, "hunger is gnawing at me" and "having butterflies in the stomach". However, although we often use this kind of concrete description, the knowledge that our hunger is related to a bodily state is not suspended.) Conversely, when the infant is fed, his experience is of an object, which we can identify as the mother or her milk, but which the infant identifies as an object in his tummy, kindly disposed to cause pleasant sensations. After the feed, the fullness contributes to the blissful phantasy in which a wonderful, all-satisfying object is contained within. Through the phantasy of projection, the "bad" object is externalized, and through the phantasy of introjection, the "good" object is internalized. These defences relate to bodily processes in which substances (milk, faeces) pass through the ego boundaries. For example, the expulsion of excrement gives rise to bodily sensations that are interpreted as objects passing out of the internal world into the external. At a later stage, however, phantasy is less connected with bodily sensations, and with the onset of the "depressive position" (described below), the internal world becomes populated with more symbolic, rather than concretely felt, objects.

It is valid to question how the concept of unconscious phantasy relates to Freud's theory of the primary and secondary processes. In many ways, the Kleinian concept cuts across the boundaries between these two modes. This has led to criticism from those who wish to uphold the distinction between primary process thinking, characterized by the work of condensation and displacement, as in the logic and symbolism of dreams, and secondary process thinking, which respects the categories of space and time and is essentially linguistic, obeying the rules of formal logic. In Klein's metapsychology, unlike Freud's, unconscious phantasy is a primary, central activity. It is constantly working with *perception*, modifying as well as being modified by it. (This will be emphasized later by Ehrenzweig in his account of creativity.) Phantasies become increasingly complex with intellectual, emotional, and physical development. They are not only manifested in dreams, but underlie the form and the content of thinking, perception, and creativity. This supposes a conception of time and of mental activity that, according to orthodox psychoanalysis, is not supposed to occur in the unconscious, or in the first year of life. To counter these objections, Isaacs quotes passages from Freud that suggest that the view of a psychic apparatus possessing only a primary process is a fiction (see Freud, 1900a), and that some organization of functioning of the unconscious does exist. Isaacs claims that to allow oral wishes in the first year with conscious memory of the experiences—as Anna Freud had described in her writings—but to deny the function of phantasy, is theoretically inconsistent.

An important concept, linked to that of unconscious phantasy, is the idea of the "inner world". According to Klein, it is

> a complex object-world, which is felt by the individual, in deep layers of the unconscious, to be concretely inside himself, and I therefore use the term "internalised objects" and an "inner world". This inner world consists of innumerable objects taken into the ego, corresponding partly to the multitude of varying aspects, good and bad, in which the parents (and other people) appeared to the child's unconscious mind throughout various stages of his development. Further, they also represent the real people who are continually becoming internalised in a variety of situations provided by the multitude of ever-changing experiences as well as phantasied ones. In addition, all these objects are in the inner world in an infinitely

complex relation both with each other and the self. [1988a, pp. 362–363]

This inner world is, thus, a complex interaction between both inner and outer experience, but Klein stresses that it is the strength of the inner, unconscious phantasies that will determine just how aspects of the external world will become internalized within, or projected from, the psyche. There is a particularly poignant semi-autobiographical essay by Walter Pater that evokes beautifully "that process of brain building by which we are, each one of us, what we are"—the structuring of the child's inner world that Klein described some half a century later. Pater described how his protagonist, Florian, recaptures memories about his long-forgotten childhood home and the way that the material objects of his past and the feelings associated with them "had actually become a part; inward and outward being woven through and through each other into one inextricable texture" (Pater, 1878 [1898], pp. 147–169). Pater described this process by which "we see inwardly"—in Kleinian terms, it is our our inner phantasies informing and structuring our perception of outer objects and creativity. Klein writes in 1940 that when Freud formulated the notion of the superego as an internalization of the child's identification with the parents during the Oedipal phase, he was describing the notion of an inner world, under the sway of inner figures that represent both parts of the self and objects in the world. However, as we have seen, Klein believed that the superego was formed much earlier than Freud supposed, and that the mechanisms of projection and introjection exist from birth, leading to the "institution inside ourselves of loved and hated objects, who are felt to be 'good' and 'bad', and who are interrelated with each other and with the self: that is to say, they constitute an inner world" (Klein, 1988a, p. 362). These figures go to make up the superego, which Freud recognized as the voices and the influence of the actual parents established in the ego.

Klein's concept of the inner world is dramatically illustrated by her 1929 paper, "Infantile anxiety situations reflected in a work of art and the creative impulse". This is one of the few examples of her own aesthetic judgement at work, albeit motivated to explicate an aspect of her clinical theory. This paper is the first of the three in which Klein discusses artistic material—the other two being "On identification" (1955), and "Some reflections on the Oresteia" (1963). In it she gives an analysis of Ravel's operetta, *The Magic Word*, based on a Berlin newspaper review of its performance in Vienna. (For a reappraisal of Klein's paper, see Hindle, 2000.) Klein elaborates the dramatic preoccupation of the child's mind; the vivid way in which inner objects, the furniture of the mind, actually become personified and take on a dramatic life of their own. She points out how these inner figures of the child's world form a kind of narrative full of persecutors, feared and attacked, which is enacted on the stage, with an ensuing poignant state of pity. What is particularly striking is Klein's vivid account of the child's world, revealing an intuitive insight into the phantasy life of the child, one that is less apparent in the harsh, terse style of her clinical writings. At the start of the story, a little boy is denied oral gratification by his mother, who tells him that he will "have dry bread and no sugar" in his tea. This leads him to fly into a rage. He becomes aggressive and turns hostile towards objects inside his home: he breaks china, tries to stab a pet squirrel, and then he attempts to wrench the pendulum from the grandfather clock. However, the things he maltreated now take on a persecuting and malevolent life of their own: the armchair refuses to let him sit in it, the stove spits out a shower of sparks at him. The child tries to escape outside but wherever he goes, there are threatening and hostile forces directed towards him—there has been "a rent in the fabric of the world". The whole world of the little boy becomes turbulent, claustrophobic, and terrifyingly confused. However, the boy notices a squirrel that has been bitten; instinctively he takes pity on it and binds the wound. The child whispers the "magic word"—"Mama"—and the whole world changes towards him. All the creatures that have hated him are now kindly disposed towards him. He is restored to the human world of kindness and helping. Even the little animals cannot refrain from themselves calling out, "Mama" (Klein, 1988a, p. 211).

Klein's description of the little boy's world is one of the few instances when we see her actually "interpreting" an artwork; however, as with Freud, psychoanalytic theory takes priority, for she is concerned with the artwork only to the extent that it illustrates her theory of the inner world. But, where Freud (and the psycho-biographers) probably would have tended to interpret the story in terms of the writer's psychic life, or vice versa, Klein's account focuses on the ongoing psychic dynamics of the world of unconscious phantasy and the importance of the reparative drive for an accurate perception of reality. The focus is less on a piecemeal analysis of individual symbols than on a broader account of how the play itself represents the child's lively inner realm. Through her analysis of the opera, Klein also shows how the inner and the outer worlds are closely meshed: indeed, it would seem that the inner world largely supervenes on the outer realm, for the child's perception of his real mother depends on his capacity to acknowledge the reality of his inner world—in this case, his destructive attacks and aggressive impulses. The urge to restore wholeness brings about a major shift in the child's perception of the world, and in its perception of him.

After her analysis of the operetta, Klein concludes this paper by referring to an article by Karen Michaelis, titled "The empty space", which gives an account of the painter Ruth Kjär, whose painting—according to Klein—symbolized a working through of inner emptiness and depression, enabling the painter to mourn her dead mother. Here, for the first time, we see Klein linking the movement from aggression to the need for restitution (also illustrated by the operetta story), specifically with a process of visual creativity. Before Ruth had begun painting, there had been no evidence of any pronounced creative talent. According to the article, at times she was subject to bouts of depression and despair, described by Michaelis (and quoted by Klein) as follows:

> there was only one dark spot in her life. In the midst of the happiness which was natural to her she would suddenly be plunged into the deepest melancholy. A melancholy that was suicidal. If she tried to account for this, she would say something to this effect: "There is an empty space in me, which I can never fill!" [1988a, p. 215]

When a picture was removed from her lounge wall (it belonged to her brother-in-law, who was a professional painter) leaving an empty space, this released a huge wave of depression in Ruth, which, says Michaelis, seemed to coincide with the emptiness within her. However, the day after the picture had been removed, Ruth decided that she would buy some artist's materials, although she had not the faintest idea of how to use them, so that she could fill the persecuting, empty space on the wall with a something of her own. Apparently, when her husband returned home in the evening, he was confronted by a painting of a life-sized, naked negress, and he found it very hard to believe that it was actually her work! He asked his brother (the painter) to see it for himself, and he thought that it could only have been painted by an experienced painter. According to the article, after this successful first attempt, Ruth went on to paint several other "masterly" pictures and had them exhibited to the critics and the public.

Klein reflects on the meaning of the "empty space" within Ruth, connecting it with the feeling that there was something lacking inside her body. Klein relates this inner emptiness to what she had defined in her earlier (1929) paper, as the "most profound anxiety experienced by girls . . . equivalent of castration anxiety in boys". According to her theory, the little girl's sadistic wish to rob her mother of all the good things inside (father's penis, mother's babies) and to destroy the mother herself gives rise to the anxiety that the mother will retaliate and rob the little girl of the good things inside her body (especially phantasied children), and she fears that her body will be damaged and destroyed by mother's retaliatory attacks. In seeking an illustration for these ideas, Klein looks at the kinds of pictures that Ruth felt compelled to paint after the first picture of the negress. It is significant that they were all portraits of women—her sister, her mother, and also one of an old woman. Klein quotes Michaelis's description of these last two portraits, first the old woman and then the one of her mother:

> And now Ruth cannot stop. The next picture represents an old woman, bearing the mark of years and disillusionment. Her skin is wrinkled, her hair faded, her gentle tired eyes are troubled. She gazes before her with a disconsolate resignation of old age, with a look that seems to say: "Do not trouble me any more. My time is so nearly at an end!"

> This is not the impression we receive from Ruth's latest piece of work—the portrait of her Irish-Canadian mother. This lady has a long time before her before she must put her lips to the cup of renunciation. Slim, imperious, challenging, she stands there with a moonlight-coloured shawl draped over her shoulders: she has the

effect of a magnificent woman of primitive times, who could engage in combat with the children of the desert with her naked hands. What a chin! What force there is in her haughty gaze! The blank space has been filled. [Klein, 1988a, p. 217]

Michaelis's verdict implies that, through the painting of her mother, not only has the "empty space" of the canvas been filled, but also Ruth's inner emptiness (depression) has been worked through via the act of painting.

Klein regards it as obvious that the desire to make reparation, to make good the injury psychologically done to the mother as well as to restore herself, was at the root of Ruth's compelling urge to paint. Klein interprets that Ruth's picture of the frail old woman expressed "the primary, sadistic desire to destroy" her mother; "to see her old, worn out, marred" is also the cause of her need to represent her in full possession of her strength and beauty. By doing so, says Klein, "the daughter can allay her own anxiety and can endeavour to restore her mother and make her new through her portrait". Klein also adds that she has found in her analysis of children, "when the representation of destructive wishes is succeeded by an expression of reactive tendencies, we constantly find that drawing and painting are used as means to *restore* people" (*ibid.*, p. 218, my italic).

Klein's "Infantile anxiety situations" is a very significant paper, both from a clinical perspective and in terms of laying the foundation for a Kleinian aesthetic, as later taken up by Segal and others. For the first time she connects creativity with deep early anxieties, construing the urge to create as arising from the impulse to restore and repair the injured object after a destructive attack. She also looks specifically at visual creativity for the first time and at its relationship to depression and the desire for reparation. A few years later, this idea was to have a significant place in her theory of the depressive position, foreshadowing further formulations. For example, the observation that, in development, fear of an attacking mother gives way to fear of losing a real, loving mother, anticipates exactly Klein's later account of the change in anxiety content from the paranoid–schizoid to the depressive position. Through her analysis of Ravel's operetta and the artist Ruth Kjär, Klein was able to make connections between aggression, depression, and the ensuing desire for repairing a world damaged by one's own hostility. She demonstrates how a work of art can vividly depict the dynamics of the inner world and unconscious phantasy without recourse to knowledge (which may be either implied or empirical) of the artist's history. When greater attention is paid to the relationship between inner and outer realms, together with the implications of the child's sadistic and aggressive attacks directed to the mother's body, psychoanalytic criticism does not have to concern itself with unlocking the mysteries of the artist's psyche, nor does it have to regard the artwork as if it were a network of symbols waiting to be deciphered. The concept of the inner world remains a major theme in Klein's work, and lies at the heart of a Kleinian approach to art and aesthetics. Indeed, as Hinshelwood emphasizes, "art is an other world, and . . . it is the internal world described by Melanie Klein" (1989, p. 434).

The paranoid–schizoid and the depressive positions

As early as three months old, the child begins to recognize that the bad mother who frustrates him, and whom he has destroyed in phantasy many times, is also the good mother who tenderly meets his needs. It is this recognition that good and bad object are actually one that lies at the heart of what Klein calls the "depressive position" (Klein, 1935). By helping to alleviate the intensity of paranoid anxiety, loving parents may help this integrative process along. Nevertheless, Klein seems to understand the internal integration of the good and bad parental imagos as a normal developmental sequence, driven by the child's increasing cognitive maturity rather than by environmental factors. The depressive position involves both fear and concern regarding the fate of those whom the child has destroyed in phantasy. (It should be noted that while Klein, in her attempt to maintain continuity with Freud and Abraham, sometimes used the term position as though it were equivalent to a developmental stage, this is actually not the case. Her term "position" implies a psychological state of affairs, or relationship to objects, that can be returned to at any time.) The child attempts to resolve his depressive anxiety through reparation: the mother and others are repaired through restorative phantasies, and actions that symbolize love and reparation. If depressive anxiety is strong enough, it might lead the child to employ defences characteristic of the paranoid–schizoid position, such as splitting the mother once again into good and bad. By making mother bad, the child avoids his own guilt and depressive anxiety—these arising from the feeling that he has destroyed what he loves and needs.

The task of the child in the depressive position is to establish a solid relationship with good internal objects. On this foundation the rest of the ego is built. If the child fails to do this, he will be permanently vulnerable to depressive illness. New, more sophisticated defences emerge with the depressive position. In the paranoid–schizoid stage, the primary defences against persecutors are the splitting of good and bad objects, idealization, and violent expulsion, associated with projective identification. The depressive position entails the emergence of manic defences, particularly in its earliest stages. As Segal notes, dependence on the object and ambivalence are denied: the object is controlled omnipotently in phantasy and treated with either triumph or contempt, so that its loss is not so painful or frightening (Segal, 1973, p. 80). Sometimes, Klein refers to this as "manic reparation". This must be distinguished from reparation proper, which is not a defence against paranoid–schizoid and depressive anxieties, but, rather, expresses genuine concern for the object *qua* object. Whereas paranoid anxiety involves fear of destruction by persecutors, depressive anxiety fears for the fate of others—real and imagined—in the face of the child's own aggression and hate. As a result of his hostility, the child fears that he has damaged and destroyed all that is good in the world, as well as within himself. The child attempts to lessen guilt and anxiety through phantasies and actions, directed primarily towards the mother, that are restorative in nature. The child tries to recreate the other it has destroyed, first by phantasies of omnipotent reparation, later by affectionate and healing gestures towards real others, constituting the drive towards creative effort.

The kinds of depressive anxiety experienced by the child change as the depressive position is worked through. At the early stages of the depressive position, the love and concern for others seems primarily motivated by fear that the phantasied destruction of the good objects will also destroy the self. However, the concern for the fate of the object soon comes to reflect a genuine concern for the object as a separate entity, which Klein sees as stemming from the child's gratitude for the love it has received from his mother. The loss of a loved person is an experience that can reactivate early depressive anxiety later in life. (In her biography of Klein, Grosskurth [1987, pp. 215–216] observes that the sudden death of Klein's eldest son, Hans, in 1933, probably contributed to her interest in mourning and depression.) Freud argues that the work of mourning consists of reality testing in which the mourner comes to accept that the loved one is no longer there, but that life is still worth living. Klein adds a further perspective: the loss of a loved external object reactivates earlier depressive anxieties, in which the mourner fears he will lose his good internal objects as well. The mourner thus finds himself confronted with a catastrophic double loss, in which the threatened loss of his good internal objects leaves him exposed again to primitive paranoid fears of persecution. The reality testing that Freud talks of must be enlarged to include the vicissitudes of the inner world in order to determine if one's inner objects are secure and complete, even if the external ones have gone. If the mourner has worked through his original depressive position sufficiently well to do this, the experience of mourning can be of psychological benefit. In normal mourning, Klein says

> the individual is reinstating his actually lost loved object; but he is also at the same time re-establishing inside himself his first loved objects—ultimately the "good" parents—whom, when the actual loss occurred, he felt in danger of losing as well. It is by reinstating inside himself the "good" parents as well as the recently lost person, and by rebuilding his inner world, which was disintegrated and in danger, that he overcomes his grief, regains security, and achieves true harmony and peace. [1988a [1940], p. 369]

Although the paranoid–schizoid position precedes the depressive position, these positions actually coexist, or rather alternate, throughout life. Even quite normal individuals may show an ego organization characteristic of the paranoid–schizoid position when confronted with stress and loss, a manifestation that is not the same as regression to a previous developmental stage. Thus, one is not necessarily diagnosing a serious mental disorder by saying that an individual is operating in a paranoid–schizoid way, even though the emergence of a full-blown paranoid–schizoid position in an adult could be classed as a psychosis. In fact, Klein seems to have changed her view on the "positions" as time went by, as Meltzer points out. Where she had written of overcoming the depressive position, her later work emphasizes its attainment or preservation (Meltzer, 1978, pp. 10–11). This change of emphasis captures the essence of the depressive position more clearly. It is a developmental achievement that must be defended and regained throughout life, because stress, as well as depression itself, reinforce and activate the paranoid–schizoid defences.

Klein did not fully elaborate her views on the paranoid–schizoid position until 1946, eleven years after her formulation of the depressive position, even though she placed it as developmentally a prior phase. Klein characterizes the earliest organization of the defences as the "paranoid–schizoid position" in order to stress both the way in which the young child's fears take the form of phantasies of persecution and the way he defends against persecution by splitting, a schizoid phenomenon. Through splitting, the child attempts to defend against the dangers of bad objects (that is, phantasies) by keeping these images separate and isolated from the self and the good objects. Ronald Fairbairn, an "Independent" psychoanalyst working in Scotland, had used the term "schizoid position" in 1941 to describe the way in which the infant's ego splits almost at birth into loving (idealizing) and hating (persecutory) aspects (Fairbairn, 1952, pp. 28–58). Earlier, Klein herself had written of the way in which aggression is split off from love and experienced as paranoia. In 1946 she linked Fairbairn's phrase with her own, calling the earliest developmental stage the "paranoid–schizoid position" in order to stress the co-existence of splitting and persecutory anxiety, one that stems from the operation of the death instinct. Freud had argued that while the infant may experience anxiety, he does not and cannot fear death, because he does not yet have an ego. Klein argued, however, that there is sufficient ego at birth for the child to fear death, which it experiences as a fear of disintegration in the face of its own hatred: "The terror of disintegration and total annihilation is the deepest fear stirred by the operation of the death instinct within" (Segal, 1981, p. 116).

To defend against this anxiety, the infant projects the death instinct outward. However, since even the youngest infant is capable of primitive phantasies involving various part-object relationships, this projection creates a hostile externalized object—the "bad breast"—that seeks to destroy the infant. Much of Klein's work with adults sought to reactivate, and subsequently to integrate, incredibly primitive images, such as the phantasies of Mr B, "in whose phantasies the bad breast bites, penetrates and soils"—a projection of Mr B's own sadism. What Mr B had in fact done was to project not merely his anxieties and impulses, but also aggressive parts of his own body into the bad object, which then came back to haunt him (*ibid.*, p. 119). Here is the foundation of the process that Klein called "projective identification". The object is wounded by an aggressive thrusting into the object of a part of the self that was felt as bad. It is this part of the self that comes back to attack the self in the paranoid–schizoid position. Projective identification, however, also has its benign aspects, notably developed in the work of Bion and Segal, who emphasize its importance in the development of the capacity to think and communicate. As we shall see below, this mechanism plays an important role in creative and aesthetic experience.

In the paranoid–schizoid position, the infant projects outward not only his own aggression but also his primitive love, which, through interaction with unconscious phantasy, creates a good object—what Klein calls the "good breast". Here we see the source of what is at once valuable, yet also very problematic, in Klein. The real parents and their reactions to the infant, whether loving or frustrating, have relatively little to do with this process. According to her theory, the bad breast and good breast, rather than being primarily responses to parental frustration and love, are generated internally. The aim of the infantile ego at this stage is to introject and identify with its ideal object, while keeping the bad objects away via a continuous process of projection and externalization. Segal notes that while the good object is usually perceived to be whole and intact, the bad object is fragmented into a series of persecutors. This is partly because the bad object represents externalized parts of the ego fragmented under the pressure of the death instinct, and partly because the oral sadism directed against the bad object leads to the bad object being seen as bitten into small bits (*ibid.*, p. 117). The infant's foremost anxiety at this stage is that his persecutors will destroy him and his good object. The primary defence is not so much projection (already used to create good and bad objects and externalize them) but splitting and idealization, in which the infant holds the good and bad objects rigidly apart, as though they exist in separate psychic worlds that never touch. Idealization reinforces this splitting process, in which the good breast is seen to be all good, and sometimes all powerful, so that he can provide secure protection against the persecutors (in the form of a manic, omnipotent defence).

Though fixation at the paranoid–schizoid stage is characteristic of schizophrenia and other severe emotional disorders, it should not be seen as primarily pathological, but as a crucial step in emotional development by which the infant learns to overcome his fear of disintegration by introjecting and identifying with the good breast. Splitting, in this sense, is an absolutely essential step in learning to differentiate good from bad. Primal splitting and idealization require a delicate balancing. In the case of too little, the child is unable to protect himself from his own aggression and lives in constant anxiety that his bad objects will overcome his good ones and destroy the self. Too much separation, however, will prevent the good and bad objects from ever being seen as one, an insight—the result of normal development—that is the foundation of the depressive position, and (according to Kleinian theory) of all creative and artistic endeavour.

Innate envy

In *Envy and Gratitude* (1988b) Klein approaches the problem of creativity from a new angle. Here she posits that the first object experienced as manifesting creativity is the feeding breast, and she also describes the detrimental effect of excessive envy on creativity. If the anxiety associated with the paranoid–schizoid position is not too great, one will naturally enter the depressive position. However, it is not merely anxiety but also envy that stands as a barrier to the integrative process associated with the depressive position. Indeed, Klein is the first psychoanalyst to make envy a key psychoanalytic concept. For Klein, it is an oral- and anal-sadistic expression of the death instinct and has a constitutional basis.

Klein cites Crabb's *English Synonyms* in her distinction between envy and jealousy, where "jealousy fears to lose what it has; envy is pained at seeing another have that which it wants for itself". Klein adds that the jealous person wants to exclude another from the source of good, as occurs with the Oedipus conflict, for example. Envy is also distinguished from greed, where the latter is "an impetuous and insatiable craving, exceeding what the subject needs and what the object is able and willing to give". At the unconscious level, greed is accompanied with phantasies of scooping out and devouring the breast—i.e., destructive introjection. Envy seeks not only to rob in this way, but also to put bad parts of the self into the mother, in order to spoil and destroy her: in "the deepest sense this means destroying her creativeness" (Klein, 1988b, p. 180). Frequently it does so out of sheer spite, for if the envious person cannot have all the good himself, then no one else shall have it either. In this case, envy serves a defensive function. If the good is destroyed, then there is no reason to feel the discomfort of envy. Shakespeare's Iago is a good example of the envious personality at its most psychopathic extreme. His cruel pursuit of the progressive downfall of Othello, Cassio, Desdemona, and other innocent third parties, is motivated purely from his hatred and resentment of their goodness. Iago says of Cassio, that he has a "daily beauty in his life / That makes me ugly" (Shakespeare, *Othello*, 5.1. 20). The innate quality of envy is pointed out by Iago's wife, Emilia, who says that there are some who are "not ever jealous for the cause / But jealous for they are jealous: 'tis a monster / Begot upon itself, born on itself" (*ibid.*, 3. 4. 58–60). Iago's spiteful plan to blacken Desdemona's purity, turning "her virtue into pitch" (2. 3. 351), is an excellent example of the desire to spoil an object because of its goodness. Indeed, he wishes to pervert her "goodness", by creating out of it "the net / That shall enmesh 'em all" (2. 3. 353).

Envy is very depleting, because it drains the world of its goodness. Too much of it interferes with the primal split between the good and bad breast, and the building up of a good object becomes virtually impossible, in that even the good is spoiled and devalued precisely because it is good. The individual is left isolated in a world of persecutors with no good objects to rely on, around which to consolidate the ego. Likewise, Iago does not trust anyone: he suspects that he has been cuckolded by Othello; he does not trust his wife, and he feels threatened by Cassio's position of authority. Iago thus has no "good inner object" with which he can identify. All goodness perceived in others is regarded as alien and persecuting, and it is because he cannot posses their goodness that he actively seeks its destruction.

Klein makes the point that envy is probably the worst of all emotions because it destroys all sources of creativity and value both in the self and in the world. It also disrupts the process of reparation, associated with the depressive position. Because envy hates goodness, the envious person does not feel guilt at aggressive impulses directed towards the good object. It is thus at odds with the task of restoring the object to wholeness, since doing so would only enhance envy by reinforcing the recognition that the good lies outside the self. As a result, the child destroys his good objects and loses the ability to distinguish between what is good and what is bad. This heightens feelings of persecution; thus, envy bars the successful working through of the depressive position, as well as the strengthening of the ego. Excessive envy produces a vicious circle: the more the good object inside is spoilt, the more depleted the ego feels, and this, in turn, increases envy even more. Perhaps the most ironic expression of envy occurs in what is called the "negative therapeutic reaction". In this situation, patients are unable to accept the help of the analyst because they see the analyst as having something good to offer. It is as though the patient must stay ill in order to deny that the analyst and his interpretations have any use.

Envy's effect on the creative capacities of the individual and on the capacity to experience aesthetic pleasure has implications not only for the production of art, but also for art criticism. Klein writes that:

> My psychoanalytic experience has shown me that envy of creativeness is a fundamental element in the disturbance of the creative process. To spoil and destroy the initial source of goodness soon leads to destroying and attacking the babies that the mother contains and results in the good object being turned into a hostile, critical and envious one. The super-ego figure on which strong envy has been projected becomes particularly persecutory and interferes with thought processes and every productive activity, ultimately with creativeness.
>
> The envious and destructive attitude towards the breast underlies destructive criticism which is often described as "biting" and

"pernicious". It is particularly creativeness which comes the object of these attacks [. . .] Constructive criticism has different sources, it aims at helping the other person and furthering his work. Sometimes it derives from a strong identification with the person whose work is under discussion. Maternal or fatherly attitudes may also enter, and often a confidence in one's own creativeness counteracts envy. [Klein, 1988b, p. 202]

We will see later, in the work of Bion and Meltzer, that envy of one's own creativity, and also envy of the created work itself, may be a significant factor in artistic inhibition and appreciation. Klein's theory of envy has also helped to illuminate the vicissitudes of critical practice—both from the point of view of the artist as his own critic, and also the consequences of envy for the perception and evaluation of the art-object. Roger Money-Kyrle has drawn attention to the function of envy in both artist and critic. He believed that artistic activity is never completely free from envy, both of other artists' achievements and of the creative parts of the self. It may be a powerful spur to personal achievement, as well as a potential source of persecutory anxieties that inhibit or impede success. He writes that

> Since no one . . . is wholly free from envy, the internal saboteur is never wholly absent. If present only in a small degree, it may act as a spur; and I think that, even when too strong to be directly opposed, it can sometimes be cheated. There are, for example, over-modest artists who disclaim the creative originality which their work in fact displays. The price they pay for their success is that they must never admit or enjoy it; for if they did, it would desert them. More often, however, the presence of a powerful saboteur inside results in failure. And if, as seems likely, people seldom attempt success in art unless they are aware of some technical ability, most failures probably spring more from attacks of inverted envy than from lack of potential skill. [Money-Kyrle, 1961, p. 116]

Klein's theory of envy (and gratitude) has also been of significance in the aesthetics of philosopher, Richard Wollheim, who concludes, however, that "it goes without saying that we shall not find powerful chronic envy within the orbit of art. Envy of such order makes creativity impossible" (Wollheim, 1987, pp. 231–232).

Overview of Klein's contribution

In short, Klein's development of Freud's metapsychology enabled great leaps to take place in both clinical theory and in psychoanalytic aesthetics. Klein's and Segal's accounts of the processes of symbol formation and unconscious phantasy reach deep into the heart of the meaning of meaning itself. In addition, Klein's account of the inner world enriched the language of classical psychoanalysis and elaborated the way in which psychic functioning, ostensibly the world of the imagination, structures our relationship to the external world. The implication of this inner world was to assign it the concrete significance of a place, the space where meaning is generated—and the prototype of this space is the child's perceptions (i.e. phantasies about) the mother's body. This was to be of great importance in the aesthetics of both Stokes and Wollheim.

In his essentially neuro-physiological account of the mind, Freud did not find a place for the inner world, and this prevented him from coming very close to the nature of mental health, for his Darwinian model of the mind could only address itself to mental illness and the causal factors implicated in this. Freud also had difficulty, because of his basic mechanistic model, in thinking of emotionality as being central to mental life, and had no language that could effectively describe the nuances of affective experience. As with symbols, Freud could only think of emotionality in a Darwinian way, as a relic of primitive forms of communication, and therefore tended to confuse the experience of emotion with its communication, thus treating it as an indicator of mental functioning rather than as a function itself—akin to a noisy "ghost-in-the-machine".

Klein's work gave an entirely new significance to the concept of phantasy: that unconscious phantasies were transactions actually taking place in the internal world—a communication not only between inner and outer, but a negotiation between inner objects, too. This also gave a new meaning to dreams, which could not be viewed merely as a process for allaying tension in order to preserve sleep (Freud, 1900a). In Klein's view, dreams could be regarded as part of a dream life that was going on all the time, awake or asleep, effectively cutting through the primary–secondary process distinction and revising the relationship between conscious and unconscious modes of functioning. In many ways, unconscious phantasy can be regarded as "dreaming while awake". In effect, this transformed psychoanalysis from its status as a Baconian science aiming at explanations leading to absolute truths and laws into a Platonic account, which is essentially a descriptive approach, attempting to observe and describe phenomena that were infinite in their possibilities because they were essentially imaginative and not just neuro-chemical elements of "mental energy" within the brain.

Klein also elevated Freudian psychoanalysis into a Manichean account of the mind where there is an ongoing battle between the psychic forces of love and hate, life and death, fragmentation and integration, the vicissitudes of the struggle in the inner world between the "good breast" and the "bad breast", all of which structure the developing ego and have profound consequences for adult life. This transformed psychoanalysis into a model that could approach the social and organizational relationships not just intrapsychically (literally, the "gang in the mind") but also in terms of the external world. It was Bion (1961, 1970) who was to extend this aspect of Klein's thinking most fully. More recently, Alford (1989) has attempted to link Kleinian insights with the critical social theory of the Frankfurt School.

Throughout this chapter, I have tried to show the importance Klein gave to the attainment of the depressive position and its relationship to earlier, more primitive mental states characterized by paranoid–schizoid defences and phantasies. I have suggested that a large part of Klein's preoccupation with depression, loss, persecution, and envy, was greatly bound up with her own traumatic experiences and the hostilities she encountered in both her personal and in her professional life. However, her most powerful theme, throughout her writings, teaches us that adult life cannot flourish without the secure internalization of the depressive position, and the integration and recognition of external reality that this encompasses. Indeed, Klein associated all cultural and creative capacities with the achievement of the depressive position. An awareness of whole, independent objects depends upon the lessening of envious impulses, accompanied by feelings of gratitude and the capacity for "give and take". Klein writes that:

> enjoyment is always bound up with gratitude; if this gratitude is deeply felt it includes the wish to return goodness received and is

thus the basis of generosity. There is always a close connection between being able to accept and to give and both are parts of the relation to the good object and therefore counteract loneliness. Furthermore, the feeling of generosity underlies creativeness and this applies to the infant's most primitive constructive activities as well as to the constructiveness of the adult. [1988b, p. 310]

The capacity for gratitude in the growing child counterbalances and heals the depleting effects of the impoverishing, envious forces in the psyche. The destructive implications of envy, and the damage it can wreak on the creative and aesthetic capacities, became developed more fully in the later critical writings of Adrian Stokes, as well as British School analysts such as Hanna Segal, Wilfred Bion, Donald Meltzer, and Roger Money-Kyrle. Through their writings, the Kleinian account of innate envy has gradually become established as a significant critical tool in psychoanalytic aesthetics, illuminating the way destructive and depleting forces within the psyche are implicated both intrapsychically in the creative process, and intersubjectively in the dynamics of aesthetic response, including within the practice of art criticism itself.

Note

1. In writing this chapter on Klein, I am indebted to Grosskurth (1986) and to Hughes (1990) for the biographical and historical background. For the clinical perspective, I have drawn on Segal (1973, 1981, 1986, 1991) and Meltzer (1978, 1981).

CHAPTER THREE

The development of Kleinian aesthetics

"See now they vanish
The faces and places, with the self which, as it could, loved
Them. To become renewed, transfigured, in another pattern"

(Eliot, 1936, *Four Quartets*: *Little Gidding*, III)

In this chapter I shall explore the development of Kleinian aesthetics through the work of the psychoanalyst Hanna Segal, one of Klein's pupils, and the art critic and historian, Adrian Stokes. Their combined contribution lays the foundation of what can be described as a "traditional" Kleinian aesthetic: an approach to art which, as we shall see, regards the attainment of the depressive position as central to aesthetic and creative experience, binding it to a specific ethical commitment.

As we explored in the previous chapter, during the late 1940s and the 1950s Kleinian concepts were beginning to open up a whole new perspective on the relationship between the developing mind and its relationship to internal and external objects. Freud had always been always interested in the creative achievements of human beings and coined the term "sublimation" to denote the transmuting of basic instinct for biological satisfaction into an exalted form of conduct and civilized achievement in the "sublime" and non-physical world of symbols. For Klein, however, creativity was a much more involved process. It was seen not as the simple transforming of an instinct, but an infinitely more complex activity involving the concept of reparation, play, and unconscious phantasy activity, together with the synthetic function of the life instincts. The emphasis was shifting away from psycho-sexual phases to the phenomenology of the ego's relationship to primary objects (the mother's body), under the sway of the life and death instincts. This approach allowed better understanding of the changing ego-structure and its relation to the perception of the world. This, together with an emphasis on symbolization as a sublimatory, *developmental* activity and the formulation of the concept of the depressive position, enriched psychoanalysis with new tools for understanding the location and genesis of creativity, together with a concept of aesthetic value, which, in the Kleinian account, is inextricable from the emergence of the moral sense.

It was largely through the pioneering work of Hanna Segal that these insights were applied to the domain of art and the understanding of creativity. After discussing Segal's contribution, I shall describe how Adrian Stokes's seven-year analysis with Klein and his acquaintance with the psychoanalytic world greatly enlarged his critical project and enriched his critical writing with an evocative language and new conceptual tools.

The aesthetics of Hanna Segal

As noted in the earlier chapter, Klein contributed only three papers that touched on artistic material and did not develop an aesthetic theory as such. Like Freud, her interest in art related to the way it could illuminate and clarify certain aspects of her psychoanalytic theory that she was interested in at the time. It was Klein's pupil and close ally, Hanna Segal, who was the first to fully elaborate a Kleinian aesthetic. Other clinicians, such as John Rickman, Ronald Fairbairn, Paula Heimann, and Ella Sharpe, were early contributors to the development of a British School aesthetic, deploying both Freudian and Kleinian insights. Rickman (1940) and Fairbairn (1937) focused on the formal aspects of art and the nature of aesthetic experience; Heimann (1942) looked at the "problem" of creativity and sublimation; Sharpe (1930, 1935) examined the contrasts between artistic and scientific creativity, and the role of libidinal experience in creative development. In all these writers, there is an emphasis on the formal aspects of art and the non-neurotic aspects of creative thinking, as opposed to a focus on more orthodox themes, such as symbolic content analysis, pathography, and the tendency to view creative activity as maladaptive. See Rank (1932) and Sachs (1942). However, when Klein came to formulate her theory of the paranoid–schizoid position, a number of these thinkers distanced themselves from her, including Heimann and Sharpe.

During the 1940s and 1950s, Segal (along with Kleinian coworkers such as Wilfred Bion) contributed to the pioneering of the psychoanalysis of schizophrenics. She was especially interested in the disturbance of *symbol formation* in schizophrenia. Her observations confirmed the implications of Klein's original working hypothesis that the fixation point for psychosis lay in the paranoid–schizoid position and was related to an impaired capacity to form symbols (Segal, 1950, 1957). This interest in symbols and their failure to become established, led Segal into the domain of aesthetics and she focused on the attainment of the depressive position as the *sine qua non* of both successful symbol-formation and artistic activity.

Segal's "A psychoanalytic approach to aesthetics" (1952) was first read to the British Pyschoanalytic Society in 1947, and it is here that the Kleinian aesthetic is first articulated in theoretical form. In this important paper, Segal points out that in the past, psychoanalysis, through its discovery of unconscious phantasy life and symbolic processes, had made possible psychological interpretations of art works, such as Freud's analysis of Leonardo. Other papers have shown how the latent content of universal infantile anxieties are symbolically expressed in art works: examples are Freud's "The theme of the three caskets" (1913f), Jones' "The Madonna's conception through the ear" (1914), and Klein's "Infantile anxiety situations" (1929). Such psychoanalytic approaches, however, left unaddressed the "central problem of aesthetics" which, Segal says, concerns the nature of "good" art and what distinguishes it from other human activities, and especially "bad" art.

Freud gave an account of how the artist's phantasy life shapes his creation, but failed to give an adequate account of why we should derive pleasure from listening to such daydreams. His suggestion is that we derive pleasure and a release of tension from seeing our own deepest phantasies expressed for us. As I pointed out in Chapter One, Freud was not interested so much in the formal qualities of art as in their symbolic content. In his essay on Leonardo, for example, he makes no claim to understanding why Leonardo was a great painter, because to do that he would have to know more about the sources of creativity, the "innermost secret" as yet untapped by psychology.

Segal believes that Klein's concept of the depressive position enables us to "isolate in the psyche of the artist the specific factors which enable him to produce a satisfactory work of art" and will "further our understanding of the aesthetic value of the work of art, and of the aesthetic experience of the audience" (Segal, 1986, p. 186). Using some clinical material and examples from literature, she elucidates two major concerns of aesthetics: the distinction between successful and unsuccessful art, and the nature of the audience's aesthetic experience. She recapitulates the process that Klein described: the infant's movement from the fragmentation of the paranoid–schizoid position (a world essentially composed of part-objects split into ideally good and overwhelmingly persecutory), to an awareness of the people around him as whole persons. The child comes to see the whole object as having both good and bad qualities. This whole object, says Segal, "is loved and introjected and forms the core of an integrated ego". However, because of this situation, the infant now feels a new kind of anxiety. The persecution he felt from his bad objects now becomes a fear of *loss* of the loved whole object, both in the external world and inside him. The sadistic phantasies are still active at this stage and threaten to destroy and fragment the object both from the inner and the outside world. According to the Kleinian view, it is the memory of the good situation when the ego contained the whole object, together with a realization that the child's own sadism is responsible for the destruction of the object, that evoke the wish to restore and *recreate* the lost, damaged object, both outside and within the ego. At this stage, a more acute sense of inner and outer reality develops, so from this perspective, artistic (reparative) activity cannot be viewed as regressive and neurotic. Indeed, the urge to restore, repair, and recreate the world anew is inseparable from the development of a realistic relationship to the external world, and this lies at the heart of subsequent "authentic" creativity.

But this pathway from fragmentation to integration is not without obstacles. If depressive anxieties are not tolerated and there is a lack of confidence in the capacity to restore the object, then the loved object is felt to be irretrievably lost. This frustration may result in the object being fragmented into persecutors, and the "internal situation is felt to be hopeless". What Segal (following Klein) calls the manic defences are activated to protect the ego from feelings of loss. These involve a "denial of psychic reality, omnipotent control, and a partial regression to the paranoid position and its defences: splitting, idealisation, denial, projective identification" (*ibid.*, p. 188).

In a later paper, Segal describes in more detail the kind of artistic creation characteristic of the manic defence, exploring the "shadowy area in which originate both the psychotic delusion and the artistic creation" (1986 [1974], pp. 207). This touches on a theme that also concerns Milner (1952 [1987]), Winnicott (1953), and Ehrenzweig (1967), but these writers prefer to stress the *positive* aspects of the manic experience. As we shall see in Chapter Six, illusion is regarded by these writers as an essential aspect of all symbol formation, vital for psychological development and creativity. However, Kleinians do not credit illusion with a constructive, developmental role, and they regard such experience as omnipotent, involving a denial of reality bordering on the pathological and inimical to creativity. Later, we will see how these differences were implicated in the Klein–Winnicott debate in 1951 over the status of Winnicott's "transitional object"—a concept that highlights the *benign* experience of illusion (as opposed to "delusion"), grounding healthy psychic development. Segal stresses that one of the major tasks of the artist is to *create a world of his own*. Even when he believes that he is faithfully reproducing the external world, the artist is, in fact, using this world to rebuild his inner realm. Segal cites Proust as a good example of an artist compelled to create by the need to recover his lost past, and, in *Remembrance of Things Past*, he describes the process of his own creativity. All Proust's lost loved objects (his parents, his grandmother, and his much loved

Albertine) are recaptured and brought back to life—indeed, according to the Kleinian view, it is only these lost or dead objects that can be made into a work of art. Elstir the painter says, "It is only by renouncing that one can re-create what one loves", implying "that a creation is really a *re-creation* of a once loved and once whole, but now lost and ruined object, a ruined internal world and self" (Segal, 1986 [1952], p. 190).

It must be borne in mind that the movement from the paranoid–schizoid to the depressive position is by no means a "stage" that, when worked through, remains secured. It remains a challenge throughout life. Indeed, the Kleinian analyst Wilfred Bion (1962) believed that there is an ongoing oscillation between paranoid–schizoid fragmentation and depressive reintegration which is a necessary part of creative living. He designated this movement as "PS↔D", and, as I shall explore in the next chapter, linked it with the philosophical writing of Poincaré and the insights of Keats. Like Bion, Ehrenzweig (1967) also emphasized the creative rhythm between fragmentation and reintegration, but thought that between these two extremes there lies something else, a "manic-oceanic" phase, which acts like a "receiving womb" to hold the fragmented reality in suspension before its eventual reintegration.

If the depressive position is not fully worked through, Segal observes that artistic inhibition is likely to result in the production of an "unsuccessful artistic product" (art that is too "slick", a decorative prettification, is regarded as inauthentic). To illustrate this, Segal gives clinical examples of artists who have suffered inhibitions in relation to their work because of an incapacity to work through depressive anxieties. One example concerns a young girl, "A", with a talent for painting, but whose rivalry with her mother made her give it up. After some analysis she began doing decorative work and handicrafts, but realized, however, that this was not "real" painting, as it failed to be "moving and aesthetically significant". The girl would deny in a manic way that this caused her concern. When Segal interpreted these unconscious sadistic attacks on her father and the resulting depression from the internalization of this mutilated and damaged father, the patient recalled a dream. The girl, in the dream, had seen a picture in a shop that represented a wounded man alone in a forest. She felt quite overwhelmed with emotion and admiration for this picture and thought that it represented the essence of life. If only she could paint like that, she would be a truly successful artist. Segal interpreted that if "A" could fully acknowledge the depression over the wounding and destruction of her father, she would then be able to express it in her painting and achieve "real art". Because of her excessive sadism and resulting despair, it was impossible for the patient to do this. The manic denial of her depression led to the delusion that all was right with her world. The dream showed not only the girl's sadistic attacks on her father, but also "the effect on her painting by her persistent *denial of depression*" (1986 [1952], p. 191, my italics). According to Segal, this denial of depression led to a "superficiality and prettiness" in her artwork—the denial of her dead father and the ugliness and conflict she felt were not allowed to disrupt her ordered work.

Segal notes that patient "A" suffered from sexual difficulties as well as creative blocks; this points to the "genital aspect involved in artistic creation", which is of great importance because

> Creating a work of art is a psychic equivalent of pro-creation. It is a genital bisexual activity necessitating a good identification with the father who gives, and the mother who receives and bears the child. [*ibid*., p. 192]

(The genital aspect of creativity has also been emphasized by writers such as Stokes, Ehrenzweig [1967], and Meltzer [1973].)

Segal wonders whether there exists a specific factor in the psychology of the successful artist that would differentiate him from the unsuccessful one. According to Freud (1911b) what distinguishes the neurotic from the artist is that the latter finds his way back to reality again, and moulds his phantasies into another kind of reality. Segal adds that the artist has an acute reality sense in two ways: first, towards his own inner reality, which is not confused with the external world; and second, the artist is acutely aware of the reality of his *medium*. The artist must become highly sensitive to the nature, needs, limitations, and possibilities of his material, be it words, paints, stone, clay, or wood. The neurotic as well as the "bad" artist, uses his material in an omnipotent, magic way. The "real" artist is aware of both his inner world and the nature of his medium, which he is able to work upon to express his phantasy. The artist, like the neurotic, must suffer depression, but the artist reveals a greater capacity for tolerating anxiety. (As we shall see in the next chapter, this capacity to tolerate painful experience plays a crucial role in Bion's theory of thinking, and he formulates it in terms of Keats's "negative capability".) Although the artist withdraws into his inner realm of phantasy, he is more able than most to communicate and share his vision. Thus, he makes reparation, not only to his own internal objects, but to the external world as well.

Segal wonders whether this new light on the psychology of the artist can help us to understand the aesthetic pleasure experienced by the audience. Does it help us to understand the link between the artist's own "mental constellation" and that of his public? What makes a work of art a satisfactory experience? Freud himself recognized that there was something about the artist's state of mind that was implicated in the aesthetic experience of the audience; indeed, he comes nearest to the Kleinian account when he observes that

> what grips us so powerfully can only be the artist's *intention*, in so far as he has succeeded in expressing it in his work and in getting us to understand it. I realise that this cannot be merely a matter of *intellectual* comprehension; what he aims at is to *awaken in us the same emotional attitude*, the same mental constellation as that which in him produced the impetus to create. [Freud, 1914b, p. 212]

But, as we have seen earlier, Freud does not pursue this observation, for his emphasis on the *content* of phantasies rather than their structure precludes him from linking aesthetic experience to the objective, formal qualities of the object. Freud was certainly aware of an aspect of artistic experience that Kleinian theory was able to develop more fully. Segal, for example, does this when she observes that the "aesthetic emotion proper" is

> the pleasure derived from a work of art and unique in that it can only be obtained through a work of art, is due to an *identification* of ourselves with the work of art as a whole and with the whole internal world of the artist as represented by his work. In my view, all aesthetic pleasure includes an *unconscious reliving of the artist's experience of creation*. [Segal, 1986, p. 198]

In classical tragedy, for example, the spectator identifies himself with the author, the whole tragedy, and with the author's inner world. The spectator is able to face the ruin and devastation of the central character because the artist has himself faced the reality of his own broken inner world, and, despite this pain, has been able to create a unified work of art. Out of all the chaos and destruction, the formal qualities of the work (unity of time, place, and action) bring together the fragmented parts of the inner world and demonstrate that out of destruction comes wholeness again. Thus, through the creation of his art, the artist faces his depressive anxieties, and allows his audience to experience their own—but in a *bearable* way. The "perfect form" of the artwork allows a reintegration to take place, harmonizing the chaotic content of the artwork, which reflects the fragmented inner world.

Segal makes explicit what was only touched upon in Klein's thinking, construing the infant's awareness of his own destructiveness and the ensuing drive for reparation as lying at the heart of all artistic activity. The value and integrity of an object (and object-relationships) are negotiated through the infant's struggle with manic as well as depressive anxieties and a successful working through of these emotions depends upon on the child's acknowledgement of his own aggression, and the ensuing guilt at the damage he has done. This activates the specific phantasy of reparation—the urge to repair what is felt to have been irrevocably destroyed, and, thus, the desire to restore the lost, loved object (primarily, the mother) is the essence of all creative achievement. At the height of the paranoid–schizoid position, where aggressive and destructive phantasies are at their zenith, the sense of whole objects is lacking. The object tends to be split into ideally good elements on the one hand, and persecuting elements on the other. This means that the object is not seen as a valuable, self-sufficient object entire unto itself. With the onset of the depressive position, however, the good and bad part-objects become gradually integrated into a sense of whole objects, with good and bad aspects. This is a fundamental epistemological achievement for the child, when he perceives that the *one* object can manifest very different qualities (both frustrating and gratifying ones), but still retains its identity and wholeness. However, this a painful recognition, for it means that the child perceives that not only is his love directed towards his loved object, but also his aggression. This is why, in the early stages of the depressive position, there is still a tendency to regress to the more primitive paranoid–schizoid defences (splitting, projection, and idealization), in order to preserve the phantasy of an ideal object, untouched by hate and aggression. In the depressive position, experiences become less ideal or persecutory and are perceived more objectively. There is a recognition of the object's "goodness", coupled with a lessening of envious impulses and depleting splitting mechanisms, and this becomes the emotional basis for authentic art and creativity.

The Kleinian stress on the object's wholeness means it is better equipped than classical Freudian aesthetics to address the nature of what comprises the formal elements of beauty. For it is through the formal characteristics of the artwork that we gain a sense of wholeness: the frame, the handling of the materials, and so on. In this way, the artwork stands apart as an intact world of its own, while it might bear witness to terrifying, fragmented, and hostile elements. Kleinians would evaluate an artistic production through their perception of the artist's relationship with his medium. Like the infant, he or she must acknowledge the "otherness" of the object. "Authentic" (as opposed to omnipotent) creativity must necessarily involve the struggle with external reality—the artist's materials, and probably the burden of artistic tradition, too. This latter aspect focuses more on the oedipal drama, as described in Bloom (1975). The value of the artwork will greatly depend on the constellation of anxieties, defences, and phantasies that shaped the creation of the artwork; it is these mechanisms that are directly implicated in the formal elements of the artwork and to which the spectator responds in the aesthetic encounter. Despite the fact that a work of art may bear witness to destruction and chaos (Picasso's fragmented women, for example), Segal argues that the very process of creating an artwork speaks of the artist's capacity to acknowledge his aggression and fragmentation—to restore the chaotic experience to us in a bearable form.

John Rickman (1940) also connected the beautiful with the whole object, while Sharpe (1935) considered beauty essentially as *rhythm*, the rhythmical movement of the body that creates a feeling of continuity and pleasure—the life force itself, perhaps. When Segal analyses the term "beautiful", she concludes, however, that it is "but one of the categories of the aesthetically satisfying". She does not equate "good" art with beauty, or "bad" art with what is "ugly". She believes that *both* beauty and ugliness must be present for a full aesthetic experience. Beauty is the expression of the life instinct, and ugliness is the expression of the destructive force of the death instinct (Sachs, 1940). As in psychic health, there must be an awareness of *both* aspects. All successful (authentic) art must embody the deep experience of the artist—that is, his depression, the working through of which lies at the heart of all artistic creation. Indeed, it is not unusual to find that deeply moving art often stirs feelings of both rapture and melancholy. Klein, of course, was the first to make explicit the link between the working through of depression and artistic creativity, when she described in her 1929 paper how the painter Ruth Kjär worked through the loss of her mother through the painting of her portrait.

In the Kleinian view, the capacity to experience beauty arises from the struggle between life and death impulses. The link between beauty and death is traditionally fairly well acknowledged, particularly in the writings of the nineteenth-century aesthetic critic Walter Pater (whose influence is apparent in Freud's 1910 essay on Leonardo), and a number of commentators have drawn attention to the awesome, even terrifying, aspects of great beauty, an experience that seems to embody the fearful experience of depression and death. According to the Freudian analyst, Hans Sachs, this is because the static, eternal element in beauty is a manifestation of the death instinct. Pater (whose critical writings made considerable impact on the development of Adrian Stokes's thinking) was also acutely sensitive to the relationship between beauty, terror, and death, and it is a theme that he often returns to throughout his writing. For instance, he perceives in Leonardo's work the "interfusion of the extremes of beauty and terror" (Pater, 1873, p. 104), and regards it as an image which "from childhood we see . . . defining itself on the fabric of his [Leonardo's] dreams". Pater also notes the artist's preoccupation with the woman's "unfathomable smile, always with a touch of something sinister in it" (*ibid.*, p. 124), and notes how the "fascination of corruption penetrates in every touch [the] exquisitely finished beauty" of Leonardo's *Medusa* (*ibid.*, p. 106).

Although Segal remained the main exponent of traditional Kleinian aesthetics, she subsequently modified her views on a number of issues. Following the work of her colleague, Elliott Jacques, Segal came to see an important difference between a "pre-mid-life" and a "post-mid-life" type of creativity. The former kind of artist seeks more of an *ideal* object, and, post-mid-life, seeks the re-creation of a more *independent* object (Segal, 1986, p. 204; see also Jacques, 1965). The impact of the "mid-life crisis" on creativity also concerned Ehrenzweig (1967). He believed that middle age is a time when we tend to lose contact with deeper, unconscious mental levels. But, rather than interpreting this loss of contact as the result of a "drying-up of mental life, a necessary effect of the ageing process due to a lowering of psychic tension" (*ibid.*, p. 290, he argues that our increased powers of abstraction "may be due to a third and last cyclical advance and eventual recession of the death instinct in our mental life" (*ibid.*). According to Ehrenzweig (and aligned with the work of Jung), it is a challenge to which we must respond in order to remain "totally sane" (*ibid.*). Segal, also in line with Stokes, came to emphasize more the role of the idealization arising from the paranoid–schizoid position (Segal, 1991). Stokes (1965) argued that the artist seeks a point at which he can sustain simultaneously an *ideal* object merged with the self, and an object perceived as *independent*, as in the depressive position. This shift of emphasis has been inspired by developments in Kleinian theory, such as those pioneered in the late 1950s and early 1960s by Wilfred Bion. His re-evaluation of the positive, communicative role of paranoid–schizoid mechanisms, such as splitting and projective identification, has had a major impact on our understanding of the capacity for thinking, and how it may fail to develop (*ibid.*, p. 265).

The Kleinian contribution to psychoanalytic aesthetics thus represents a very important step forward, supplementing Freud's rather narrow account of aesthetic and cultural value. For Freud, artistic and cultural experience are viewed as being essentially neurotic, wish-fulfilling, regressive activities, with relatively little value in themselves, apart from being consolation for instinctual renunciation, helping to preserve both psychic and social equilibrium. Unlike the Kleinian account, cultural life has little constructive role to play in emotional and intellectual development, or in reality testing. Freud, who would "scorn to distinguish between culture and civilization" in *The Future of an Illusion* (1927c), left no space for an account of cultural experience that preserves the sense of it being a thing-in-itself, a source of enrichment and communication. For Freud, culture is a "thin veneer", the barrier separating our civilized selves from the chaos of unrestrained libidinal impulses. Our tendency towards neurosis is the price we pay for this renunciation. Freud thereby reduces culture to a compromise formation that barely makes up for our loss, but enables us to preserve the social organization through an inhibition of our sexual and aggressive instincts. His view of culture could be considered a bleak one; however, it could be said that the Kleinian world-view is equally pessimistic about human nature. The Manichean emphasis on good and bad, love and hate, as well as the grim, deterministic view of an innate envious impulse, suggests that we are far from Rousseau's "noble savage". Klein's and Freud's views on human nature both resonate with the sixteenth century philosopher Thomas Hobbes's belief in our fundamental aggression and destructiveness, which the social bond keeps in check for our self-preservation. For Freud, all cultural and artistic achievement arise from repression; for the Kleinians, they arise out of the depressive urge to repair a damaged inner world; culture is an atonement for destructive attacks on our primary object, the maternal body.

It is a problem for psychoanalysis that it tends to view cultural and artistic activity in terms of intrapsychic defence mechanisms, which somehow become implicated within the social domain. Indeed, Marxists criticize psychoanalysis strongly for reducing the social into the private, intrapsychic realm, and this is perhaps one of the reasons why Marxist and psychoanalytic theory have not been wholly compatible. As we shall see in Chapter Seven, the art critic Peter Fuller viewed his book *Art and Psychoanalysis* (1980) as an attempt to harmonize the insights of both Marxism and psychoanalysis. Looking back on his work some years later, he felt that perhaps his hopes were misguided. Although psychoanalysis seems unable to offer a broadly social theory of human needs and behaviour, the work of the British psychoanalyst Donald Winnicott (1971) offers a non-reductionist account of culture. His is the first psychoanalytic attempt to find space for creative and cultural experience. As I shall explore later, he believes that creative and cultural experience are essential to our psychic development and well-being. For Winnicott, culture is a thing-in-itself, reducible neither to "repression" (Freud) nor "reparation" (Klein).

There can be little doubt that the depressive position plays a significant role in aesthetic and creative activity. But perhaps Segal and orthodox Kleinians tend to over-emphasize and perhaps even idealize the depressive position as being the locus of all aesthetic value and creative experience. What Segal fails to emphasize is the broadly creative element in *all* unconscious phantasying. Kleinians would argue that phantasies other than that of reparation and restoration are essentially omnipotent, inimical to the recognition of whole objects, and hence to the creation of art. We shall see later how the "orthodox" Kleinian aesthetics, articulated mainly by Segal, differs in some important respects from other contributors such as Milner (1952 [1987]) Meltzer and Harris Williams (1988) and Ehrenzweig (1967).

I shall now consider the way in which Kleinian insights significantly enriched the critical project of Adrian Stokes. In brief, Stokes correlated the two traditional aspects of artistic labour—its "carving" and "modelling" modes—with the depressive and paranoid–schizoid positions, respectively. His use of Kleinian theory enabled him to transcend the conventional conception of artistic activity as a series of *linear* progressions through time into what is essentially a *spatial* history of art. I shall begin by sketching the background to his thinking, particularly the impact of Pater and Ruskin on his approach to art and critical writing, bearing in mind how his encounter with psychoanalysis enhanced not only his critical vocabulary, but also his own creative achievements.

Adrian Stokes and psychoanalysis

> The form is mechanic when on any given material *we impress a predetermined form, not necessarily arising out of the properties of the material* [. . .] The organic form, on the other hand, is innate; it shapes as it develops itself from *within*, and the fullness of its development is one and the same with the perfection of its outward form. Such is life, such the form. [Coleridge, 1960, p. 198]

> . . . for the material in which he [the literary artist] works is *no more a creation of his own than the sculptor's marble.* [. . .] the art of the scholar is summed up in the observance of those *rejections demanded by the nature of his medium.* [. . .] For in truth all art does but consist in the removal of surplusage, from the last finish of the gem-engraver blowing away the last particle of dust, back to the earliest

divination of the finished work to be, lying somewhere, according to Michelangelo's fancy, in the rough-hewn block of stone. [Pater, 1895, p. 16]

The contribution of Adrian Stokes is of a very special kind. He is a unique figure in this study, combining a successful career as an art historian, critic, painter, and poet with the added experience of being in analysis with Melanie Klein for several years. (The analysis began in January 1930 and continued until 1937. Analysis resumed for a short time in 1947 after the break-up of his first marriage to the painter, Margaret Mellis.) His beginning analysis in 1930 coincided with five years of particularly intensive creation, during which time he wrote five books and over thirty articles. In addition, he took up painting in 1936, just at the time when he was establishing himself as an original writer with something very specific to say. When asked why he had decided to take up painting at this particular moment of his career, Stokes would answer that he began painting because he felt there was no one else around prepared to paint the kind of painting that he thought ought to exist. In addition, he became a prolific poet in the late 1960s, and a collection of his poems, together with an introduction to his life and work, was published soon after his death in 1972.[1]

The analyst Eric Rhode, who was a close friend of Stokes, has spoken about the impact psychoanalysis made on the art critic. Apparently psychoanalysis benefited him in a number of ways: "he began to write once more, and his writings began to realise the promise that before had only been hinted at" (Rhode, 1973, p. 813). (Rhode finds Stokes's first two books, *The Thread of Ariadne* (1925) and *Sunrise in the West* (1926), "incoherent to the point of being unintelligible", by comparison with Stokes's more systematic and evaluative method in *The Quattro Cento* [1932].) Psychoanalysis made an important contribution to his personal sense of creativity as well as helping to refine his ideas about art. Indeed, the two are so intertwined it is difficult to say where his creativity ends and his "theory" of art begins. For example, Wollheim writes that "for him, the theory of art, the experience of art, came to form an indissoluble triad . . . manifesting . . . 'identity in difference'" (1980, p. 31). In an illuminating article, Carrier (1973) examines Stokes's theory of art with regard to the aesthetics of Gombrich, Goodman, and

Wollheim. During his twenties, Stokes avidly read Ruskin and Pater—the two critics who relate to Stokes most directly in terms of style and sensibility—and his writings abound with undercurrents and allusions to their writing. According to a number of commentators, Stokes is the direct heir to the tradition of Pater's and Ruskin's aesthetic and their "evocative" criticism. (For a detailed account of Stokes and the tradition of aesthetic criticism, see Bann [1978, 1980] and Read [2003].) In *Stones of Rimini*, for example (a title with obvious Ruskinian resonances), although the great Victorian sage is not explicitly mentioned, he was certainly an omniscient, ever-present figure during Stokes's trip to Italy in 1925. In his diary entry of 9 May 1925, Stokes writes, "Ruskin must have been a eunuch although a great man. [. . .] He lashes me daily, hurls at me Stones of Venice" (quoted in Bann, 1988, p. 138). Stokes never completely detached himself from the influence of Ruskin and Pater, which was not altogether benign, although there is a change in theme and emphasis in his later years. (Cf. Bloom's [1975] Freudian analysis of the artist's oedipal struggle with tradition. It helps to illuminate Stokes's grappling with his precursors, Ruskin, Pater, and perhaps also Freud.) The Sitwell brothers, whom Stokes says were "the first to open my eyes", were another shaping influence (Arts Council of Great Britain, 1982, p. 52). Stokes spent time holidaying with them in Italy, and it was during one of these visits, in 1927, that he was introduced to Ezra Pound. The influence of Pound's "carving" conception of poetry and their mutual interest in Sigismondo Malatesta helped to shape Stokes's fascination with art and architecture. For example, Stokes writes in *Stones of Rimini* that the "*Sigismondo Cantos* of Ezra Pound have long inspired me" (1978 [1934], p. 189). For an exploration of the relationship between Pound and Stokes, see Smith (1980) and Read (1999).

It was psychoanalysis, however, that was to become an increasingly significant factor in both his personal development and his career as writer. From his days at Oxford he had expressed much enthusiasm for Freud, an interest motivated not from intellectual curiosity alone, but one that probably stemmed from deeper, emotional concerns. Richard Wollheim tells us that Freud's *Interpretation of Dreams* (1900a) and *The Psychopathology of Everyday Life* (1901b) had made a particularly deep impression on Stokes in his early twenties (Wollheim, 1974, p. 317. For a brief biography of Stokes, see Bann, 1980; also useful are Read's entries on the Internet [see References section for details]). Stokes had apparently suffered from debilitating bouts of depression in his adolescence and during his years at Oxford. The chance meeting on the steps of the British Museum in 1928 with Robson-Scott (who had been at Rugby with him and was the translator of Freud's *The Future of an Illusion*) thus provided Stokes with much needed literature on the subject as well as giving him the opportunity to engage in lengthy discussions with Robson-Scott. This led to a seven-year analysis with Klein, which began in January 1930, soon after Robson-Scott had introduced Stokes to Ernest Jones (the President of the British Psychoanalytical Society at the time). Jones in turn introduced him to Klein, who had newly arrived from Berlin with a growing reputation for her pioneering work with children.

Even before his sessions with Klein began, Stokes was deploying psychoanalytic ideas in his work. As with Freud in his essay on Leonardo, he appears to have drawn no distinction between the analysis of *art* and the analysis of the *subconscious*. Thus, in 1930, Stokes writes that every detail of Giorgione's *La Tempesta*

> can be interpreted as of direct symbolical significance. I write "can be" rather than "is" not because I doubt the interpretation to be offered, but because I dislike to limit Giorgione's preoccupation. The defect of any analysis, however, in battering down the shades of conscious, semi-conscious, and unconscious intent, must be endured when the object is four centuries away [. . .] Freedom in all hierarchical barriers down, natural affinities, Giorgione expressed very strictly—the moment was so vivid—in terms of lassitude. Quiet observation had a supreme, a lyrical content. The only worthy discipline in such quiet commands utter relaxation, the discipline of precise images. [Stokes, 1978 (1930), p. 491]

Stokes was to refine his method considerably over the years in his numerous critical writings. But, in this reconciliation of "utter relaxation" with "discipline", "preoccupation" with "observation", and the achievement of "lassitude" through the removal of "hierarchical barriers", it is surely not too fanciful to trace in these examples Stokes's own hopes for psychoanalysis (though they are also a good description of Giorgione's merits).

References to Freud and Klein appeared in his art writings only after the war. It appears that he needed to assimilate the impact of psychoanalysis fully before he could acknowledge it. Eric Rhode says that "it was not until 1955, with his study of Michelangelo, that he risked generalising about the connection between psychoanalysis and art" (1973, p. 813). Similarly, Wollheim recalls that Stokes "didn't want to be a theoretical writer about art in the light of psychoanalysis", and that the first way in which psychoanalysis affected him was the way in which it "both coloured the sensibility and gave him a way of describing sensibility" (*ibid.*). As a number of his close friends and colleagues suggest, Stokes remained wary of divulging too much about his own analysis and the more personal aspects of his sessions with Klein. However, in an early review of Klein's *The Psycho-Analysis of Children* (1932), Stokes expresses some interesting views about the ethics and technique of analysis. He insists that psychoanalysis does not set out to "change" the patient:

> Analysis does not assault values, nor dispute them. It leads us to view life differently only so far as we have viewed it with an overplus of anxiety. The quantitative and qualitative aspects of each person's vitality remain unique. [Stokes, 1933, p. 527]

We gather from the conclusion of this review that he wished to conceal his relationship with Klein, pretending to have learned only from her preface "that Mrs Klein had settled in England" (*ibid.*, p. 530). One could take this as an expression of his wish for discretion and privacy concerning his analysis.

Stokes's "Envoi", the end piece to *Venice* (1945a), is very much his psychoanalytic "messenger". Here we read the first coherent statement of a philosophy based implicitly on the psychoanalytic theories of Freud and Klein, preparing us for the books to follow, which explicitly acknowledge their debt to psychoanalysis. The following extract has a particularly strong Kleinian emphasis:

> Mental as well as physical life is a laying out of strength within, rivalry, as it were, with the laid-out instantaneous world of space. To project is to distort. [. . .] We carry with us all the time the certainty of life and death, a relationship parallel to the interdependence of subject and object. [. . .] Mental processes, unknown

in themselves, obtain entry into consciousness through speech. Symbolic substitution even before speech, is natural to the infant. The basis of all speech is substitution, the basis of all projection. To create is to substitute. (1978 [1945a], p. 138)

Then, in the autobiographical *Inside Out* (1947), evocatively subtitled "An essay in the psychology and aesthetic appeal of space", Stokes strikes the Kleinian keynote of his thinking. The reader will encounter in this little book (and also in *Smooth and Rough* [1951]) a poignant blend of autobiography and criticism, invoking the vicissitudes of Stokes's Edwardian childhood experience, his travels to Italy and their shaping of his aesthetic perception. The book begins with the statement that "In the nursery, that is where to find the themes of human nature: the rest is working-out, though it also be the real music". This voices his firm commitment to the Kleinian belief in the confluence of infantile experience with adult life—one that informs not only the content of his writings, but also his unique approach to writing about art. The subtle blend of psychoanalysis, autobiography, art history, and criticism create a kind of writing that builds upon the evocative criticism of Hazlitt, Ruskin, and Pater. But it also adds psychoanalytic perspective to their insights, which allows a deeper exploration of the relationship between critic, artwork, and spectator/reader, thereby enriching the vocabulary of criticism, where "there is no clear distinction between the physical description of the work and the spectator's response to it", and the "texture of his writings is analogous to the texture of our actual experiences of art" (Sylvester, 1961).

There seems, in fact, to have been a natural reciprocity between his psychoanalytic interests and his own intense powers of fantasy, and Rhode is no doubt right in surmising that, from *The Quattro Cento* onwards, "whole sorts of thought processes were derived from analysis in his books". For example, Lawrence Gowing recalls that

> The fantasy in his thought was far closer to the surface of day to day conversation and observation than in anybody else I've ever talked to. I remember going to Bertorelli's one evening, and a Negro came in and sat down opposite us with his back to the fluorescent tube in the window. Adrian said: "He's taken the violet out of his

skin and hung it up behind him like a hat". This was a beautiful and typical perception of pragmatic ingredients as fantastic elements which was quite new to me. [Gowing, 1973, p. 815]

Stokes's essay "Living in Ticino" is a particularly poignant and eloquent example of his penetrative imaginative power expressed through evocative prose. He blends Proustian personal recollection with philosophical reflection on the nature of memory and time. Memories of family life, an Edwardian childhood, his reappraisal of the past after re-marriage, and thoughts on Italy as a symbol of security and rebirth are intertwined. The essay speaks of the power of the image to fuse a multitude of polarities: space and time; sight and sound; past and present; loss and gain. The relationship between mood and creative perception is evoked through a web of diverse and suggestive imagery: the recollection of the bonfire at his old family home; the sound of bells on a Sunday morning; the security of a canopy of shade at a cafe in Locarno; a huge storm in Genoa; a lighthouse flash seen from afar; a kitsch Edwardian bowl (Stokes, 1964).

After the Second World War, Stokes's writings began to address wider cultural and environmental issues, believing that psychoanalysis, as a humanistic discipline concerned with *value*, could offer insight and the possibility of change. However, as Stokes's work broadened to accommodate wider spheres, his readership narrowed. Many of those who had admired his earlier work now claimed to be "baffled and alarmed by his use of psychoanalytic ideas". Indeed, the eminent Sir Geoffrey Faber had thought him the greatest prose writer of his generation, but Faber and Faber "dropped him like a hot potato" (Rhode,1973, p. 815; the Tavistock Press, specializing in psychoanalytic literature, agreed to publish his later work). Sir Kenneth Clark was one influential art historian who distanced himself from Stokes's psychoanalytic writings, complaining that Stokes had let psychoanalysis "carry him too far" (Arts Council of Great Britain, 1982, p. 8). We do know that in 1947, after the break-up of his marriage to the painter Margaret Mellis (one of whose works is featured on the dust-jacket of *A Game That Must Be Lost*), he resumed psychoanalysis briefly, before moving to Switzerland and marrying Ann, the sister of his first wife. His autobiography, *Inside Out*, resonant with Kleinian themes concerning human nature and his own childhood experience, was published in the same year; and it would seem reasonable to suggest that it was not only an account of aesthetic sensibility, but also a form of self-analysis. However, unlike the memorative/backward-looking writings of Hazlitt, Ruskin, and Pater, Stokes was able to use his psychoanalytic experience to *de*-idealize and integrate his childhood experience, rather than splitting it off (as his forebears seem to have done) into an idyllic paradise, or an idealized past wherein lies the key to creative apperception, but remaining separate from the starker realities of adulthood. (In particular, see Hazlitt's scattered references to an idealized childhood in his *Table Talk* [1891]; the early chapter of Ruskin's *Praeterita* [1885–1889]; and Pater's curious semi-autobiographical essay, "The child in the house" [1878].)

The close relationship between Stokes's aesthetic criticism and his experience of psychoanalysis has also been examined by Stephen Bann, who considers how this can be viewed in the light of a broader perspective—the development of a uniquely British critical tradition that has its roots in the evocative criticism of Ruskin and Pater (William Hazlitt could also be included in this genre). Bann contends that it would not be "too fanciful to imagine that the English aesthetic critics were in some sense working a furrow parallel to Freud's, and . . . Stokes would have found it only natural to step from one to the other" (see Bann, 1988, p. 136). Perhaps it would be true to say that Stokes has most in common with Freud and psychoanalysis through his distinctive kind of writing, a style that draws deeply upon his imaginative and evocative powers, linking a number of images and aspects of human consciousness. For Stokes, psychoanalysis seemed to be a way of life, a *raison d'être* informing the very texture of his own perceptions and emotional responses, rather than the canonical application of psychoanalytic theory to art and aesthetics, a tendency perceptible in some writers who have deployed psychoanalytic ideas in their work. (Compare the art criticism of Peter Fuller [whose work will be explored in Chapter Seven of this book], who has been criticized by Wright [1984, p. 92] for validating his interpretations by "freely quoting from a wide range of texts of the object-relations school, combining them to suit his purposes". This rather omnipotent use of psychoanalytic theory is very different from Stokes's method, which is perhaps more truly "psychoanalytic" in the sense of that it embraces a a multiplicity of resonances, layers, and meanings; a kind of writing that is not "about" psychoanalysis in any mundane sense, but is informed by its spirit.)

Despite a number of his loyal followers falling by the wayside, Stokes continued to immerse himself in psychoanalytic thinking, and by 1956 had founded the Imago Group. It was known as the Imago Society, and aimed to discuss areas of mutual interest from a Kleinian perspective. Membership was open to both practitioners and non-practitioners who had experience of analysis. Members included Richard Wollheim, Donald Meltzer, Wilfred Bion, Roger Money-Kyrle, John Oulten, Wisdom, and Stuart Hampshire. The Group was dissolved in 1972. A few years later it reformed for a period as the New Imago Group, with Donald Meltzer, Martha Harris, Margaret and Michael Rustin, Eric and Maria Rhode, Lisa Miller, Meg Harris Williams, and Alan and Judith Shuttleworth, among others. A number of Stokes's published papers and writings appear to have been read first to this group: for example, Part II of *Painting and the Inner World* was conceived first as a dialogue between Stokes and the Kleinian analyst Donald Meltzer, during one of the meetings. Papers included: "Listening to clichés and individual words"; "Psycho-analytic reflections on the development of ball games, particularly cricket"; "On being taken out of oneself"; "Primary process, thinking and art"; "Psycho-analysis and our cultures". These papers are collected in Stokes (1973). The dialogue with Meltzer, "Concerning the social basis of art", is reprinted in Stokes (1978) 219–235, and in Meltzer and Harris Williams (1988), pp. 206–226.

Carving, modelling and Kleinian theory

I shall now turn to what must be one of Stokes's most significant contributions to aesthetics and art history: a theoretical stance that harmonizes the conflicting claims of Pater's idealism on the one hand, and Ruskin's materialism on the other, into a coherent account of aesthetic experience supported by the psychological insights of Melanie Klein and her School (see Wollheim, 1974, 1980 for his useful elucidation of Stokes's theoretical development). Of course, Stokes was not the first to base an art history on such an opposition. Behind his distinction between carving and modelling lies a fundamental polarity that can be traced through the whole history of art. (The late nineteenth-century art historian, Wölfflin, based his classic work *The Principles of Art History* [1915] on the interplay between a series of opposing elements of perception, or "five categories of beholding": the linear *vs.* the painterly; Renaissance *vs.* Baroque; "open" (atectonic) *vs.* "closed" (tectonic) form; absolute clarity *vs.* relative clarity; multiple *vs.* uniform unity. Wölfllin's approach was concerned with *form*; he adopted a positivist methodology that implicitly critiqued the Burkhardtian approach, which regarded art objects as the expression of an age. Wölfflin, however, was keen to isolate the cultural ethos and the visual tradition from any sense of the artistic personality.)

Stokes's theory of carving and modelling is essentially a spatial history of art in that it is not confined to a linear historical progression. "Modelling" and "carving" were terms that enabled Stokes to cut across historical boundaries and artistic forms, linking artworks from a number of different epochs and media. Through their celebration of the carving aim, Stokes could show the commensurability of, for example, the sculptor Agostino's work with that of the architect Laurano, together with the painters Piero della Francesca, Giorgione, Bruegel, Chardin, Cezanne, and the modern sculptress Barbara Hepworth.

In the following section, I hope it will become clear, through the contribution of Kleinian object-relations theory, how Stokes became well equipped to address the interplay between the artist and his medium, together with the relationship between the spectator–critic and the artwork. Indeed, in his approach, Stokes saw no essential difference in the relationship between artist and medium, and spectator and artwork, for, according to Kleinian theory, the same intrapsychic processes are at work in *all* object relationships.

In *The Quattro Cento* (1932) Stokes outlines the chief characteristics of the art that concerns him. (As the subtitle of the book suggests, Stokes is writing "a different conception" of the Italian Renaissance; indeed, what turns out to be an essentially *spatial* history of art. His own term "Quattro Cento" designates a certain *kind* of artistic activity that transcends temporal boundaries; it does not refer to a specific historical moment, as does the original word

"Quattrocento". Interestingly, the onomatopoeic quality of the words "Quattro Cento" itself suggests calm proportion and equality of stress, values which are central to the spirit of Quattro Cento art.) The first of these characteristics is "love of stone"—but this "love" of stone is not the same as "attention to" stone, which refers more to an artist's omnipotent use of the medium. The "stone-struck" artist relates to the stone as if it were alive (unlike Michelangelo, he says, who forced his material into life); he is sensitive both to its potential as a medium and to its capacity to realize his own fantasies—i.e., its content. The Quattro Cento artist treats his medium as if it were an independent entity that actually contains living figures, and desires that the stone should "realise its own life". An art born out of the love of stone exhibits "stone-blossom", which Stokes compares with the feature he calls "incrustation". These two are not the same, for whereas stone-blossom *grows out* of the work, incrustation has been *added* from the outside. But they do have in common the negative property that "they never give the effect of having been put there, just like that", and the more important property of being "in a tense communion with the plane" that shows them off. Stokes identifies beautifully the dynamic interplay between these two characteristics, as he perceives them, in Verrocchio's *Lavabo*:

> First of all, there is the use of coloured stone, the porphyry arch framing the whole, and the serpentine central disc; also the dark colours of the huge lip of the cup. These make the white marble luminous, and lead the eye to the shadows at the junction of the surfaces, to where, for instance, the bat wings, ribbed and ending in claws like an umbrella, cling to the urn. Hence the feeling of incrustation, *surface into surface,* and also of *growth from within* (witness the oak wreath)—of stone blossom. [Stokes, 1978, p. 73, my italics]

Stokes then identifies "mass", or "mass effect", which is again introduced by way of a contrast. He juxtaposes the massiveness of the "scenic" effect valued by Roman and Baroque artists (for example, Luciano Laurana's courtyard at Urbino—"the greatest feat in mass effect known to me") with a linear treatment of space such as we perceive in Brunelleschi. The architecture of the latter displays for Stokes a "perfect neatness"—implying a frigidity that would appeal to one "who wished to be civilised in a mountain fastness", contrasted with the freer-spirited Luciano who "left [his stone] rough" (*ibid.*, p. 133). The effect of mass is directly visual, making no appeal to touch or to tactile memory: "mass effect" is directed only to the "quickness of the eye" and "allows the immediate, the instantaneous synthesis that the eye alone of the senses can perform" (*ibid.*, p. 134). Stokes imaginatively likens architecture that exhibits this characteristic to the immediacy in the wide open face of a rose. In "Pisanello" (1930), Stokes observes that the example of a Quattro Cento artist refutes Pater's dictum in *The Renaissance* that "all art constantly aspires to the condition of music", stressing that art has nothing to do with time, rhythm or with process. It discloses itself *instantaneously*, thus: ". . . purely visual matter is dissociated from noise as well as from silence, from past, present and future. Things stand expressed, exposed, unaltered in the light, in space. Things stand" (Stokes, 1978, p. 135).

The third aspect of Quattro Cento art is *perspective*—once more the "love" rather than its "use" as characterized by those un-Quattro Cento Florentine artists. Stokes conceives of perspective in a rather different way from that to which we are accustomed. Rather than conceiving of it as primarily a visual aid, Stokes sees it as a device that offsets the side-effects of representation. For any attempt to render a three-dimensional space on the flat (representational painting), or deep space in a shallow space (representational relief), lends itself to a powerful attack on that surface. When depth is gouged out, Stokes notes that the artist will attempt to cover this up by the use of "finish"—a prettification that is in vain because the tension of the plane will have been destroyed. The "love of perspective" is important here, for it gives the artist a way in which he can accommodate and contain (perhaps also make reparation for) the inherent dangers in spatial representation. If the single plane has to be given up, equivalence is restored through a multi-planed picture in relief, where the gradations are progressive rather than sudden. (Ehrenzweig [1949, p. 98] makes a similar point that the "introduction of perspective into painting was not a cool and rational discovery of a more 'correct' and realistic representation", and that through the "distortions of perspective", the "terrible mutilations to the human body" must have produced great emotional shock on contemporaries. He believes that the "double meaning" of perspective must have been more apparent for the Renaissance artists: its "surface" meaning was the triumph of a scientific world-view; its deeper meaning expressed the ambiguity of the unconscious mind, based on corporeal phantasies. Today, however, perspective has been more or less fully "rationalized" as the correct representation of the world.)

The fourth characteristic is the most subtle. Wollheim perceives that Stokes's word "emblematic" illustrates nicely a very important aspect of Quattro Cento art (1974, p. 321). Although the word is used literally, Stokes also uses it in a metaphorical, more creative way, drawing together the sense of the process by which an inner state is objectified—the manifestation or revelation in the external world of what is essentially subjective. In matching inner world experience with that of the outer world, the artist has not followed a set of preconceptions or rules—there is an "exuberance" where the fit between inner and outer has been "thrown out" spontaneously. The term "emblematic" thus evokes the sense of something that can be seen meaningfully only if it is perceived as the outcome of an engagement with the material.

At the time of writing *The Quattro Cento*, Stokes had no way of unifying these characteristics. It was not until *Stones of Rimini* (1935) that he was able to integrate them with the phenomenon of "carving". Stokes developed this term, extracting it from its familiar context—the opposition between carving and modelling practices enshrined in traditional art theory. Although Stokes does refer to the two activities in *The Quattro Cento*, its fuller possibilities are as yet unrecognised; here the distinction is used in its traditional sense, referring to actual artistic practice. Indeed, as Stokes began to develop his ideas in *Stones of Rimini*, the traditional deployment of the terms "carving" and "modelling" created more confusion than clarity. For instance, Stokes observed that some pure Quattro Cento art, such as Donatello's bronze relief work on the base of *Judith*, was in fact modelled. Stokes also noted that some Northern Italian sculptors were very un-Quattro Cento in the way they quite literally carved their stone. In *Stones of Rimini*, we are concerned with suggestiveness and metaphor: the "imaginative meanings that we attach to stone and water" (1978 [1935], p. 187), and Stokes sets out to "attack the vital though confused distinction between carving and modelling" (*ibid.*, p. 229). Inspired primarily by the bas-reliefs of Agostino, he refines the use of the distinction, using it metaphorically, referring to a process or an activity that depicted "the two main aspects of labour" involved in artistic production. These two activities also represent what is and is not Quattro Cento in Renaissance sculpture and architecture. (To illustrate this distinction, compare the "modelled" work of Donatello with that of the "carver" Agostino. See http://www.artcyclopedia.com [accessed 2 July 2007] for examples of these artists' work.)

Stokes sums up the distinction thus:

> whatever its plastic value, a figure carved in stone is fine carving when one feels that not the figure, but the stone *through the medium of the figure, has come to life*. Plastic conception, on the other hand, is uppermost when the material with which, or from which, a figure has been made appears *no more than as so much suitable stuff for this creation*. [Stokes, 1978, p. 230, my italics]

To carve is essentially to polish, for both bring to life that which "already exists in the block". Indeed, the careful polishing of the stone is like "slapping the new-born infant to make it breathe"—a powerful image with echoes of Klein!

To conclude: the activity of carving is judged not only by the artist–medium interaction, but also through the impression that a carved work makes on the viewer. Stokes emphasizes that it is an essentially spatial experience; form is unemphatic and carefully graduated. Every part "is on some equality with every other part", recalling "a panorama contemplated in equal light by which objects of different dimensions and textures, of different beauty and emotional appeal, whatever their distance, are seen with more or less the same distinctness, so that one senses the uniform dominion of an interrupted space" (*ibid.*, pp. 247–248). As the word "panorama" suggests, visual values are very much intertwined with those found in good landscape. Indeed, Stokes was especially responsive to the Mediterranean landscape, just after sunset, when "things stand".

Now we shall look at what "modelling" entails. Stokes writes:

> That with which you model in sculpture is as much a material as the as the stone to be carved, but with modelling activity, the ... plastic material has no "rights" of its own. It is a formless mud used, very likely, to make a model for bronze or brass. Modelling is a much

more "free" activity than carving. The modelled shape is not uncovered but created. This gives rise to freer treatment, free in the sense that it is a treatment unrestricted by so deep an imaginative communion with the significance of the material itself. The modeller *realises* his design with clay. Unlike the carver, he does not envisage that conception as enclosed in his raw material. [*ibid.*, p. 235].

Unlike the stone-lover, who "woos" his stone into being, the modeller, treats his medium merely as such suitable stuff for his own creation, giving free rein to his desires and fantasies rather than communing with its independent qualities. From a Kleinian perspective, we could characterize the modeller by his largely omnipotent unconscious phantasies, as contrasted with the specific phantasy of recreation or reparation, which is closer to the carving mode. (Cf. Hinshelwood's "traditional" Kleinian critique of Winnicott's theory of creativity, where

> the creation of phantasies of an omnipotent kind . . . is not part of aesthetic appreciation or endeavour. The latter comes from the creation of a specific kind of unconscious phantasy, the phantasy *of* creating and recreating (reparation) which no longer has omnipotent qualities. I think this is an important distinction: the *creation* of phantasies (in both Klein and Winnicott) and the phantasies *of* creativity (Klein only). [Personal communication, 12 June, 1990])

Like carving, the modelling or plastic conception is judged in terms of both the artist's relation to his medium and the effect on the viewer. The modelled work often "betrays a tempo", a strong rhythmic quality or "mental pulse" appealing to our kinaesthetic and tactile senses. The carved work, however, increases the viewer's spatial awareness—temporality becomes spatiality. Examples of modelled work include the "rapid content" of Rodin's sculpture, the "calligraphic omnipotence" of Far Eastern pictorial art, and the "supremely personal, supremely aesthetic" touch of the Baroque artists (1978, pp. 31–179).

Stokes also applies the distinction to drawing and painting. The ground for this is prepared in *Stones*, when he suggests that the painter–carver will pay careful attention to the flat surface of his medium and will "emulate the tonal values which the actual carver reveals on his surfaces, more or less equally lit, of his block" (*ibid.*,

p. 236). But it is not until *Colour and Form* (1937) that he gives an extensive and detailed exposition of this application. *Colour and Form* is particularly significant in Stokes's theoretical development, because it is here that he effectively frees the concept of carving from literary and technical restrictions by extending much further from its traditional architectural and sculptural origins into the domain of painting. Although Piero had been there from the start as a Quattro Cento artist, Stokes now felt able to identify much more precisely the characteristics intrinsic to a whole kind of painting that exhibited the essential quality or qualities he had found mainly in the work of fifteenth-century architects and sculptors. The book also bears witness to an important development in Stokes's career—his own experience of painting. It distils a number of years of thought and discussion, mainly with his mentor, the painter Adrian Kent, who had been with Stokes on a painting holiday to St Ives, a favourite haunt for artists.

So how does Stokes apply carving–modelling values to painting? Essentially, a kind of painting in which the carving aim is realized is one in which vitality is attributed to the surface of the canvas and the painter dedicates himself to its preservation. An exact parallel is drawn between the vitality with which the canvas is endowed and the potential life that the carver attributes to the stone and then tries to reveal. But vitality can only be preserved if colour determines form, or where colour serves as a "principle of creation". But not just any use of colour to shape form will suffice as the analogue to carving. First, colour must be used so as to provide a *total organization* of the forms that a picture contains. It must not be used just to balance or offset adjacent forms. Stokes talks of chromatic relations being "reversible", meaning that the terms of such a relation must be mutually enhancing, and one must not act merely as a foil to the other. For this to be realized, Stokes advises the use of *near-complementary* colours, where "at least one colour is neutralised and the other perhaps changed from the normal tone value of its hue". The carver–artist chooses colours "which do not so much aim . . . at a featureless inter-annihilation, but which point constantly to a common root that nourishes them both". For example,

> in a certain brown and olive green there is a common yellow to yellow orange parent. They are brothers rather than rivals [. . .] And

because of this, their difference, which each one enhances in the other as if voluntarily, appears all the more remarkable. They have a common ground, a family tree to which they both return for nourishment. [Stokes, 1978, *II*, p. 47]

It is through this device that "identity in difference" is achieved in a painting. Stokes was to develop this classic concept by linking it through "carving" with the Kleinian account of the depressive position as a mode of experience which celebrates the recognition and tolerance of otherness: in short, a mutual enhancement based on co-operation and interchange. This he opposed to the destructive competitiveness that he associated with the modelling mode, linking it with part-object or paranoid–schizoid relationships (*ibid.*). As we shall see in Chapter Seven, Wollheim develops Stokes's account and suggests that the use of near-complementaries has a "special binding effect" which helps to secure the sense of *corporeality* in painting.

The second feature of colour-carving entails that colour must be used in such a way as as to suggest that each form has its own inner light. This effect he calls *luminosity*, and he contrasts it with the use of colour to represent reflected light or light used as a source of illumination. Finally, the total organization of colour must reveal itself all at once—"in a fraction of a second". Forms must not be "groped for", and Stokes approvingly cites Vasari's comment that Giorgione's painting could be seized in "una sola occhiata" (see www.artcyclopedia.com, accessed 2 July 2007, where you will find these illustrations). The chromatic immediacy of forms is analogous to mass in architecture or relief, and it is this that ensures painting a primarily (but not exclusively) visual character. All together, by describing these characteristics, Stokes was able to demarcate a tradition of carving in painting as something that transcended the frontiers of chronology as well as of art form. The first painter, in his view, to fully realize the carving conception was Piero, followed by Brugel, Chardin, and Cezanne. In later writings Stokes was to include de la Tour, Vermeer, and Picasso.

Stokes did, however, come to recognize the more positive aspects of the modelling experience; and the next step is to consider the interaction of the carving and modelling modes in both sculpture and painting. In "Carving, modelling and Agostino", after describing the essential opposition of carving and modelling, Stokes then emphasized their *interdependence*, and the same applied to his later accounts of painting. Taken in isolation, the modes refer to the essence of two extremes, but in practice they coexist (in varying proportions), one mutually sustaining and complementing the other. Thus, plastic conceptions have been "realised pre-eminently in stone as well as in plastic materials" and the prevalence of the plastic aim in European carving is "proof of the importance of stone in European art" (Stokes, 1978, I, p. 237). Stokes is keen to show how certain periods in history tend to emphasize one mode more than another. In the Renaissance, for instance, the "love for stone" was particularly intense and an infusion of modelling values served to enhance those "values proper to stone". Modelling may *vitalize*, as well as devitalize, the carving aim (*ibid.*, p. 238). Even Agostino, Stokes's carver *par excellence*, is an "offspring of Florentine modelling". For, "unless he had learned his trade in the Florentine school, he could never have developed so facile and flowering a technique, nor attained such a naturalism". Stokes admires the infusion of modelling into the carving aim so long as it "enhances the layer formation of the stone" (*ibid.*, p. 247). Although the carving mode is perceived to be the mode *par excellence*, modelling gradually gains in importance and stature. Wollheim remarks that

> what had in earlier books appeared as the lesser or the more negative tradition in art, the tradition of modelling, in which you produce an object which is very sharply or harshly differentiated internally and therefore doesn't stand apart from oneself quite so much, comes into its own in the later writings: it is increasingly celebrated in the notion of the enveloping character of art, the incantatory character of art. [Wollheim, 1973, p. 815]

In order to understand more fully the way in which carving and modelling are linked to create a unity and value in aesthetic experience, I shall now look at the important way in which Kleinian concepts informed and enlarged Stokes's project and how, in the light of developments in the British School (especially through the work of Bion) he came to review his theory of modelling. Stokes's urge to unite the concerns of psychology, history, and the formal aspects of art into a coherent critical discourse developed into an ambitious project that culminated in the publication of six small volumes by the Tavistock Press between 1955 and 1967. These books undertook, both in general and in many points of art-historical detail, to correlate the two modes or processes—the "two main aspects of labour" that Stokes had come to think of as all-important within the making of art—with the two psychic attitudes or "positions", the two fundamental kinds of relationship, that Klein and her colleagues had come to think of as underpinning our intellectual and emotional development. Stokes's overall task was to link the carving mode with the tendency to relate to whole-objects, and the modelling mode with those relationships that emphasized part-objects. (To recap briefly: the two fundamental object-relationships that Klein and her co-workers described were the "paranoid–schizoid" and the "depressive" positions. The first of these psychic attitudes is one in which relations to part-objects, or objects not felt to be wholly independent of the individual, dominate. The second is one in which relations to whole objects, or objects experienced as independent, self-sufficient, and separate, are ascendant.) Of course, within the part of psychoanalytic theory to which Stokes appealed, the two psychic attitudes initially belong to a developmental or *historical* account of individual psychic development; i.e., the infant passes through a stage of part-object relating and gradually progresses to whole-object perception. But, as we have seen, Klein stressed that although these are historical stages, they are potentially active within us throughout our lives. They refer to *existential* states—modes of perception and behaviour. Indeed, this collaborated very well with Stokes's ever-increasing awareness that the carving and the modelling modes were never to be found in isolation.

In correlating the two kinds of relationship with the two kinds of art, Stokes was centrally concerned to show how each kind of art was adapted to symbolize the benign aspect of the relationship it mirrors, or its characteristic satisfactions. But he was also to insist that the darker aspect of the relationship was not ignored. So, the modelling mode celebrates the oceanic feeling, the "invitation in art" to merge with the object, but it also finds a place for the splitting and the attacks that accompany it. The carving mode celebrates the self-sufficiency of the whole object, but there is also a place for depression, the painful recognition of the otherness of objects.

It is not hard to see the suitability of the carving mode to express what Stokes terms "the joyful recognition of self-sufficient objects". It all depends on those qualities already outlined in earlier writings: the love of the material, the attention to texture, and the reciprocity of form, the use of inner light, and the even progression of surfaces. It was the suitability of modelling to the part-object relationship that proved more difficult for Stokes to work out fully, but its perception is crucial to an understanding of the new value that he eventually came to assign to modelling. This re-evaluation came out of a prolonged and intensive study of certain great works, which seemed to have epitomized for him the essence of this dual activity. The artists he turned to were Michelangelo, Turner, Monet, and, much later, Rembrandt. Stokes not only reassessed the value of modelling, but gained a deeper sense of how *both* modes are implicated from the very start. In *The Invitation in Art* (1965) Stokes develops the notion of modelling to include a number of aspects that he had tended to regard as less wholesome than those of their carving counterparts. Central to this new theory is an aspect that he calls the "pull", the "envelopment factor", the "incantatory process", and, canonically, "the invitation in art". Most of us are familiar with the way in which art has the capacity to take us out of ourselves, to pull us into the work. Certain kinds of subject matter tend to do this (depictions of reverie and elemental scenes, for example), but Stokes also looked at how *form* was able to facilitate this effect. He formulated how the pull is heightened just when the form is least integrated, when the surface has been greatly attacked, with heavy emphasis on depth and harshest chiaroscuro. Stokes also distinguished between the modeller's compulsion to create a manic kind of unity through form and/or subject matter, and the kind of harmonious integration characteristic of the carver.

The new theory of modelling takes into account the work of Klein's colleagues in the British School, pioneered by Bion (1962), whose work increasingly emphasized the *communicative* aspects of projective identification and its role in symbol formation. Projective identification is what Klein had regarded as an essentially depleting defence mechanism, involving omnipotent phantasies of manic fusion with the part-object, thought to be inimical to the forces of creativity. As we shall see in the next chapter, Bion was to show how this mechanism of projective identification, via the "container–

contained" relationship, establishes a vital link between the mother's unconscious and that of her infant, without which there could be no development of the thinking apparatus, no ability to learn from experience, and certainly no capacity for empathic and imaginative identification—arguably essential aspects of artistic activity and the aesthetic encounter.

The work of Bion and his close colleague and pupil Donald Meltzer enhanced and largely revised traditional Kleinian aesthetics and its understanding of creativity. As we have noted, Segal and Stokes did not differentiate between creativity (reparation) and the aesthetic sense: they regarded both as arising from the successful working through of the depressive position. However, Bion (1970) and Meltzer and Harris Williams (1988) emphasize that the capacity for aesthetic experience (which they regard as inseparable from the evolution of truth and the moral sense) is innate. This means that rather than being an *outcome* of the depressive position, it is the aesthetic capacity itself that precipitates the movement from the fragmentation of the paranoid–schizoid position to the recognition of whole objects in the depressive position. (It is interesting to note that Segal remains loyal to the "orthodox" Kleinian stance, and that even in her most recent work [Segal, 1991] no reference is made to Donald Meltzer's significant contributions to Kleinian aesthetics.) Consequently, their work has had great import not only for our understanding of aesthetics and creativity, but also for the nature of critical practice itself.

Note

1. See Stokes (1981). Since Stokes's death in 1972, there have been many contributions published relating to Stokes's work that, following a retrospective exhibition of his paintings at the Serpentine Gallery in 1982 and the three-volume publication of his critical writings (1978), have helped to secure Stokes's reputation as a significant "critic of our time" (Wollheim, 1959a). Despite the preoccupation with deconstructive and postmodernist critical stances in recent decades, a number of respected aesthetes, critical thinkers, and cultural historians (such as Stephen Bann, Richard Wollheim, David Carrier, Andrew Forge, Laurence Gowing, and the psychoanalyst Eric Rhode) have enhanced

our comprehension of Stokes's significance to humanist studies and to our present day environment, which Stokes himself found increasingly alienating, possibly even sanity-threatening. For a very recent collection of scholarly articles that pay homage to Stokes's significant contribution to aesthetics and cultural history, see Bann (2007); Hulks (2001, 2006); Carrier (1997); Read (2003). I would also refer the reader to the website devoted to scholarship about Stokes's work, www.pstokes.demon.co.uk (accessed 15 January, 2008).

PART III
DEVELOPMENTS IN THE BRITISH SCHOOL

CHAPTER FOUR

The legacy of Wilfred Bion

> "Meaning is revealed by the pattern formed and the light thus trapped—not by the structure, the carved work itself"
>
> (Bion, 1991, Book I)

Over the past forty years, Bion's work has influenced a number of thinkers—practitioners and non-practitioners alike—who are concerned with art and creativity. Since this book was first compiled, Bion studies have flourished, and there are now available a wealth of books and articles in English and other languages. For example: Symington & Symington (1996); Sandler (2005); Bleandonu (1994). Jacobus (2005) is one of the few who have explored the connection between Bion's ideas and philosophical aesthetics. This chapter will look at Bion's development of Freud's and Klein's metapsychology and the impact of his ideas on current aesthetic debate, largely developed through the work of Donald Meltzer and his step-daughter, Meg Harris Williams.

The evolution of Bion's work begins with his early papers on schizophrenia in the 1950s, which were the basis of the elaboration of a more sophisticated "theory of thinking", developed in 1962.

His earlier writings (pre-1970) attempt to place psychoanalysis on a more "scientific" footing, using various analogies mainly taken from mathematics, geometry, biology, physics, and chemistry. These methods of exposition, however, largely fell short of Bion's expectations, and in his pursuit of a new universe of discourse we see him gradually shifting away from the scientific to the more aesthetic and mystical (religious) vertices, drawing upon an impressive array of philosophers, poets, and mystics, including Sophocles, Plato, Meister Eckhart, Kant, Shakespeare, Milton, and Keats.

It seems that once Bion had removed the "mathematical scaffolding" of his writings, a new era began (Meltzer, 1978, p. 30). He said himself that the "latency period in his creativity" ended when his fully worked out theory of thinking was presented in 1962, two years after Klein's death. This includes his last theoretical work, *Attention and Interpretation* (1970); his two-part autobiography, *The Long Weekend* (1982) and *All My Sins Remembered* (1985); and the three-part, semi-autobiographic, science fictional account of the mind, *A Memoir of the Future* (1975–1979, republished by Karnac Books, 1990).

The richness of his later writings offers a very different kind of approach—one that demands much patience and effort on the reader's part and may provoke extreme reactions in an unsuspecting first-time reader. His writing is difficult to follow and often irritatingly obscure, as he constantly refers to a wide range of mathematical, philosophical, theological, mythical, and literary sources that enrich his ideas, but can also create an air of obscurity for those who are unfamiliar with the intellectual terrain coupled with his eccentric style of writing. Bion's later work becomes progressively more mystical, relying on the reader's own aesthetic appreciation of the "underlying pattern" in his often puzzling, but always challenging, writings. Indeed, he has been referred to as "one of the rare mystics of ours or any time" (Grotstein, 1981, p. 33). Perhaps it is because of their somewhat off-beat, eccentric approach that Bion's later writings have been taken less seriously—regarded by some as offering interesting but rather impractical psychoanalytic tools, and dismissed more severely by others as the quasi-religious ramblings of a crank. Donald Meltzer (a close friend and colleague of both Klein and Bion), his wife Martha Harris, and her daughter Meg Harris Williams (a writer and artist), have been most helpful in making Bion's ideas more explicit and accessible. Together with the psychotherapist and writer Margot Waddell, these commentators have made important contributions to a post-Kleinian aesthetic, deploying Bion's insights in relation to a variety of artistic and cultural issues and his model of the mind. The art critic Peter Fuller (discussed later in this book) became particularly interested in the post-Kleinian developments in British School thinking and deployed the ideas of Bion, together with those of Milner, Rycroft, and Winnicott, in the analysis of American abstract painting, especially that of Robert Natkin and Mark Rothko.

New directions in a Kleinian account of aesthetic value and the creative process were pioneered largely by the work of Bion in the 1960s and 1970s. Meltzer, Bion's chief exponent, continued to develop a very distinctive theoretical stance, and devoted much effort towards demystifying Bion's ideas. *The Apprehension of Beauty* (1988), written in collaboration with Meg Harris Williams, is a significant contribution to a "post-Kleinian" aesthetic, linking the work of Bion explicitly with philosophical and literary, as well as developmental, concerns. For, according to Meltzer, Bion has brought together the art and science of psychoanalysis and placed it on a foundation no longer isolated from other fields that deal with human mentality—psychology, sociology, history, philosophy, theology, the fine arts, anthropology, and palaeontology. Bion is seen as evolving not psychoanalytic theories, but theories about psychoanalysis as a *thing-in-itself*, in the Kantian sense, from what the analyst experiences; linking psychoanalysis with the broad sweep of humanitarian endeavour, and placing more value than any of his predecessors on the supreme value of the self.

The evolution of Bion's work

Bion's distinguished career began early. At seventeen, he joined the army Tank Regiment to fight in the First World War, and was awarded the DSO for his efforts at the battle of Cambrai. *The Long Weekend 1897–1919* (1982) is the first of a two-part autobiography, and gives a vivid account of his wartime experiences and their effects upon his development. He put his wartime experience to evocative use, comparing the position of an analyst in the consulting room with that of the soldier on the battlefield, who has to retain the capacity to think while under fire. Bion saw the consulting room as a potential battlefield where the analyst must try to *think about* (contain) his patient's responses or attacks, rather than blindly projecting and expelling them. This demands great discipline and "negative capability".

In 1918 he was demobilized, and then went to read Modern History at Oxford, where he fell under the influence of the philosopher H. J. Paton, who introduced him to the work of Kant and to other philosophers, such as Plato, Hume, and Poincaré. This philosophical input was to exert a powerful influence on his later metapsychological formulations. In 1924, he went to study medicine at the University College Hospital in London. By 1929 he was qualified, and had achieved the Gold Medal for Clinical Surgery in 1930. The influence of the distinguished surgeon Wilfred Trotter was to inspire Bion's interest in groups and herd instincts. Bion's preoccupation with psychology flourished, and was strengthened by the training analysis that he began with John Rickman, a prominent member of the British Psychoanalytic Society, who was later to introduce Bion to Melanie Klein and suggest that he be analysed by her. Bion's analysis with Rickman was interrupted by the outbreak of the Second World War. During the war he was made Officer-in-Charge of the Military Training Wing at Northfield Military Hospital for six weeks: his task concerned the rehabilitation of officers suffering from shell-shock and other nervous problems. In this short time he was able to bring the effectiveness of group work into serious consideration. His classic study *Experiences in Groups* (1961) traces the development of his ideas from his pre-psychoanalytic days to his later involvement with Freudian and Kleinian thinking.

In his Introduction to *Experiences in Groups*, Bion emphasizes that the psychoanalytic approach through the individual, and his own approach via the group, are dealing with "different facets of the same phenomena". These two ways of seeing provide the practitioner with a rudimentary "binocular vision". Bion states that the observations tend to fall into two categories: the Oedipal situation, relating to what he calls the "pairing" group, and the other, which centres on the myth of the Sphinx, relating to the withholding and subsequent revealing of knowledge. He also stresses the significance of the Kleinian theory of projective identification, and the interplay between the paranoid–schizoid and the depressive positions. It is with these two sets of theories in mind (Freud's and Klein's) that he goes on to tackle the nature of groups, and his account was to offer new ways of bringing psychoanalytic theory to bear on issues outside the consulting room, to illuminate the wider social, political, and cultural domain. Bion suggests that no individual, even in isolation, can be considered as marginal to a group or as lacking the active manifestations of group psychology, even when the conditions that demonstrate this do not appear to be present. Freud's theories (especially that of the Oedipus complex) show the importance of the family group in the development of every human being. Klein's work, particularly her hypotheses about early object relations, psychotic anxieties, and primitive defences, allow us to understand that the individual does not only belong to a family group from the start of life, but also that his first contact with his mother and other persons from his surroundings exert a profound influence over his subsequent emotional development. The psychotic anxieties aroused in relation to the first objects are reactivated in various adult situations. The individual must establish contact with the emotional life of the group, which poses a dilemma of evolution and differentiation owing to having to face the fears associated with *change*.

At the Tavistock Clinic, Bion worked with small groups of patients to help clarify group tensions. He stressed the importance of the emotional reactions of the observer, who is often made to experience certain projective identifications from members of the group who wish to cast him in the role of (say) teacher, consultant, or parental figure. Bion deals with this by refusing to take on such roles assigned to him by the group. He describes the group's resulting exasperation, confusion, and anger as he objectively and impassively witnessed their behaviour, noticing that there often followed a reinstatement of some willing—and usually authoritative—person who would be prepared to carry out the roles designated to him or her, depending on the "basic assumption" of the group. Bion also became aware that there were different forces at work within the group that seemed to pull in opposite directions. The groups that congregated to carry out a specific task showed attitudes and methods that did not seem conducive to the achievement of the proposed aim. These were manifest in the intellectually barren conversations during the sessions, in the loss of critical judgement, and in the disturbances in the rational behaviour of its members—all of which did not correlate with the ability and intelligence of its members outside the group situation. Solutions to the problems within the group were not found by using methods attuned to reality. The group situations were heavily charged with emotions that exercised a powerful influence on its members and seemed to orientate them without their awareness of this happening; moreover, the members did not appear to want to examine these situations.

Bion concluded that there are two main tendencies potentially operating in a group: one is directed toward the accomplishment of the task, and the other seems to oppose it. Work is obstructed by a more primary, regressive activity, characteristic of the id-function. Bion introduces specific terms that describe these common features observed in various experiences. The most important are his concepts of *basic assumptions, group mentality*, and the idea of the *work group*. The idea of "basic assumptions" clarifies the concept of group mentality. The term refers to the existence of a common, unanimous, and anonymous opinion at any given moment. Basic assumptions are shaped by intense emotions of primitive origin and are powerful examples of the workings of unconscious phantasy. Their existence helps to determine the organization that the group will adopt and also the way in which it will approach its tasks. The group culture will always show evidence of the underlying basic assumptions active at any given time. The underlying emotional impulses in a group are often irrational, working in unconscious ways, and often opposed to the conscious rational opinions of the group members, yet they express a shared phantasy of an omnipotent or magic type as to how to achieve the group's goals.

Bion is perhaps best known for his work on groups; yet the inroads he made into the understanding of psychosis and the study of thinking have probably been the most profound contributions that he made to psychoanalysis. The 1950s were an important period in the development of Kleinian theory and practice, because Klein's ideas about psychotic anxieties and defences were tested with severely ill patients who were mainly diagnosed schizophrenics. A further goal was to see how far psychotic patients could be analysed without changing the essentials of the psychoanalytic method. The analysis of psychotic patients produced new material, and significant pioneers included Hanna Segal and Herbert Rosenfeld. All three thinkers agreed on the feasibility of the psychoanalytic method in treating psychosis, and found impressive substantiation of Klein's views that the fixation point for schizophrenia was in the paranoid–schizoid position. All found confirmation of her ideas on projective identification, the early and persecuting superego, the pain of depressive anxiety, and the retreat from it using the manic defences and those relating to the paranoid–schizoid position. The papers published by Bion on psychosis follow chronologically from his work on groups and these writings (1950–1962) were brought together in his *Second Thoughts* (1967) and, as the title suggests, were reviewed in the light of further developments in his thinking, going beyond the examination of Klein's theories. He began to take an interest in the difference between the normal and pathological experience of the paranoid–schizoid position, which led on to a distinction between projective identification used to evacuate and fragment mental contents, and projective identification as a form of *communication* that could influence the recipient and could in turn be influenced by him. This analysis of psychotic thinking and the role of the paranoid–schizoid position led him to formulate a theory of thinking and creativity that is quite possibly one of the most original we have today.

Bion, thinking and creativity

Bion's theory of thinking, formulated in 1962, was founded on this work and on some other earlier notions, in particular his concept of "linking", derived from observations of psychotic behaviour in the consulting room. In his paper "Language and the schizophrenic" (1955) and in *Second Thoughts* (1967), Bion described the attacks on the ego itself, which represented the experiences that Klein (1946) had regarded as the effects of the death instinct arising from within—the feeling of falling to pieces. Bion emphasized, in particular, an attack on the awareness of internal reality. It is the *links between mental contents* that are attacked by the schizophrenic, and Bion observed that language is not being used as a form of verbal communication but rather to project the envious, greedy, and hostile split-off parts of the self into others, including the analyst. Freud had also outlined this process when he studied severe obsessional neurosis, but Bion emphasized its violent quality.[1] The result is that the schizophrenic lives in a fragmented world of turbulence, with unusable, primitive ideas in his mind—ones that cannot be used for thinking:

> All these are now attacked until finally two objects cannot be brought together in a way which leaves each object with its intrinsic qualities intact and yet able, by their conjunction, to produce a new mental object. [Bion, 1967, p. 50]

He adds that the destruction of these connections and conjunctions leads to the patient feeling as if he is "surrounded by minute links which, being impregnated now with cruelty, link objects together cruelly". Bion called these particles "bizarre objects" and later, "beta elements"—raw, unprocessed sense data that cannot be assimilated and symbolized by the ego as "food for thinking". The effect is akin to what Freud (1911b) termed a "world catastrophe", or what analyst Edna O'Shaughnessy describes in terms of

> a disaster for mental life which is not then established in the normal mode. Instead of thinking based on the reality principle and symbolic communication with the self and with other objects, an anomalous enlargement of the pleasure ego occurs, with excessive use of splitting and projective identification as its concrete mode of relating to hated and hating objects. Omnipotence replaces thinking and omniscience replaces learning from experience in a disastrously confused, undeveloped and fragile ego. [1981b, p. 183]

Bion took these observations much further and established a formal theory. He envisaged the thinking apparatus as the "container–contained", with the mind's coupling activity based on an *innate predisposition* to conceive of the link between a container and its contents, typically the nipple in the mouth or the penis in the vagina. The attack on the link between two internal mental objects is also an attack on the *internal parent couple*. Because of the connotations of the oedipal couple, the conjoining of two mental objects is felt not only to arouse envy, but to be the basis for internal mental creativity. This is also known as the "combined parent figure" (see Hinshelwood, 1989, p. 240). Meltzer (1973) was to develop this point, seeing the fount of personal creativity as due to the depressive reconstruction of the internal couple in realistic intercourse, as opposed to the sadistic and violent coupling characteristic of more primitive mental states. The coupling of penis and vagina, or mouth and nipple, was taken by Bion to be the prototype of the way mental objects are put together, one inside the other. Thus, putting experiences into thoughts, and thoughts into words, entails a repeated chain of linking processes modelled on physical intercourse between two bodily parts. With this model, Bion went on to investigate the nature of thought itself—the mating of a "preconception" (an innate "expectation" in the Kantian sense) with sensory realizations. He drew attention to the epistemophilic impulse (which Klein had herself noted), which he called "K". The K-link works alongside the love (L) and the hate (H) impulses, forming the basis of relationships to objects (including the relationship and cross-fertilization of ideas in the mind) that establishes meaning and respect for the integrity of these objects. The container–contained relationship is operated upon by the dynamic influence of the paranoid–schizoid (Ps) and depressive positions (D), plus the "selected fact"—akin to a catalyst. This process he termed "Ps↔D", with the double arrow suggesting an ongoing oscillation between the two positions. However, working against the positive links in this process, Bion stressed that there were also negative anti-links of $-L$, $-H$ and $-K$. These are the antithesis of healthy relating to objects, and work to annihilate and corrupt meaning and psychic reality. Creativity is thwarted by the destructive forces that fragment positive links to objects, and this results in an impoverishment of psychic life.

Bion's contribution to the understanding of creativity is thus intrinsic to his theory of thinking. It supplements the view of "traditional" Kleinians, like Segal, by placing value on the essential *interdependence* of processes of fragmentation and integration, which he regarded as essential to all creative thinking. He used Klein's concept of the paranoid–schizoid and depressive positions to illustrate the ongoing relationship between disintegration and reintegration that is an essential part of the creative process. Where Klein emphasized the negative aspects of the paranoid–schizoid position and placed the depressive position at the heart of successful development, Bion saw the fragmentation and splitting in the paranoid position as a necessary aspect of human experience. Thinking involves the dismantling of previous views and theories, allowing the formation of new ideas. In changing one's way of thinking, the container has to be dissolved before it is reformed. Bion regarded the effort of dissolution as having the quality of a small psychic *catastrophe*, a "going-to-pieces". It was therefore a movement into the paranoid–schizoid position. The reforming of a new set of views and theories is a synthesizing move, like that of the depressive position. The sense of catastrophe seems to start when the infant first screams, and Bion thought the intuition of it was probably older than life itself: a memory of the explosive force that created the universe, carried within the molecules of our bodies. The process of tolerating the upheaval caused by the new idea requires the kind of strength that Keats called "negative capability". (Indeed, Bion often referred to a passage by Keats in which he wrote that a "Man of Achievement" was "capable of being in uncertainties, Mysteries, doubts, without any irritable reaching after fact and reason" [Keats, 1958, p. 193].) In this context, creative effort can therefore be viewed as an ongoing process, on a small scale, of movements to-and-fro between the paranoid–schizoid and depressive positions.

The implications of Bion's ideas for aesthetics have been noted in both Segal's and Stokes's later work. Stokes, for example, talks of the "sense of fusion" combined with "otherness" at the heart of authentic aesthetic experience. A similar emphasis on the link between disintegration and re-integration in artistic activity can be found in Ehrenzweig (1967).

Bion was also influenced by Poincaré's account, in his *Science and Method*, of the process of creation of a mathematical formula. Bion noted that it "closely resembles the psycho-analytical theory of paranoid–schizoid and depressive positions adumbrated by Mrs Klein". Poincaré writes:

> If a new result is to have any value, it must unite elements long since known, but till then scattered and seemingly foreign to each other, and suddenly introduce order where the appearance of disorder reigned. Then it enables us to see at a glance each of these elements in the place it occupies in the whole. Not only is the new

fact valuable on its own account, but it alone gives a value to the old facts it unites. Our mind is as frail as our senses are; it would lose itself in the complexity of the world if that complexity were not harmonious; like the short-sighted, it would see only the details and would be obliged to forget each of these details before examining the next, because it would be incapable of taking in the whole. The only facts worthy of our attention are those which introduce order into this complexity and so make it accessible to us. [cited in Bion, 1962, p. 72]

Bion takes this to be a model of *all* creativity—the way in which seemingly disparate, chaotic elements accumulate around a "selected fact": a process that gives new meaning to both the chaotic elements and the fact selected. For Bion, this "selected fact" is an *emotional* experience.

Bion's theory of thinking and creativity marks a major step forward in psychoanalytic theory. For, not only does it provide psychoanalysis with its first account of thoughts (the "contained"), and the thinking apparatus created to think them (the "container"), and their relationship to the thinker, it also radically reorientates psychoanalytic theory into the mainstream of western epistemology. Bion moves away from Freud's mechanistic biological reductionism into a philosophical sphere, invoking the pre-determinism of Kant and Plato. He supplemented Freud's instinct theory with Plato's theory of inherent forms, pure thoughts (what Bion called "thoughts without a thinker") and Kant's *a priori* assumptions (things-in-themselves). His conjecture is that pure thoughts exist long *before there is a mind to think them*. According to his theory, they are drawn from passivity into disruptive energies by the sense organ of consciousness as the latter is stimulated by events in the external and/or internal world. A mind is needed to think these thoughts. (Grotstein notes that Bion's version of Descartes's "cogito ergo sum" would probably have been "I am, therefore I have thoughts without a thinker which demand a mind to think about them" [Grotstein, 1981, p. 15].) According to Bion (following Freud), it is in response to the pressure of thoughts that the thinking apparatus evolves. This begins when the infant projects his uncontainable fear, discomfort, and anxiety into the mother, who acts as a container for the child's fears. The mother is able to receive these projections and modify them so that the infant can introject the fear but in a "detoxified" form.

Bion introduces the terms "alpha function", "alpha elements" and "beta elements" to designate certain aspects of this process. Alpha function refers to the ability to *create meaning* out of raw, unprocessed sensory data, which he called beta elements. The mother's "reverie" is her alpha function, and represents the ability to modify her child's tensions and anxieties. The mother and the child form a "thinking couple", which is the prototype of the thinking process that continues developing throughout life. (Bion decided to use Greek symbols and mathematical language to express his ideas because he felt that ordinary language was too saturated with preconceptions. By using a terminology removed from familiar language, Bion hoped to allow the analyst's own experience to fill the terms with his own meaning derived from personal experience.) Alpha function works on the unprocessed beta elements and transforms them into alpha elements in a way similar to a chemical transformation—indeed, Bion compares it to the digestive process, thinking being "alimentary". The beta elements (which are fit only for projection and splitting) are so modified that they become absorbable and, quite literally, *food for thought*. Alpha elements represent the link between our innate preconceptions (intuitions) and our raw experience of the external world. They form the building-blocks of thought upon which more complex systems can be built. Ultimately, Bion saw psychotic experience as the result of failure by the mother to contain her infant's fear of dying. Perhaps the mother was psychotic herself, or depressed, and unable to contain and modify her child's fears. In this situation, all the infant's anxiety is projected into the mother, and instead of being contained and modified by her, the fears are returned to the child but now in a heightened form. The establishment of alpha function is impeded and thinking seriously impaired. The task of the analyst treating a psychotic is similar to that of the mother who contains the infant's projections without being destroyed by them. The re-establishment of the patient's ability to tolerate anxiety and frustrations depends on his ability to make use of the analyst's own alpha function. When the patient's own alpha function is re-established and his anxieties contained, then the whole process of normal thinking can begin.

Bion's concept of the container–contained relation was to have significance not only for Kleinian thinking, but for psychoanalytic theory generally. It added the possibility of the psyche's adaptability and re-established the importance of external reality, which had been lacking in Kleinian psychology. His model of the analytic encounter has similarities with that of Winnicott, who saw the analyst as taking over the role of the environment–mother that first failed the child; it allows for the importance of the individual's relationship to his environment and the importance of the mother's adaptability to respond intuitively to her infant's needs.

The re-mapping of mental space

Following on from the work of Melanie Klein, there has been much interest in the British School in the exploration of the nature of inner space in both its positive and negative realizations. As Bion points out, traditional Kleinian formulations relied upon a visual image of a space containing all kinds of objects. One of Klein's most significant contributions to psychoanalysis was her account of the *inner world*, especially the concreteness of internal reality and the internal objects that comprise it (Bion, 1970, p. 8). The mother's body is regarded as the first "container" into which the infant projects his love and his hate, and correspondingly perceives the inside of the body to contain a whole host of very concretely-felt objects— whether hostile or benign depending on whether the paranoid– schizoid or depressive position is in the ascendant. Klein's account of the mechanisms of projection had been derived from the common-sense account of three-dimensional space, and this depended upon a space into which was projected parts of the personality that have been split-off. The degree of fragmentation, together with the distance to which these fragments have been projected, is thought to be an indication of the extent of mental disturbance or normality.

It was Bion's great contribution to highlight the communicative, empathic role of projective identification, and its prototype in the infant–mother relationship (Bion, 1962). Through the mysterious activity of the mother's *reverie*, the infant's split-off anxieties (projections) are contained, detoxified and returned to the infant, who introjects them, but now in a modified form: "unthinkable anxiety" and "nameless dread" have (through mother's reverie or "alpha function") become bearable. The notion of the mother (and specifically her breast) as a container that the child himself takes in, Bion believes is the prototype of all thinking and creativity—the "thinking breast" becomes for the infant the "container for the sum of meanings". As we have seen, his concept of PS↔D elevated Klein's account of "positions" from their libidinal, economic framework to a psychic mechanism that actively fills the container with meaning. There is an initial schizoid fragmentation followed by an eventual depressive reintegration, centring around what Bion calls (after Poincaré) the "selected fact". The prototype for this is the nipple; it may be an image, or a thought around which the new meanings can converge and organize themselves. It resonates with what Stokes called the "image in form" (1966), and also links with Ehrenzweig's (1967) account of the "hidden order" emerging from the "manic–oceanic womb" of undifferentiation after an initial schizoid breakdown (see Chapter Five). However, it must be emphasized that, for Bion, the "thinking breast" is essentially an *internal* object—it is not "self-created" in the sense of Winnicott's account of "hallucinatory wish-fulfilment", which postulates that the child imagines that he has magically created the breast because it is presented to him at the time of his needing it.

In *Attention and Interpretation*, Bion suggests that such geometric concepts as lines, points, and space "derived originally not from a realization of three-dimensional space, but from the realizations of emotional life". They are also "returnable to the realm from which they emerged". He believed that the geometer's conception of space derives from the experience of "the place where something was", and so it can be returned to make sense of psychic experiences such as the feeling of "depression" which is, says Bion, "the place where a breast or other lost object was", or the space where "depression or some other emotion used to be" (1970, p. 10). (It is useful to bear in mind this "geography of inner space" when we explore Fuller's analysis of Rothko's "backward journey into the limitless expanse of space" in Chapter Seven.) Bion argues that, despite our association of them with everyday expressions, there is an essential difference between the geometer's space and that characteristic of *mental* images. In the latter, an infinite number of lines may pass through any one point (multi-dimensionality) but if one attempts to represent such a visual image by points and lines on paper, then there would be only a finite amount of lines. Bion says that this "limiting quality" inheres in all representations of three-dimensional space that approximate to the points, lines, and space of the geometer—who had to "await the invention of Cartesian co-ordinates before he could elaborate algebraic geometry" (1970, p. 11). Such limitation, however, does not inhere in mental space until the attempt is made to represent it in *verbal* thought. Bion postulates mental space as a thing-in-itself that is essentially unknowable, pre- or non-verbal, but that can be represented by non-discursive thoughts, including phantasies, dreams, memories (alpha elements). There is a conflict between the impulse to leave the intuition unexpressed and the impulse to express it. The restrictive element of representation (verbal, pictorial, mathematical) obstructs its transformation; it will not be able to capture the full quality of the initial experience. Yet, the individual who lacks the capacity to map a realization of their inner space is in a state analogous to "having pain without suffering it" (perhaps this is what Mrs Gradgrind meant when she remarked in *Hard Times* that "there is a pain somewhere in the room but I am not quite sure where it is"!); "not understanding planetary movement because the differential calculus has not been invented"; "not being conscious of a mental phenomenon because it has been repressed".

The creative, adaptive individual who has what Keats termed "negative capability" can tolerate the frustration without seeking for a substitute for thought: in Winnicott's terms, he can hold the paradox without a "flight to split-off intellectual functioning" (1971, p. xii). Intolerance results in the splitting and projection of beta elements, which are "not thinkable" but can only form "bizarre objects" suitable for evacuation. This takes place in a mental space that has no visual images to fulfil the functions of a co-ordinate system; there is "no conception of containers into which projection and introjection could take place and the mental representation of space is felt as an immensity so great that it cannot be represented at all" (Bion, 1970, p. 12). Such a state Bion compares to "surgical shock"—where the dilation of the capillaries in the body increases to the extent that the patient may "bleed to death in his own tissues". Bion adds that

> Mental space is so vast compared with any realisation of three-dimensional space that the patient's capacity for emotion is felt to be lost because emotion itself is felt to drain away and be lost in such immensity ... [What may then] appear to the observer as thoughts, visual images and verbalisations, are actually debris, remnants or scraps of imitated speech ... floating in a space so vast that its confines, temporal as well as spatial, are without definition. [1970, pp. 12–13]

Through the psychoanalytic process, the patient gradually evolves the capacity to make use of words, points, and lines of sensuous space for the understanding of emotional (psychic) space—and this involves the toleration of frustration, acceptance of the limitations of external reality, and the lessening of omnipotence, all which are necessary (Bion implies) in the process of transformation of non-sensuous intuition into its sensuous realization. According to Bion, the (successful) analyst becomes the container for the patient's content and also provides a content for his container.

Although I have not yet discussed Winnicott's account of the "potential space" (to be explored in Chapter Six) it is interesting to compare it briefly at this point with Bion's ideas about mental space. Although they are both "post-Kleinians" in the sense of being pupils of Klein who pioneered new developments that largely went beyond her paradigm, there are important differences, which relate, in my view, to Bion being more of a "Kleinian" than Winnicott. (Fuller [see Chapter Seven] regards both Winnicott and Bion as "post-Kleinian", and theoretical differences tend to be submerged when looking at aesthetic issues. But some Kleinians [e.g., Hinshelwood] hesitate to call Bion a "post"-Kleinian at all. For a more detailed discussion of this point see Glover [1989].) Bion's conception of inner space concerns the *inner* world, one which arises from what he calls "Ultimate Reality" or "O"—that which

> stands for the absolute truth in and of any object; it is assumed that this cannot be known by any human being; it can be known about, its presence can be recognised and felt, but it cannot be known. It is possible to be at one with it. That it exists is an essential postulate of science but it cannot be scientifically discovered. No psychoanalytic discovery is possible without recognition of its existence. [Bion, 1970, p. 30]

This "O" can only be apprehended when there is no memory, desire, knowledge, or understanding. Indeed, he says that it is the religious mystics who have probably come closest to the experience of it. From a literary and philosophical perspective, he likens it to Milton's "void and formless infinite", Huxley's "Divine Ground of Being", Plato's Ideal Forms, and Kant's Noumenon. It represents the gap in knowledge, the emptiness from which all existence comes; and Bion acknowledges that this may appear terrifying, chaotic and annihilating. (It also links, in my view, with the symbol of the *empty circle* that became a prominent symbol in Milner's patient Susan's drawings, as well as in Milner's own personal set of visual metaphors. She refers to it as the direct "non-symbolic" experience of the undifferentiated matrix of bodily awareness. Milner's account [in contrast to Bion] sees this almost solely in terms of its creative and transformative potential.) Winnicott's theory of the "potential space" is essentially a benign concept of the interaction between child and mother. Unlike the Kleinians, Winnicott did not believe in the existence of an innate instinctual clash between love and hate, indeed, he saw no unconscious phantasy operating from birth—thus re-focusing (or avoiding!) the Kleinian emphasis on the innate sadism and destructiveness of the earliest infantile phantasies, and replacing it with a far more beneficent conception of the earliest weeks of life. Having said this, however, Winnicott's theory, developmentally speaking, could be viewed as fundamentally achieving much the same thing as Bion's account of the breast as the first "container" for the child. Indeed, in a number of correspondences, Winnicott argues that what Bion is saying is virtually the same as himself, albeit cloaked in more abstract form (see his letter to J. O. Wisdom, Winnicott, 1987, p. 159).

Bion's mental space is multi-dimensional, vast and infinite, with no direct correspondence with sensuous reality. It is therefore quite a move away from Klein's account of the inner world—which is, prototypically, based on the child's phantasies concerning the mother's body and its contents, assuming a conception of three-dimensionality, and populated with concretely experienced objects. But, unlike Winnicott's account of the space *between* mother and child, the psychic experience of this *inner* space has potentially persecuting and threatening aspects, in that it can be perceived (during mental disturbance, for example) as an alien, hostile void or emptiness. The threat of being engulfed by this space is akin to the feeling of "falling forever" (Meltzer, 1978), of having no boundaries to contain fear and anxiety, and the result is a psychic catastrophe—what Bion calls "catastrophic chaos" and "nameless dread". Indeed, as we shall see below, Fuller regards the negative, persecutory aspect of inner space described by Bion as highly significant for the understanding of the spatial dynamics of Rothko's work.

Donald Meltzer and "aesthetic conflict"

Donald Meltzer, an American child psychiatrist, came to London in 1954 especially to train with Mrs Klein, and he remained in analysis with her until she died in 1960. His consolidation of Bion's work on thinking and experiencing, from which Meltzer created his own psychoanalytic epistemology, together with his systematic tracing of the development of the work of Bion and Klein from Freud and Abraham's metapsychology (Meltzer, 1975), helped to establish him as one of the leading members of the Kleinian Group. (During the latter part of his career, his views on the training of psychoanalysts brought him into conflict with the strict methods of the British Psychoanalytic Institute and he left the Society; consequently he is regarded by more orthodox Kleinians as a somewhat a controversial figure.) His contribution to the understanding of creative and aesthetic experience and its developmental role is a particularly significant development in post-Kleinian thought.

Meltzer's contribution to aesthetics is broadly humanistic, stressing the importance of creativity and the aesthetic capacity for human growth in its most far-reaching sense:

> It seems somehow fitting that the mind should discover its own beauty only after it has discovered the beauty of nature and of man's works that bear witness and extol it. In this respect the growth of the individual's aesthetic awareness mirrors the evolution of the race, in its transformation of weapons into tools, in its gradual move from anthropomorphism to understanding nature, in its even slower development from possession and exploitation to responsibility for the world. [Meltzer & Harris Williams, 1988, p. xiii]

In *Sexual States of Mind* (1973), Meltzer explores the origins of sexuality, following psychoanalytic theory from Freud and Abraham through to Klein and Bion. In the process, he traces the origins and the nature of creativity, arguing that the paradigm of the creative act is the harmonious bringing together of partners in intercourse. (This is also significant in his analysis of the relationship between artist and viewer, where "there is an exact parallel in the sexual relationships between individuals". The art-viewer is involved in processes of introjection and projection between himself and artist, via the artwork which can be of either a perversely masochistic, sadistic sort or of a more constructive, nourishing nature, depending on whether destroyed objects/parts of the self or more loving ones are being communicated.) Here he makes an original contribution to a post-Kleinian account of creative achievement, supplementing Segal's more traditional view of creativity. Where she emphasizes the depressive position as giving rise to both the creative impulse and the aesthetic sense, Meltzer's later work stresses that the capacity for aesthetic experience comes much earlier, and (following Bion) might even be present before birth. His view does not differ too significantly from Segal's; both see it as arising from the shift in perception and values accompanying the depressive position. Segal, in attributing authentic creativity to the specific phantasy of reparation, does not give any further account of how the phantasy comes into being, or of what distinguishes it from the omnipotent phantasies characteristic of the paranoid–schizoid position and of manic-defence inauthentic creation.

Meltzer develops this Kleinian account of creativity much further, seeing it, and indeed the whole structure of the personality, as given by the *internal parents combined in loving and constructive intercourse* (as opposed to a sadistic, destructive, and hostile one). This combined parent figure forms the basis of the ego ideal, tempering the more punitive elements of the earlier, harsher superego. The introjected internal parents, says Meltzer, exist as a godlike presence inside each person, and from them derives a sense of creativeness that can inspire the individual to his own constructive and creative efforts. It is the fount of all subsequent creative achievement, without which there can be no phantasy of genuine creation or reparation.

Meltzer makes an important point when he asserts that "psychoanalysis discovers that creativity is, for the self, impossible". All creativity comes "as in a dream and is a function of internal objects of . . . the individual artist-scientist" (Meltzer & Harris Williams, 1988, p. xiii). The main problem for the development of creative and aesthetic sensitivity is the struggle between his or her aesthetic sense and the "forces of philistinism, Puritanism, cynicism and perversity—what Bion called "−K"—an external as well as an internal force that undermines psychic reality and truth. Indeed, this struggle between love of knowledge and the escape from the "truth" (about ourselves and the external world) is one of the themes informing *The Apprehension of Beauty*, with its celebration of "the beauty of the method by which the mind . . . operates upon the emotional experiences of our lives to give them a representation through symbol-formation that makes thinking about these experiences possible"—what Meltzer regards as the heart of the psychoanalytic process itself (*ibid.*).

Meltzer and Harris Williams' central concept in this book is that of "aesthetic conflict", and they discuss aesthetic experience and its vicissitudes from a number of perspectives—in art, development, and violence. Aesthetic conflict is the struggle between the ravishment that the baby is felt to experience in the presence of the mother's outside, of the formal qualities of breast and face, and his mistrust of her inner world. It "can be most precisely stated in terms of the aesthetic impact of the outside of the 'beautiful' mother, available to the senses, and the enigmatic inside which must be construed by creative imagination". Beauty, a property of the "ordinary beautiful devoted mother" (as in Winnicott's "good-enough mother"), is thought of as a quality having the power to elicit a passionate response (passionate in the sense of involving all of Bion's L, H, and K links), and the capacity for this response is thought of as an innate property of the human mind of the "ordinary beautiful baby", although some people may "recoil violently from it".

In many ways, this conflict resembles that over the absent object, but it is essential to recognize that the authors think of the aesthetic conflict as concerning the *present* object—"it is the human condition" where

> the lover is as naked as Othello to the whisperings of Iago, but is rescued by the quest for knowledge, the K-link, the desire to know

rather than to possess the object of desire. The K-link points to the value of desire itself as the stimulus to knowledge, not merely as a yearning for gratification and control over the object. *Desire makes it possible, even essential, to give the object its freedom.* [ibid., p. 27, original italics]

One consequence of this formulation is that Melanie Klein's scheme of the paranoid–schizoid position being *succeeded by* the depressive position is no longer tenable. Instead, conflict concerning the present object is held to *precede* conflict over the absent object, and

the period of maximal beatification between mother and baby arises very early, soon to be clouded by varying degrees of postpartum depression in the mother and . . . the baby's reaction against the aesthetic impact. [*ibid.*, p. 26]

The use of the image of the infant's retreating into the cave in reaction against the dazzle of the sunrise may be seen as the most explicit statement of a Platonist current in analytic thought that begins with Melanie Klein's idea, in *Envy and Gratitude*, that the inborn capacity for love is a precondition for a good feeding experience, and, as we have seen, this is developed further in Bion's theory of innate preconceptions.

Evidence for these formulations is adduced throughout *The Apprehension of Beauty*, from the clinical material of patients in widely differing states of development and from the work of poets and other imaginative writers. The mutual enrichment that is possible between analysis and art is evident in the integration of the two authors' contributions. Passages from the poets are quoted as being particularly felicitous expressions and embodiments of crucial manifestations of that inspiration which, in its reliance on the creativity of the internal parents, goes beyond the "useful productivity" in which received knowledge is appropriately applied. At the same time, Harris Williams gives examples of the encounter between the critic and the work of art that embody the features of engagement with an aesthetic object, and many of the formulations concerning the task of the critic are directly applicable to the analytic situation. The authors emphasize the "mystery of private spaces", one that they repeatedly contrast with *secrecy*, the latter relating more to the projection of curiosity and feelings of exclusion and to the stimulation of the intrusive curiosity that culminates in violence. Meltzer argues that the sense of mystery and wonder inspired by the idea of the mother's inner world and the parents' "nuptial chamber" can be at best unevenly sustained: oscillations between the sense of awe and intrusiveness, between knowledge as exploration and knowledge as control, between Bion's "knowing" and "knowing about", are traced in Harris Williams' analysis of the attitude of *Hamlet*, just as in Meltzer's story of a little girl patient who was severely damaged at birth. Violence, both mental and physical, is seen as an extreme form of the impulse to violate the privacy of the parents' private space; the impulse to do violence to the baby that is the issue of this nuptial chamber provides the link with the perversions.

One of the ways in which the aesthetic impact of the mother, with its challenge to pride and envy, is felt to be made more bearable, and the imaginative relation to her private spaces therefore more tolerable, is delineated in a chapter "On aesthetic reciprocity". Here it is shown how a mother's failure to experience anything about her damaged little girl as beautiful was linked to the child's mechanical, intrusive, and controlling "knowledge about" the parental intercourse, while the apprehension of its mystery could evolve through the therapist's acknowledgement of the child's genuine drive towards exploration and enquiry. Thus, it is emphasized that the baby's initial response to the mother is to do with what it can perceive, while that aspect of "babyishness" that elicits the mother's aesthetic response is to do not with the baby's formal qualities, but with its potential for development. (This links with the observations of some possible consequences where there has not been adequate containment of the conflicting responses to the object: for instance, psychosomatic symptoms when this impact can no longer be evaded [see the chapter "The recovery of the aesthetic object"], or the avoidance of thought and meaning in favour of sensory experience that Frances Tustin (1972, 1981) described in autistic children.) As Meltzer has said elsewhere, the development of an analysis is furthered if the analyst can keep in mind that he is "presiding over a process of great beauty".

This mental attitude, and the potentiality for symbolization and the apprehension of meaning that it generates, is also what characterizes the critic who engages with a work of art in such a way that *he himself is open to transformation*. Meg Harris Williams suggests a number of qualities expected from a sympathetic critic. First, there must be

> some ability to tolerate the uncertainty of the cloud of unknowing aroused by the confrontation with the aesthetic object, without irritable reaching after fact and reason; some capacity to look steadily at the subject until eventually a pattern emerges. [Meltzer & Harris Williams, 1988, p. 181]

That is, the critic should be more concerned with "knowing" than with the academic kind of "knowing about" (*ibid.*). Second, we should expect "some means of verbal expression which, however inadequate it may be, is nonetheless in intention geared towards receiving the inherent expressiveness of the art-symbol, rather than superimposing the critic's preconceptions" (*ibid.*, p. 181). Third, and most importantly (though most elusive to define or locate), there should be some overriding sense that the critic's encounter with art constitutes one of his life's formative experiences: that is, to use Bion's terms, an identifying with the evolution of "O", "O" being the "absolute essence", or "central feature" of an emotional situation, translated by Bion and others as the "state of being in love".

Commitment should be to a *process* rather than to interpretation: the language of aesthetic criticism should be such as to make it possible to generate new realms of meaning through exploration and discovery, based on "passionate congruence" between the forms of the inner self and those of the aesthetic object (*ibid.*). Form and verbal imagery are seen as essential manifestations of the symbolic activity by means of which the emotional experience embodied in the work of art is contained, rather than as some kind of clothing that may be removed or analysed away in order that a secret meaning may be "got at" (Cf. Roland Barthes' essay on the phenomenon of striptease, where he claims that the archetype of woman is "desexualized at the very moment when she is stripped naked" [1973, p. 91]).

Harris Williams quotes extensively from the work of Adrian Stokes—the critic *par excellence* who exhibits the qualities outlined above—to show how a psychoanalytic criticism may be based on a spatial model in which the viewer both incorporates and is enveloped by the work of art, and is impinged upon by its surface and by its depths. Such a mode of criticism involves "thinking with" the work rather than "thinking about" it: tracing the formal qualities of its composition in such a way that meaningful resonances are set up within the critic, who then seeks to find a symbolic form that may convey these to the reader. The work of art "does not yield the *meaning* of its message . . . to the viewer who has not committed *himself* for observation and exploration" (Meltzer & Harris Williams, 1988, p. 183). Indeed, such an approach is equally fruitful with poetry and with visual art. The careful attention of a "practical criticism" to the quality of the words and their sounds in *On Westminster Bridge* evokes an image of the evolving relation between the poet and the scene he is contemplating that is analytically meaningful in the terms of this book, though very far from being a "categorisation of art's phantasy contents". The relevance of such a position to the analytic situation is particularly acute—for example, it corresponds to the difference between an analytic interpretation that elucidates or, alternatively, "explains away".

A critical approach to any work of art that involves a "translation" of its central ideas leads to a rather barren exposition. Instead, for the reader–viewer, "thinking with" the artwork enables an enriched degree of complexity in our experience of it. The greatness of a work of art consists in the encompassing and embodying of conflicts, the tracing of which it is the task of criticism to evoke—but not necessarily *resolve*. This kind of reorientation of perspective is mirrored in the shift that Meltzer describes as taking place in a dream of a patient (a poet). The patient seemed to

> shift his perception of beauty from the idealised good object to the *struggle itself*, including the malign and random, along with the good, as participants in the drama, and thus in the love of the world. [*ibid.*, p. 3]

We will return to some of these themes in the conclusion to this book.

Psychoanalysis as an art

Although Bion's first models of the mind were firmly within the scientific and mathematical domain, he grew increasingly aware of the limitations of his scientific vertex. I would like now to give an overview of the direction that his later writing took, for this has important implications for both clinical theory and the status of psychoanalysis itself. In *Elements of Psychoanalysis* (1963) and *Transformations* (1965) we see him gradually moving away from his preoccupation with science as explanatory, towards a descriptive, evocative, and *aesthetic* conception of psychoanalytic thought. His writings from the mid-1960s are liberally scattered with analogies from the visual arts and literature. Bion stressed that it was the *visual sense* that lies at the core of unconscious phantasy, and he describes the phenomenology of the analytic encounter more and more in terms of visual and aesthetic analogies. For example, in *Transformations* (1965), he writes that when he thought he grasped his patient's meaning it was often "by virtue of an *aesthetic* rather than a scientific experience" (p. 52). In this book, Bion uses a new way of describing the actual process of transformation that occurs in the analytic session—and this also evokes Bion's method of communicating to the wider community. The model constantly invoked in *Transformations* is that of the landscape painter transforming a scene of poppies in a field into pigment on canvas meant for public viewing. Another image he uses to describe the analytic encounter is that of the lake reflecting trees disturbed by the wind, and the viewer seeing only the water, recalling Plato's image of the cave: emotional reality distorted by emotions that block the patient's realization of becoming "O" (his designation of the Truth—akin to Platonic Ultimate Reality).

Elements and *Transformations* may be seen as ambitious experiments aimed at describing a method of psychoanalytic observation using mathematical devices and rules. It becomes clear by the end of *Transformations* that Bion has realized that this language is no longer adequate. He arrives at the rather humble conclusion in this book that what constitutes meaning in the session is the "opinion of the analyst". What he is beginning to show us is that the scientific formulation of psychoanalytic elements and their transformation is not one belonging to a causal chain arrangement, but rather a pattern of problems like a poem or a picture, available only to *aesthetic* intuition. We also see his growing emphasis on "Truth"— which he regards as being as necessary to the psyche as food is to the body. Truth has an aesthetic dimension that is an essential part of the analytic encounter. The love of knowledge, together with love itself, are seen to be one and the same, invoking Keats' poetic dictum that all we need to know, and all we *can* know, is that "Beauty is Truth and Truth Beauty". (Keats also wrote that "what imagination seizes as beauty must be truth". Keats and Bion are pointing to a kind of "truth" by which we live: an aesthetic truth, directed particularly towards apprehending the interplay between the forces of good and bad, as opposed to the correctness of intellectual statements about things. According to Keats, truth was particularly linked with the question of justifying good and trusting to it in the face of destructive and evil elements that abound. In Bion's terms, this involves faith in Ultimate Reality, 'O', which demands our capacity to tolerate potentially catastrophic change and unknowing without resorting to impoverishing and destructive defences. Bion links this capacity to Keats' "Negative Capability".) It is the love of *truth*, coupled with an *aesthetic sense*—functions of the analyst's personality, his training and experience, together with his ability to form an *opinion* of what is happening in the consulting room—that are the focus of the analytic encounter.

In his last theoretical book, *Attention and Interpretation* (1970), Bion casts off the mathematical and scientific scaffolding of his earlier writings and moves into the aesthetic and mystical domain. He builds upon the central role of aesthetic intuition and Keats' notion of the "Language of Achievement", which "includes language that is both a prelude to action and itself a kind of action; the meeting of psycho-analyst and analysand is itself an example of this language" (*ibid.*, p. 125). Bion distinguishes it from the kind of language that is a *substitute* for thought and action, a blocking of achievement that belongs in the realm of "preconception"—mindlessness as opposed to mindfulness. The articulation of this language is possible only through love and gratitude; the forces of envy and greed are inimical to it. This language can be expressed only when the "bondage of memory and desire" are cast off. He advised analysts (and this has caused a certain amount of controversy) to free themselves from the tyranny of the past and the future, for Bion believed that in order to make deep contact with the patient's unconscious the analyst must rid himself of all preconceptions about his patient—a superhuman task that means abandoning even the desire to cure. The analyst should suspend memories of past experiences with his patient because these could restrict the evolution of truth. The task of the analyst is to patiently "wait for a pattern to emerge". For, as T. S. Eliot recognized in his *Four Quartets*,

> only by the form, the pattern
> Can words or music reach
> The stillness. [*Burnt Norton, V*]

The poet also understood that "knowledge" (in Bion's sense of it designating a "preconception" that *blocks* thought, as opposed to his designation of a *"pre*-conception" which *awaits* its sensory realization) "imposes a pattern and falsifies"

> For the pattern is new in every moment
> And every moment is a new and shocking
> Valuation of all we have ever been. [*East Coker, II*]

The analyst, by freeing himself from the "enchainment to past and future", casts off the arbitrary pattern and waits for new aesthetic form to emerge, which will (it is hoped) transform the content of the analytic encounter.

It seems to be the case that when Bion's understanding of the mind was able to free itself from its mathematical enclosure, the aesthetic potential of his work could approach a fuller realization. The scientific vertex was unable to contain his truth, and it was the inspiration of the poets that eventually provided him with an intuitive language that was more truthful to emotional reality. It is Bion's three-volume novel, *A Memoir of The Future*, that most clearly shows the importance he attaches to the aesthetic vertex and its capacity to communicate between "discrete individuals" something that is "beyond the range of our logical, rational modes of thought". Bion believes that there may be

> something about the dramatic art "form" which is perspicuous. That might make communication possible through the barrier. I was thinking of something which I cannot support in any way that I regard as scientific unless we suppose that science develops from a germ of phantasy. [1992, p. 539]

He chose a science-fictional form because of its greater flexibility than theoretical writing in responding to truth. He observes that

"... psychoanalytic jargon was being eroded by eruptions of clarity. I was compelled to seek asylum in fiction. Disguised as fiction the truth occasionally slipped through" (1992, p. 230). In his fictional work we can appreciate the importance Bion attached to the functions and possibilities of artistic form in expressing truth. His attempt in the *Memoir* is to find an "underlying pattern" in psychic experience that can allow meaning to evolve in the face of threatening new ideas that herald catastrophic change and fragmentation of the psyche. Through the artistic form of the novel, Bion recounts his own catastrophic change (during the war) and presents us with an opportunity to submit to the forces of a new idea. The message is clear: unless we are able to accept change, which is always painful, we will never grow. The analyst's task is to enable the analysand to experience and contain (to borrow George Eliot's phrase in *Middlemarch* [1871]) "that roar that exists on the other side of silence", and to facilitate the emergence of a new and shocking pattern that can create its own boundaries. Thus, meaning and form undergo the mutual expansion and transformation which lies at the heart of creative experience.

In Book I of the *Memoir*, and in his *São Paulo* talks (1980), Bion describes this process in artistic terms by describing how a sculpture affects the observer: the "meaning is revealed by the pattern formed and the light thus trapped—not by the structure, the carved work itself". Bion is saying that the form of art, like the analytic encounter, captures meaning which lies outside its own boundaries—the concrete form can evoke forms which lie in a realm beyond—that "deep and formless infinite" described by Milton. Bion transforms the analytic encounter into one which is essentially a work of art, an aesthetic process which he likens to

> the diamond cutter's method of cutting stone so that a ray of light entering the stone is reflected back *by the same path* in such a way that the light is augmented—the same "free association" is reflected back by the same path, but with augmented "brilliance". So the patient is able to see his "reflection", only more clearly than he can see his personality as expressed by himself alone (i.e. without an analyst). [cited in Meltzer, 1978, p. 126]

From an aesthetic viewpoint, one of Bion's outstanding strengths lies in his constant striving to help others to live according to the saying "to thine own self be true". Bion, like Winnicott, emphasized the importance of the self and its need to have an understanding of its own nature. He recognized that the attainment of truth is never complete, for it cannot be experienced intellectually. It is only true while it remains unverbalized; any attempt to put it into words distorts it. Bion is telling us that we must *be* that truth. This means facing up to the truth about ourselves and *becoming* this truth—reaching "O" is closer to a mystical state than to a "cure". We infer from this that a successful analysis is one that facilitates the patient's experience of new ideas, enabling him to experience change creatively in response to these. The analyst and analysand, like the prototype of mother–baby, become a "thinking couple", and through this the patient is able—if envy and paranoid defences not too strong—to re-view his experience in a way that restores the ability to accept and to learn from new experience.

T. S. Eliot, in his *Four Quartets*, expresses a view of the relationship between meaning and experience that Bion explored in his writings and clinical work:

> We had the experience but missed the meaning,
> And approach to the meaning restores the experience
> In a different form, beyond any meaning
> We can assign to happiness. [*The Dry Salvages, II*]

The experience of meaning—and also meaninglessness—are vital for growth. The meaning might not give us any contentment, but it will be part of our being "O". Thus, it is not pleasure that we should crave but Truth, which is the vital food necessary for our psychic health. This is the essence of Bion's message, and through this he has transformed the task of analysis into something that fosters a more profound self awareness, consonant with Eastern philosophical thought. Bion's language echoes his metapsychological beliefs and he emphasized the emotional experience of his words over and above intellectual understanding. He preferred our transforming his ideas into our own experience, rather than a mindless, uncritical assimilation, and often cautioned that we should not try to understand what he said or wrote, but rather we should be receptive to our individual impressions and responses to what he said, advising his audience "not to listen to me, but to yourselves listening to me". His work has thus led to new findings and new territories for analytic exploration, and, although he must acknowledge his profound debt to both Freud and Klein before him, he has largely moved beyond them. He has placed the analyst in the position of an artist, exploring the "deep and formless infinite" of the unconscious, waiting for a pattern to emerge. (On a similar theme, Jacobus observes that

> Bion's aesthetics [. . .] have an uncanny resemblance to the experience of reading where we have to not-see what we are seeing, or to see it only in the mind's eye, in order to understand it. It is this which makes reading an emotional experiencce and links it to psychoanalytic insight. [2005, p. 253])

Meltzer's later work, largely inspired by Bion, suggests that not only do new psychoanalytic theories "organise the clinical phenomena that have been observed in a more aesthetic (beautiful?) way" (1978, p. 119), but that the beauty of the analytic encounter lies in the re-experiencing of the earliest realization of the mother's body—especially her face—which, for the infant, is essentially an aesthetic encounter, a moment of intense aesthetic impact.

From this is precipitated Meltzer's notion of *aesthetic conflict*: an ambivalence lying at the heart of deeply felt aesthetic experience, the intensity of which threatens to fragment and overwhelm the newborn child; it is that beauty which "is nothing but the beginning of terror that we are still just able to bear" (Rilke, quoted in Segal, 1986, p. 203). One of the most significant aspects of this work is the way in which words denoting fundamental human emotions and concepts—truth, beauty, awe, wonder, joy—are reinstated in a central theoretical position, as they are in Winnicott's writings, too. This contrasts with much psychoanalytic literature, where

> The absence of the vocabulary of aesthetics . . . at least in its theoretical vocabulary, is nowhere more stunningly illustrated than in Melanie Klein's *Narrative of a Child Analysis*. The terse and even harsh language of her theories, and their preponderant concern with the phenomenology of the paranoid–schizoid position, stands in astonishing contrast to the emotional, and certainly at times passionate, climate of her relationship to Richard and of his overwhelming preoccupation with the vulnerability of the world to Hitler's destructiveness and his own. [1988, p. 25]

Following the work of Bion, there has been a considerable reorientation in psychoanalysis within the British School towards the recognition of a "self"—a far richer and more sophisticated notion than the Freudian "ego", which is essentially a structural concept. This, together with an emphasis on role of aesthetic and creative capacities for development, and the belief that successful symbol formation depends on what Milner calls "a going backward in order to come forward"—i.e., the return to the infantile, narcissistic illusion of omnipotence that the infant himself has created the world—has led to a conception of the relationship between artistic practice and psychoanalysis that emphasizes the role of intrapsychic *illusion* (as opposed to *delusion*) in aesthetic and creative experience. (See also Alvarez [1992] for a clinical exploration of the inner landscape of autistic, borderline, deprived, and abused children. Her work supports a less condemning approach to manic play, regarding its importance as a sign of life and exuberance, together with the evolving of a sense of self in such children: Alvarez regards it as "a natural and necessary part of normal development" that "need not arise from narcissistic or defensive motives" [p. 173].)[1]

The dialogue between art, education, and psychoanalysis has also been greatly enriched by Meg Harris Williams, who argues that the "post-Kleinian" model, as developed by Bion and Meltzer, has eventually made the designation of "psychoanalysis as an art form a convincing and useful proposition" (1999, p. 127). Inspired by Bion's and Meltzer's contributions and her own "lifelong psychoanalytic education", she has written extensively on the interface between psychoanalysis and aesthetic modes of thinking and experiencing. Bion and Meltzer, as we have noted, helped to establish psychoanalysis's links with the humanities, which have a long history in exploring suprasensuous experience. It is the Kleinian model of the mother and baby in reverie that represents the coming-to-knowledge where the origins of symbol formation lie, and also the origins of aesthetic experience. The mother's ability to "think about" her baby helps establish the good internal thinking object for the baby: the raw sense data (beta elements) are transformed by the mother's reverie (her alpha function) into digestible experiences that the baby is able to assimilate as "food for thought"—the metabolization of projected anxieties that constitutes Bion's "learning from experience".

In line with this model, Harris Williams points out that analytic "success" is not so much about cure but rather "depends upon the patient's having sufficiently introjected a capacity for learning from experience to continue his self-analysis" (*ibid.*, p. 131). She emphasizes Bion's admiration for artistic method and how he believed it could illuminate and contribute much to the psychoanalytic method. It does this by reminding us of our actual lived experience, and also because it "unobtrusively engineers a radical change in the human mind" (*ibid.*, p. 130), akin to what Bion termed "catastrophic change"—a process of becoming present to oneself in such a way that one will never be quite the same again. It elicits a transformation through the "facts of feeling"; it is the *having* of an experience rather than its reviewing through hindsight, that marks the movement towards self-knowledge. Through tolerance of doubt and uncertainty, "a pattern will emerge". Harris Williams points out that in the post-Kleinian model, there is an interdependence between "the scientific knowledge gained by psychoanalysis and the artistic mode of attaining it", and that this view aligns psychoanalysis even more closely with philosopher–poets such as Coleridge, with his understanding of the "shaping spirit of imagination", Keats with his "vale of Soulmaking", and the "fearful symmetry" of Blake's Tyger—a powerful image of a new idea bursting forth to create catastrophic change. It is through the transference–countertransference relationship between patient and analyst that psychoanalysis seeks to re-establish learning-from-experience. For, according to Bion, however long an analysis, it is only the beginning of the process of discovery: "It stimulates growth of the domain it investigates" (Bion, 1970, p. 69).

Note

1. Hulks (2006) explores some interesting parallels between the "geometry of fear" sculptural movement that had emerged after the Second World War (characterized by the spiky, twisted, tortured , battered, alien-looking human or animal figures created by sculptors such as Henry Moore, Reg Butler, Lynn Chadwick, and Eduardo Paolozzi) and the growing psychoanalytic interest in the world of the schizophrenic and, in particular, "schizoid linguistics", largely pioneered by

Klein and Bion . Hulks draws on Bion's influential paper "Language and the schizophrenic" (1955) to explore the (overt or covert) intentions of the artist and to make sense of our reaction to such artworks. In the work of Reg Butler, for example, Hulks sees parallels in what Bion interpreted as the schizophrenic's use of language to "split the analyst" and to "create a feeling of consternation in the listener" with the "intention to extend schizophrenic perception to others" (pp. 111–112). Hulks suggests that Butler's sculptures invite the viewer to share in the experience of the schizoid condition with the intention of "spreading illness and abnormality". He observes that

> the use of schizoid linguistics in [Butler's] installed works seems to represent a further widening and deepening of this splitting strategy ... objective viewing is no longer available, since an external perspective does not reveal the work adequately; only an endopsychic pserpective is effective. As a result, the viewer becomes absorbed in the work and the schizoid engagement begins. [*ibid.*, p.112]

Note

1. I am indebted to Neil Maizels for this observation.

CHAPTER FIVE

Ehrenzweig and the hidden order of art

"To make someone love the unconscious, that is teaching art"

(cited in Milner, 1988 [1937], p. 244)

Anton Ehrenzweig's enthusiasm for the study of psychology and art was present from the very start of his academic career. At the same time, he studied law in his native Vienna and was appointed a magistrate there in 1936. Two years later he moved to London, where he lectured in Art Education at Goldsmiths' College until his death in 1966. It is interesting that in an early paper (1949) he should address the nature of guilt, a feeling that he believed was implicated in all scientific endeavour, and also in our constant need to establish causal links and reasons. This also has implications for his view of art history, explored below.

Ehrenzweig was well acquainted not only with recent developments in psychoanalysis, but also with cognitive psychology. Indeed, much of his work is a critique of what he called "academic theories of perception", and it is the Gestalt account of perception that he finds particularly unsatisfactory, largely because it fails to acknowledge the important developmental role of libidinal experience in perceptual activity. He was also familiar with the anthropological studies of Jung, Frazer, and Graves, relating their work to his study of the theme of the "dying-god"—which he regarded as the underlying motif in the psychic experience of creativity. But he came increasingly to emphasize how the insights of psychoanalysis, particularly those of the British School, corroborated his own research into the visual arts. This interchange culminates in his last book, *The Hidden Order of Art* (1967), which draws together strands of his thinking developed over thirty years of research. More explicitly than in any earlier writings, Ehrenzweig traces here the resonances and parallels between his ideas and those of a number of British School thinkers, such as Klein, Segal, Bion, Milner, and Winnicott. However, before we look at Ehrenzweig and the British School, I will examine some similarities and divergences between the aesthetics of Ehrenzweig and the ego psychologist Ernst Kris, in particular their respective development of Freud's account of the joke.

Ehrenzweig owes as much to ego psychology as he does to instinct theory. He shares some of the same preoccupations as Kris—an attention to the structural changes taking place in the ego during artistic experience, for instance. Yet he also focused on the way in which the primary process (id) worked with conscious perception (ego). In this sense, his work both parallels and draws upon a general revision of the Freudian account of the relationship between primary and secondary processes that is characteristic of post-Kleinian thinking.

Ehrenzweig, Kris, and the debt to Freud

As we noted earlier in this book, it is Freud's analysis of the relationship between aesthetic pleasure and the structure of the joke that stimulates inquiry into possible structural changes within the ego during the creative process. Both Ehrenzweig and Kris regarded Freud's theory of the joke as particularly productive with regard to aesthetics, certainly in relation to the understanding of the formal aspects of art. To a certain extent, both thinkers were concerned with structural changes within the ego during the creative process and their consequences for aesthetic experience, and thus hailed Freud's analysis of the joke as a model which could address the nature of artistic form without recourse to the psychobiography and content analysis that is generally associated with classical Freudian aesthetics. However, when we look at their respective views of perception and its relationship to unconscious processes, important differences begin to emerge. Although both thinkers are interested in the fate of the ego during the creative process, Ehrenzweig's theory focuses less upon the aesthetics of the external object (the art work itself) and more on the intrapsychic nature of creativity and associated phantasies. His work emphasizes the constructive role of unconscious perception and its relationship to the body (instinctual experience).

Ehrenzweig acknowledges that there are some similarities between his own and Kris's account of art. Kris's view that during artistic activity the artist can let his mind regress to primitive states and still remain in control is very akin to Ehrenzweig's central hypothesis, which emphasizes that the "diffuseness and vagueness and seeming emptiness of dream vision becomes in the artist's hands an exact instrument for controlling the complexity of art" (1961, p. 123). However, Ehrenzweig thought that the ego psychologists were wrong in their demotion of the creative process to, in effect, a regressive, archaic activity—Kris's dictum of "regression at the service of the ego". He argues that what is missing in Kris's concept is the insight that creativity does not merely control the regression *towards* the primary process, but also the *work of the primary process itself*. What is central to Ehrenzweig's thesis is that the primary process turns its potentially disruptive effects into constructive ones; thus, it is a highly efficient instrument for making new links and shaping more comprehensive concepts and images. The unconscious and conscious matrices are not merely linked; rather, surface thought is wholly immersed in the matrix of the primary process.

For the ego psychologists, creativity necessarily involves a regressive element; the primary process is regarded as an important but essentially primitive form of functioning. Thus, Hans Hartmann, one of the founders of ego psychology, whose work much influenced Kris, writes that the process of artistic creation is the prototype of synthetic solution, and ... this is the most important difference between it and "fantasying". Such a tendency toward "order" is inherent in every work of art, even when its content or intent represents "disorder". This is, then, another case of *"regressive adaptation"*: a mental achievement (whose roots are archaic) gains a new significance both for synthesis and in relation to the external world, precisely because of the *detour through the archaic*. [1958, p. 76, my italics]

Although there are some superficial similarities in the terms used by Hartmann and Ehrenzweig (both make reference to creative "order" and "disorder", for example), their respective approaches to nature of the primary process have a different orientation. In *The Hidden Order of Art*, Ehrenzweig makes this difference very clear. He agrees that Hartmann and Kris were right to assert that id and ego once evolved from a common undifferentiated matrix. However (possibly out of deference to the academic theory of perception put forward by the Gestalt psychologists), Hartmann and his followers did not fit perception into their model. Had they done so, Ehrenzweig thinks that they "would have wholly anticipated [his] theory of undifferentiated image-making" (1967, p. 262).

Ehrenzweig's theory of perception is integral to his general account of artistic creativity. To lend support to his claim that id and ego (ostensibly primary and secondary process functioning) work together, he deploys the Kleinian concept of *unconscious phantasy*, with its dynamic and structural aspects. For, as Susan Isaacs (1948) has pointed out, unconscious phantasy is "the mental representation of instinct". It is the bridge between the demands of the id and their representation in the conscious mind. Ehrenzweig argues that

> Unconscious phantasy life during our whole lifetime is supplied with new imagery by the ego's cyclical rhythm of dedifferentiation, which feeds fresh material into the matrix of image-making. Far from being autonomous of the id, the ego's perception is constantly at the disposal of unconscious symbolic needs. The ego is certainly not at the id's mercy. [1967, p. 263]

According to Ehrenzweig's theory of perception, the ego dissolves of its own accord in order to provide "new serial structures" in the external world as well as for symbolization of id phantasy in the inner world. However, he emphasizes that to call this activity regressive does not capture its true nature; for it is "part and parcel of the ego-rhythm which makes perception work".

Until the work of post-Kleinian thinkers such as Bion, Winnicott, Rycroft, and Milner, progress in psychoanalytic aesthetics had been halted through the relative neglect of the *undifferentiated* structure of primary process phantasy. The earlier work of Freud and his co-workers did not fully take into account the true nature of unconscious phantasy. What Freud had called primary process structures, says Ehrenzweig, are "merely distortions of articulate surface imagery caused by the underlying undifferentiation of truly unconscious phantasy" (*ibid.*). The nature of primary process condensation bears witness to this, where incompatible images interpenetrate into a *single*, all-encompassing vision. This kind of fusion, however, must be distinguished from the more familiar kind of condensation, one that Freud drew attention to in his theory of jokes. In this kind of structure, the object forms have become "concrete and unyielding", and they will partially cancel each other out because of the incompatibility of their appearance. Ehrenzweig thinks that this is why Freud's analysis of the joke mechanism did not lead to any major breakthrough in an equivalent analysis of artistic structure. For this "partial obliteration" no longer wards off the focus of our waking attention, and our unconscious perception is not actively stimulated and much of the original substance of the image is lost. True undifferentiated primary process structures, on the other hand, are fluid and freely interpenetrating, and it is only this kind of structure that can include all the ambiguity of primary process phantasy.

What Freud's analysis of the joke did well to achieve, however, was to show how its primary process structure constitutes the objective property of a "good" joke, apart from its subjective origin in the unconscious. Freud's great contribution illustrated how the primary process distorts, displaces, and condenses the structure of language, just as it does the dream. Ehrenzweig points out that it was Bion who first addressed the pathological aspect of this process in the schizophrenic. The schizoid tendency is to splinter violently language, thoughts, and even perceptual functions into "bizarre objects". The violence of their fragmentation leads to the particles being perceived as equally violent and threatening, resulting in a vicious circle of increases in splitting and violent projection.

The rhythm of creativity

In his papers of 1961 and 1962, Ehrenzweig first sets out his main thesis concerning the dynamics of art and creativity, calling for a revision in psychology and psychoanalytic aesthetic theory that, in his view, did not fit with the facts of artistic experience. He argues that although Kris

> prepared the way for recasting our concept of the primary process by suggesting that the creative mind can allow conscious functions to lapse in a controlled regression towards the primary process . . . this does not yet mean that the primary process itself is accessible to control and order. [1962, pp. 301, 317]

Kris's account of the "regression at the service of the ego" is weak because it de-emphasizes the positive, constructive role played by the id in artistic experience; he believed creativity involved an essentially primitive and archaic striving towards earlier phantasies, which themselves had to fit in with the demands of the ego for the achievement of constructive work. As we have discussed, Kris's aesthetics is grounded in the assumption that perception is removed from the sphere of instinctual (id) conflict. This implies that perception is itself not under the sway of unconscious processes, but, rather, the creative individual is somehow able to "regress" and make constructive use of id material while still remaining in control of his faculties. Here Ehrenzweig explicitly diverges from Kris in his firm belief that perception is implicated in both conscious and unconscious mental processes. He puts forward his main thesis that art has a hidden substructure, which may seem disruptive, disordered, and chaotic to conscious perception. However, working alongside the Gestalt-preoccupied conscious mind is what he calls "unconscious scanning", where our depth mind perceives the hidden substructure beneath. It is this tension between an ordered, conscious Gestalt, and the deeper structure that appears chaotic to the conscious perception, which is the essence of creative and aesthetic perception. (Indeed, Ehrenzweig suggests that his work should also be read with the same kind of "unconscious scanning".)

In *The Hidden Order of Art* (1967), he defines creativity as the "capacity for transforming the chaotic aspect of undifferentiation into a hidden order that can be encompassed by a comprehensive (syncretistic) vision", and he argues that "conscious surface coherence has to be disrupted in order to bring unconscious form discipline into its own" (1967, p. 127). However, because this "unconscious form" cannot be consciously analysed in rational terms, we must rely on our "low level sensibility" to distinguish "irresponsible arty-crafty gimmicks from truly creative art ruled by an inner necessity". Thus, for Ehrenzweig creativity is inseparable from his account of aesthetics: creative or "depth" perception is the source of authenticity, and it is the same kind of creative perception that characterizes the spectator's aesthetic experience.

In previous papers he first tackled issues he was to rework more fully and link together more comprehensively, such as the Gestalt theory of perception, which he examined critically in "Unconscious form-creation in art" (1948, 1949a) and attempted to show how it falls short of true experience. The first section attempts to develop a libidinal account of perception and aesthetic experience based on Freud's theory of sexual development. The second part of the paper looks more closely at concerns within the history of art, and he examines the nature of stylistic change in the arts, which he believes is inextricably linked to large-scale changes in human perception over the centuries. According to his theory, unconscious perception gradually becomes "revised" by succeeding generations, so that what was once regarded as chaotic, disturbing art—the "shock of the new"—gradually becomes accepted and rendered harmonious and manageable by succeeding generations of perceivers. Thus, a particular style or "period" is delineated, with recognizable, stable characteristics. This, he argues, is purely a form of secondary revision, where our conscious minds wish to create a good Gestalt that appeals to our sense of rationality and order. Unconscious chaos is replaced by surface harmony. The paper makes the point that the artist's unconscious vision tends to dissolve all differentiation and order into the "chaos of pan-genital vision". To counter this, the artist projects conscious order and beauty into the external world. Ehrenzweig argues that the scientist also projects order into the external world, but it is the order of *causal necessity* and compulsion.

The following paper, "The origin of the scientific and heroic urge" (1949b), argues that scientific explanation, either by guilt or by a compelling causality, externalizes an internal compulsion by guilt feelings from which the scientist tries to free himself. Ehrenzweig finds Klein's account of the primitive and sadistic nature of infantile phantasies very useful in the understanding the *oral* nature of guilt and its self-destructive tendencies. For do we not speak of "pangs" of guilt and "gnawing" remorse? (The German word for remorse is *gewissenbisse*, which also means "bite".) According to Klein's account, infantile aggressive wishes connected with sucking and devouring are turned inwards by the superego (under the sway of the death instinct), which then turns its oral aggression of gnawing remorse (guilt) *against* the ego. This was, of course, an important revision of Freud, who thought that the superego and its ability to arouse guilt feelings originated during the Oedipal phase. (In Ehrenzweig's later definition of creative perception as "poemagogic" phantasy this will be supplemented also by the post-Kleinian developments of Bion and of Milner.) Although the "Scientific urge" paper is concerned mainly with the relationship between the origin of guilt and the Western scientific tradition, Ehrenzweig's account of guilt and causality is also signficant for his implied view of art history (see Lyotard [1974], which highlights some of the implications of Ehrenzweig's work for the philosophy of art history). For his work continually stresses that the order of time, as we conceive it, exists only in our *surface* experience, while the *depth* mind is able to perceive without regard to this temporal ordering, and it is this illusion of temporal sequence that is perhaps the most cogent of all externality illusions. As Freud also emphasized, time is the mode in which the ego works, and this mode is externalized and perceived as an objective order in time that all natural events have to follow in the outside world. Thus, it follows from Ehrenzweig's account of guilt that any historical explanation should abandon notions of continuity, of sequential linkage, of influences—not only between one culture, school, or artist and another, but between artistic institutions and their social contexts.

A history which is freed from guilt (although Ehrenzweig does not himself express it in these terms) would present a model similar to Pater's conception of the "House beautiful", which "the creative minds of all generations ... are always building together". Here, says Pater, "oppositions cease"—like the classic-romantic distinction, for example (1895, p. 253). In effect, this means that all forms would be co-present or even *within* one another, and, consequently, at any "period" as determined by secondary chronology there could be found a large number of completely different, anachronistic or incompatible musical or pictorial objects, and transformational linkages criss-crossing throughout. The history of art would be like an historical surface, itself scanned, undifferentiated, and syncretic at every point. A (non-hidden) order would only become manifest through the operation of various blocking and channelling devices that would work to assert the predominance of one stylistic genre over another. The "secondary rationalisation" is irreversible, and, once imposed on art, the original experience is lost forever. We can, however, reinterpret art according to our own contemporary "form feeling". This may be an arbitrary ordering, but it is no more so than the rationalizations of previous generations. Ehrenzweig believes that great art is distinguished by its capacity to withstand such arbitrary manipulations of its conscious surface, and this is because its real substance belongs to deeper untouched levels. Because of this, we do not mind that we are unable to reconstruct the conscious motives of, for example, the Stone Age cave artists or of the ancient Egyptians. This unconscious, atemporal "hidden order" allows us to give meaning to the work of generations long before our own, and thus the conscious intentions of the artist seem relatively unimportant. Ehrenzweig concludes that

> What alone seems to matter to us is that complex diffuse substructure of all art. It has its source in the unconscious and our own unconscious still reacts readily to it, preparing the way for ever new reinterpretations. The immortality of great art seems bound up with the inevitable loss of its original surface meaning and its rebirth in the spirit of every new age. [1967, p. 77]

Ehrenzweig described the "articulating tendency" of the surface mind in his first book, *The Psychoanalysis of Artistic Vision and Hearing* (1953), where he is concerned with the part played by unconscious modes of perception in all creative work, both scientific and artistic. He notes the fact that we tend, in the most part, to notice compact, simple, precise forms, at the same time eliminating vague, incoherent, inarticulate forms from our perception, and points out how both William James and Freud, independently of each other, drew attention to this articulating tendency of our surface perception, while ideas coming from the lower layers of the mind, like dream visions, tend to be appear chaotic, elusive, difficult to grasp. The Gestalt psychologists, similarly, used the term "Gestalt tendency" to describe how we like to find a pattern, even in chaos. Ehrenzweig goes on to tell of how the Gestalt psychologists take art as a supreme manifestation of the human mind's striving towards articulate Gestalt; but he believes this theory has led to a *failure* to appreciate some of the most fundamental aspects of art—the "creative accident". We need only look at examples of our own reveries, dreams, and moments of absent-mindedness to appreciate that our minds do work on different levels, in an oscillating rhythm, and that when we return from an absent-minded phase it is not always easy to say what we have been thinking. Ehrenzweig points out that Otto Rank (1932) maintained that artistic creativeness involves a cyclical displacement between two different levels; yet he considered the inarticulate phase preceding the emergence of ideas as a mere interruption of consciousness, emptiness of vision. Here Ehrenzweig again refers to William James, and how he said that the creative state wrongly appears as an emptiness of consciousness only because we cannot grasp its fluid content in the precise perceptions of the conscious mind.

According to Ehrenzweig's view, the creative individual is one whose ego is *flexible* enough to undergo the temporary dissolution of its surface, rational faculties to reach deeper levels of unconscious sensing, which cannot be apprehended on a conscious level, only through a kind of secondary elaboration (this could involve the external work of art itself). Far from being mad, the artist must have sufficient ego strength (adaptability rather than rigidity) to allow a temporary dissolution of reality. Both Ehrenzweig and the British analyst Milner stress the *fear* accompanying this surrendering to (what seems to the surface, conscious ego, at least) the chaos of undifferentiation. According to Ehrenzweig, the psychotic lacks a sufficiently flexible ego to reach down to deeper undifferentiated levels, constructing rigid (schizoid) defences to protect his fragile ego from the perceived threat of disintegration and chaos— "psychosis is creativity gone wrong". The creative person, on the other hand, has a sufficiently strong ego capacity to let go of surface ordering. This suggests an implicit trust (or "faith" as Bion or

Winnicott put it) in the unconscious and its processes. (For an interesting discussion of this topic, see Eigen [1981].) Ehrenzweig concludes that any act of creativeness requires a temporary, cyclical paralysis of the surface attention. He gives an example of such temporary paralysis from an artist sketching in his background forms in a state of diffused attention, a state by which he looks at the figure and background forms in one glance. However, according to Gestalt theory, this is an impossible task. He also talks of the particular technique needed to get hold of the visions filling the creative mind (during the alleged lapse of consciousness), as a kind of absent-minded watchfulness. This brings to mind Freud's description of the analyst's "free-floating attention", and also Bion's advice to analysts to free themselves from the "bondage of memory and desire" in order to "wait for a pattern to emerge".

There is a considerable link between this kind of perception and that of mystical states, which Freud (borrowing the term from his friend, the writer Romain Rolland) referred to as the "oceanic" feeling, a state of oneness with the universe that Freud admits to not having experienced himself. Freud viewed it as a regression to the early infantile state of consciousness, when the child's ego is not yet differentiated from the external world. Hence (says Ehrenzweig), Freud claimed that the feeling of union is no mere illusion, but the correct description of memory of an infantile state otherwise inaccessible to direct introspection. Ehrenzweig explains this further by drawing on Freud's analysis of dream-thinking. He believes that the mystic feeling is explained by the surface mind's incapacity to visualize the inarticulate images of the depth mind, and his central point is that the creative process takes place in these gaps in our surface mind's activity. He goes on to point out how these rhythms of the mind can be seen as a series: ranging from the rapid oscillations of everyday thinking and perception to the slower cycle of waking and sleeping and to the even slower rhythm of creative activity in which the submerged phase may be sometimes very protracted. This also links with Bion's account of the oscillations between paranoid–schizoid fragmentation and depressive wholeness, as a necessary rhythm in creative thinking, expressed by his little formula PS↔D. In the next chapter, the relevance of this "mystical" experiencing of illusion to artistic experience will be considered in the context of Marion Milner's description of the "aesthetic moment", and also of the perceptual changes brought about by a special kind of focusing on internal body awareness.

During creative activity, Ehrenzweig believed, the *vertical* levels of the psyche—the boundaries between ego, superego, and id—become less clearly differentiated. Conscious perception works together with the id in the process of de-differentiation or "unconscious scanning", in a creative rhythm rooted in the undifferentiated matrix that forms art's hidden substructure; ego boundaries dissolve as a "manic–oceanic" limit is reached. Further to this, he thinks that there is no need to explain this oceanic fusion of imagery as a regression to a prenatal state when the child was actually at one with its mother. It might well be that a creative suspension of frontiers has already been set up and so might belong to a much later stage of development. The *productive* id can alter our perception positively; creativity is the result of the dynamic interplay between conscious ordering and unconscious scanning, which can repeatedly reorganize old images. The creative process turns "disruptive" effects into "constructive" ones. The "true" order is not at the level of the conscious ego *per se*—hence the "hidden order of art". Thus, Ehrenzweig is arguing for the existence in *all* art of a tension between surface, conscious Gestalt (secondary revision) and a hidden substructure, associated with the activities of the primary process. Indeed, there has to be a minimum of surface fragmentation to bring into action our "usually starved low-level sensibilities". To relieve his anxiety, the viewer, like the artist, has to take part in the scanning process to detect new substructures (Ehrenzweig, 1967, pp. 32–46).

In modern art (for example, cubism, action painting, and optical art) this tension reaches an almost pathological degree, where a strong conflict operates between the "depth" and "surface" elements, so that "the surface crust of mannerisms does not allow the spontaneous depth functions to breathe and so has to be disrupted totally" (*ibid.*, p. 66). According to Ehrenzweig, the modern artist attacks his own rational sensibilities in order to make room for new discoveries in artistic form. A vicious circle ensues, where the attacked surface faculties fight back, as it were, so that the spontaneous, innovative breakthrough quickly becomes "rationalized", eventually manifesting itself as a mannered, stylized device. This, in turn, stimulates further spontaneity and overthrowing of conscious ordering. The action painting of Jackson Pollock is a good example of this extreme dissociation of surface and depth function: the almost total disruption of conscious composition, and its eventual "rationalization". When Ehrenzweig first encountered Pollock's work, with its "enormous loops and droplets which dazzled the eye", it seemed to him to represent a "sudden eruption of art's unconscious substructure . . . a very direct manifestation of unconscious form principles". To avoid discomfort and to make contact with depth perception (unconscious scanning), we have to give up any attempt to integrate the patches and droplets into coherent patterns; we should let our eyes drift with no sense of temporal or spatial direction, just living in the present moment. If we succeed in evoking this dream-like state, not only does our anxiety disappear, but the picture may suddenly transform itself and lose its random appearance, and we may grasp at a previously unseen all-over "presence" rippling like a pulse across the picture plane. The vital role of this depth perception cannot be underestimated. Only this can "distinguish irresponsible art-crafty gimmicks from truly creative art ruled by an inner necessity" (*ibid.*, p. 75). This implies that the aesthetic value of an artwork is grounded in the relativity of perceptual response. Authenticity is a function of the artist's "inner necessity", and the aesthetic value of an artwork arises from the complex interplay between the unconscious perception of the artist, and the spectator's "low-level sensibility", which, by relaxing consciousness of time and space, is able to tap this hidden substructure.

However, Ehrenzweig does also suggest that it is only in very *new* art that we can fully appreciate the attack on our conscious sensibilities, and experience the kind of unconscious anxiety that he believes all artistic innovation entails. After a few years, the "inevitable defensive reaction of the secondary processes sets in". Painting in the genre of Pollock came to seem more of a deliberate exercise in the creation of decorative and pleasing patterns (*ibid.*, p. 67), and Ehrenzweig turned instead to optical art as the form *par excellence* in which "the dissociation of intellectual and spontaneous sensibilities . . . could not be more complete":

> Like serialisation in music, optical painting is a case of the intellect destroying its own modes of functioning. The single elements of an

optical composition are serialised in so smooth a gradation that the eye fails to pick out any stable gestalt pattern ... Our vision is conditioned to give up focusing and to take in the entire picture plane as a totality. It is at once directed to highly mobile and unstable patterns of pictorial space and its fluttering pulse. In this manner the initial total intellectual control of optical serialisation leads without transition directly to the experience of uncontrollable pictorial space. [*ibid.*, pp. 84–85]

He was particularly excited by the work of Bridget Riley, whose methods seemed to corroborate many of his theories concerning the interplay between different levels of perception during the creative process. He first encountered Riley's work in early 1963, at the time he would have been working on his *The Hidden Order of Art*, and wrote a critical essay on Riley's use of "pictorial space" (1965) and also (with David Sylvester) wrote a catalogue introduction to an important exhibition of her work:

One can distinguish two contrasting phases on the experience of Bridget Riley's paintings—the first phase can be called cold, hard, aggressive, "devouring", the second warm, expansive and reassuring. We sometimes speak of "devouring" something with our eyes. In these paintings the reverse thing happens, the eye is attacked and "devoured" by the paintings. There is a *constant tug-of-war* between shifting and crumbling patterns but at a certain point this relentless attack on our lazy viewing habits will peel our eyes into a *new crystal-clear sensibility*. We have to submit to the attack in the way we have to learn to enjoy a cold shower bath. There comes a voluptuous moment when the senses and the whole skin tingle a sharpened awareness of the body and the world around. [de Sausmarez, 1970, p. 30]

It is clear why Ehrenzweig was so enthused by this kind of painting, for (like his own theories) it effectively questioned the established principles of Gestalt psychology. In Riley's work there is a constant battle between surface cohesion and fragmentation of Gestalt patterns, which denies simple, balanced pictorial organization. In addition, the accompanying dazzle effects confound any attempt at focusing and resist efforts to find an easy accommodating stability. He found corroboration for the rhythmic interplay and creative tension between cohesion and disruption in the Kleinian account of the paranoid–schizoid and depressive positions: in particular, in Bion's emphasis on the oscillation between integration and fragmentation (PS↔D) that underlies not only creative thinking, but grounds all our psychic life.

Ehrenzweig describes how Riley was herself acutely aware of the tension between stability and crisis in her work. In an interview with Ehrenzweig, where she discusses her way of working, she outlines five main phases, although she adds that not *all* of these may be present in any particular work (Ehrenzweig, 1967, pp. 85–86). First, she discovers a unit that lends itself to serial transformation. Then the unit is submitted to a variety of transformations, according to the principles of serialization, that display its dynamic potentialities (such as expansion–contraction, acceleration–deceleration, directional tilting, inversion, etc.). Third, there is the arrival at the maximum "energy" involvement, and this is followed by the phase of split or dislocation, the threatened destruction of the picture plane. Last, there is a return, a process of de-escalation through a form of recapitulation, in order that the cycle of serialization be brought to an end. The question of *scale* is also crucial—both that of the unit and the total field over which it will operate. The unit must neither be so big as to become a separate entity nor so small that in a cluster it disintegrates or fuses; the total field needs to retain, when fully developed, a scale that enforce complete visual involvement. When the picture plane holds without breaking under the opposing strains, there emerges a "presence", an almost hallucinatory experience. This is the final transformation that makes the processes described above meaningful; but it is an experience that can only come about through the process of trial and error.

Ehrenzweig predicted that by the time the manuscript for *The Hidden Order of Art* would have gone into print, optical painting such as Riley's would have "lost its dazzling effect". This puts us in the interesting position of being able to personally confirm his thesis that, over time, the secondary process of rationalization will eventually transform such art into decorative textures like all other fragmentation techniques of modern art. As far as Riley's work goes, I would argue that it *has* withstood the test of time. For the dazzling effect of her work, its energy and "presence" is still sufficiently strong to suggest that its "hidden substructure" is still potentially accessible, and has (for the while at least) defied the workings of our secondary rationalisations.

Ehrenzweig and the British School

It was the psychoanalyst John Rickman, in his paper 'The nature of ugliness' (1940), who first drew Ehrenzweig's attention to the resonances between his theories and those of Melanie Klein, particularly those concerning the role of primitive, oral and anal-sadistic unconscious phantasies in psychic experience. Rickman was a member of the British School who worked closely with Melanie Klein's theories. Interestingly, it was Rickman who introduced the psychiatrist Wilfred Bion to Mrs Klein at about the same time, suggesting that he should be analysed by her!

Through Klein, Ehrenzweig became familiar with the work of other British School analysts, such as Segal, Bion, Winnicott, and Milner. His close collaboration with the latter is an index of the fruitful interchange that was flourishing between the British psychoanalytic world and the artistic domain.

Ehrenzweig became actively involved in the psychoanalytic world, contributing a number of papers to the Imago Society, writing for the *International Journal of Psychoanalysis* and the *American Imago*. He regularly attended psychoanalytical congresses and meetings, which put him in close contact with analysts from the British School. Indeed, it was at the 1953 International Psycho-Analytical Congress that he first met the analyst Marion Milner, who was to remain a close friend and colleague until his early death in 1966. Milner stresses the impact their friendship had on her own creativity, stimulating "some kind of fresh seeing". She describes him as a "writer who knows about the process of analysis from [the] direct experience" of his work with art students—specifically in textile design (1987b, p. 244). Although Ehrenzweig would have hesitated to have described himself thus (not wanting to be accused of "wild analysis", perhaps), he seemed to work very much as a teacher–therapist, attending to his student's practical needs while also trying to foster an awareness of the relationship between deeper levels of their own psychic functioning and their creativity. This is further evidenced by his belief that it was the art teacher's task "to make the student's personality more flexible and so to develop his latent creativity" (1957, p. 193).

In his analysis of artistic creativity (1967), Ehrenzweig deploys a number of key Kleinian concepts, particularly the notion of unconscious phantasy, the death instinct, and the paranoid–schizoid and depressive positions. However, we must realize that, although Klein's work was useful in explaining the first and last phases of creativity, based on her account of paranoid–schizoid and depressive anxiety respectively, Ehrenzweig felt that Klein's theory did not take into account the experience of "manic–oceanic" fusion, which he believed to be at the heart of the creative rhythm. So he turned to the insights of the post-Kleinians, making use of Bion's emphasis on the mother's containing role and her reverie, and of the ideas of Winnicott and Milner, who emphasized a primary experience of fusion with the mother that was a prerequisite for all creative experience and symbolic activity.

Ehrenzweig sees creativity as a cyclical process consisting of three interlinked phases. There is an initial *schizoid fragmentation*, where the ego undergoes a splitting; this is an experience of turbulence and disruption that is often felt to be extremely painful, even akin to a kind of death. Then a second phase, of manic–oceanic fusion, in which the unconscious prepares a "containing womb" to contain the split-off ego fragments, holding them in suspension. It is here that Ehrenzweig's account departs from Klein's schema and (in keeping with the Independents, such as Milner, Winnicott, and Rycroft) postulates a return to an illusory, manic state of oneness with the mother. However, as with Freud's libidinal "stages", Klein's "positions", or Bion's oscillation of Ps↔D, these "stages" refer not so much to a linear, historical development as to *ongoing* emotional experiences of our relationship to both inner and outer objects. They might be followed by a third phase, which Ehrenzweig links with the depressive position. In this final stage, there is a reintrojection of the fragmented parts of the psyche on a higher level of consciousness, often accompanied by acute *depressive anxiety*. As Stokes, with his emphatic Kleinian perspective has so often stated, the engagement with a medium resulting in the production of the work must necessarily involve a depressive recognition of the limitations of the real world—that the feelings experienced in the second, manic phase can never match up to expectations. For the Kleinians, the importance of acknowledging depression sets in motion the ensuing drive towards reparation. This is stressed as being essential to all (non-omnipotent) creativity and also establishes the value, the essential "goodness" of the artwork produced.

Ehrenzweig, however, does not regard this last, depressive phase as central to the creative process and (following Milner) offers an important revision of traditional Kleinian accounts of creativity. For him, it is the second, manic phase that is the most central, involving what he calls an internal "creative surrender" that is paradoxically felt to be both like a dying and a rebirth. In "The creative surrender" (1957), a paper which was written primarily as a commentary on Milner's *An Experiment in Leisure* (1937), Ehrenzweig attempts to clarify this second phase of the creative process. He explicitly aligns himself with the ideas put forward in Milner's work, and points out some of his reservations concerning Kleinian theory, particularly their stress on the depressive aspects of the experience. What interests Ehrenzweig in this paper is the imagery associated with creative activity, in particular the motif of the "dying god", which the anthropologist Frazer regarded as an unconscious common denominator in religion, art, and social growth. Although Freud had apparently read much of Frazer's work, it seemed that he preferred to view the universal theme of Western religion and social life in terms of the Oedipus complex. Yet, he also believed that a specific "oceanic" ego lay at the root of all religious experience. This is what Ehrenzweig believes to be at the heart of all creative activity, and he draws attention to Milner's (1952) insight that successful symbol formation depends on an oceanic fusion between the inner and outer worlds, and the lack of differentiation in the oceanic state leads to new "symbolic equivalences" (this is not the same as Segal's term "symbolic equation", which refers to symbols characteristic of primitive, paranoid–schizoid thinking) and hence to new creativeness.

Freud would have described the source of creativeness as the id (specifically, the Oedipus complex) and the ego condition necessary for creativity as the oceanic state; but what Ehrenzweig stresses is that Freud was wrong to see a genetic correspondence between these two aspects of creativity. Ehrenzweig argues that the Oedipus complex necessarily involves a clear differentiation between the roles of mother, father, and child, which is far from the undifferentiation of oceanic fusion. The content of the dying god image is highly undifferentiated: birth, death and love become a single theme. Robert Graves drew attention to a similar theme in his study of the White Goddess, who kills her son–lover. According to his theory, the poet must submit himself to her (suffer death through love) and in return she will be his Muse and lead him to rebirth. The sado-masochistic element of the voluntary acceptance of self-destruction Ehrenzweig connects with the "structural disintegration of imagery on the oceanic level", and it is this imagery that Milner had encountered in her own creative explorations. Both Milner and Ehrenzweig regard this imagery as primarily representative of crucial changes within the ego; it is not so much its conscious meaning but the imagery's role as a catalyst in the creative process (where much of the associated anxiety and guilt is lost) that is significant. Ehrenzweig believes that "what is felt emotionally as a surrender to self-destruction is really a surrendering to the disintegrating action of low-level imagery" (1957, p. 197). During the creative surrender a process occurs which is almost the exact reverse of what happens with secondary elaboration: the low-level imagery overwhelms the articulate surface imagery, instead of there being a victory of the conscious and rational principle. Ehrenzweig concedes that this is connected with the censorship of the id by the superego, but he wants to emphasize that it is structural changes in the ego that result in the transformation of psychic material in either direction. He says the ego could be regarded as "autonomous" in the sense that both ego tension and conflict can be described without reference to id–superego conflict. One could argue that here, at least, Ehrenzweig is closer to the ego psychologists than he is to Klein, who focused a great deal on the relationship between instinctual conflict and the persecutions of an early superego.

Ehrenzweig's account of structural roles has important consequences for his understanding of "repression". Rather than this being superego suppression of unacceptable id phantasy, it is more to do with a change in the structure of this imagery that renders it more *inaccessible* to conscious awareness. He terms this "structural repression", and believes that it explains why we know so little about low-level perceptions, whatever their content. If they do surface into consciousness, they may appear empty, as does the "dream screen". The concept of the "dream screen" has been helpful in illuminating aspects of aesthetic experience in the visual arts. It was first introduced by the analyst Bernard Lewin and has been developed more fully by Charles Rycroft (see Lewin [1946, 1948], and Rycroft [1968a]). Lewin regards it as a symbol of both sleep itself and of the breast, with which sleep is unconsciously equated. For Rycroft, however, the screen is not a component of all dreams, but a phenomenon that occurs only in dreams of those who are in a manic phase, and it symbolizes the manic sense of ecstatic fusion with the breast (mother). Milner (who was Rycroft's analyst) regards this experience of manic fusion with the breast as being related to feelings of blankness, oceanic feeling, and emptiness. In *On Not Being Able to Paint* (1950), she has stressed that these feelings are not merely an hallucinatory return to an idealized state, but are perhaps the "beginnings of something, as the recognition of depression can be" and "the blankness is a necessary prelude to a new re-integration". This primary blankness is also very close to what Bion called the "absence of memory or desire", an experience which corresponds to the Keatsian "negative capability" that Bion and Rycroft have both emphasized as being essential for imaginative and creative activity. The "blank dream" and the "dream screen" are also concepts employed by Fuller in his study of the abstract work of Natkin and Rothko in his *Art and Psychoanalysis*; as we shall see in Chapter Seven, he regards the blank dream as being analogous to states of mystical union with the universe, and argues that post-Kleinian psychoanalysis enables us to give a material explanation of religious mystical states and also the experience of "aesthetic blankness" (Fuller, 1980, p. 219).

Ehrenzweig also draws attention to the importance of ego flexibility, so that the ego can reach down from higher surface perception into lower-level imagery without fear of structureless chaos. The schizophrenic is one whose ego is less able to surrender his ego to low-level functioning. Ego rigidity therefore results in creative sterility: the schizophrenic is unable to tolerate undifferentiation, which is felt as an annihilation. This marks a new understanding of the relationship between psychosis and creativity. The classical view tended to regard the schizophrenic as being more at the mercy of his id phantasies than the healthy individual. The work of Ehrenzweig (illuminated by Bion) suggests that this not the case. What is now thought to happen with the mentally ill person is that conscious level functioning is split-off from the matrix of unconscious phantasy, which is a constant source of imaginative nourishment in the healthy individual. Indeed, the presence of rigid, highly structured, and over-concrete imagery, and the lack of a sense of animation creating a sense of deadness in the perception of the world, are well-known manifestations of the schizoid state. Such symptoms could certainly be accounted for by the split between deeper levels of emotional awareness and conscious thinking. Although a certain amount of dissociation between the "horizontal" (the surface and depth) levels of ego functioning is inevitable due to secondary process rationalization, Ehrenzweig believes that this split can be remedied by the "vertical integration" of the interplay between dissociated levels of ego functioning, and "creativity improved to the extent that the dissociation can be overcome" (1967, p. 205).

Ehrenzweig points to two seemingly contradictory features of the creative surrender that are of special importance. The surrender brings a sense of deepening reality; but at the same time it has a manic feeling, one of oceanic bliss that strangely contrasts with the imagery of death and suffering. Ehrenzweig's link between the sense of dying and the ego's de-differentiation to lower levels of functioning would make sense of this seeming contradiction. Also, the more perception is grounded in the unconscious, the more vivid it will appear to the conscious mind. When perception is cut off from unconscious levels, the result will be depersonalized vision—another characteristic of mental disturbance where the world appears flat and unreal. The emotional acceptance of death is a vital element in creativity and is also recognized by analysts as part of normal functioning. Milner regards it as essential to a healthy acceptance of reality, recalling that in Spanish bullfighting the killing of the bull is known as the "moment of truth". Segal also considers the emotional acceptance of the reality of death to be a condition of creativeness, as in her distinction of pre-midlife and post-midlife creativity that followed on Elliott Jaques's influential paper "Death and the mid-life crisis" (1965). To this Ehrenzweig would add, however, that the element of self-destruction is only experienced consciously when the ego is rigid and the descent into lower levels feels like death itself. Unlike Segal, he stresses the *absence* of depressive feeling connected with the acceptance of death. Indeed, once accepted, it is regarded as a liberation from bondage. Along with Milner and Winnicott, he emphasizes the importance of manic–oceanic fusion for successful symbol formation, marking a shift in emphasis away from the traditional Kleinian focus on the depressive position. Ehrenzweig tells us that he has

> always felt that an exclusive stress on the Depressive Position, as the source of creative activity, did not take account of the almost biological rhythm between mania and depression, where mania appears on the same level as depression, as a fundamental human attitude. [1957, p. 209]

Thus, one major characteristic of post-Kleinian aesthetics is the reappraisal of the developmental and creative role of manic fusion and omnipotence—which traditional Kleinians tend to see as a feature of primitive, "part-object" relationships. Indeed, although Stokes's earlier writings focused (like Segal) on the achievement of the depressive position as the *sine qua non* of artistic authenticity, his later contributions, such as *The Invitation in Art* (1965) and "The image in form" (1966 [1978]), viewed this state as a *necessary complement* to the depressive sense of "otherness" in art. Though unlike Stokes, who focuses on the psychic dynamics of the artist's engagement with his medium, and the consequences for both the structure of the art work and our experience of it, Ehrenzweig concerns himself more with the artist's inner experience and phantasies and especially with the importance of manic fusion in creative experience. This emphasis on the importance of the sense of "oneness", or undifferentiation, and its relationship to intrapsychic illusion is also the keynote of Milner's and Winnicott's accounts of creativity and infantile development, a theme to be explored in greater detail in the next chapter.

CHAPTER SIX

Art, creativity, and the potential space

The study of the aesthetics of the analytic encounter has become a distinguishing feature of much post-Kleinian thinking in the British School. This chapter will explore the insights of Milner and Winnicott, who both emphasize the role of creative and aesthetic experience in fostering psychic growth in both patient and analyst.

Milner's oeuvre is especially significant, for it can be viewed as an index of the way in which the psychoanalytic encounter has been seen increasingly in terms of aesthetic value, not solely as the resolution of instinctual conflict and neurosis. Like that of Stokes and Bion, it can be regarded very much as the expression of her personality. Indeed, her theoretical contribution is perhaps most fully appreciated when seen in the context of her own creative explorations and her autobiographical writing: in particular, the account of her painting activities and "doodle drawings" in *On Not Being Able to Paint* (1950), with its later appendix (1957) reviewing her struggles in the light of her subsequent analytic experience. Her writing then becomes increasingly preoccupied with what she calls (after Nietzsche) the "sagacity of the body",[1] as she explores the epistemological role of certain aspects of corporeal experience by analysing a number of her own paintings and drawings, as well as some of those produced by her schizophrenic patient "Susan". Susan's story, recounted in *The Hands of the Living God* (1969), is primarily the case history of a very ill young woman, yet it can also be considered to have made an important contribution to the study of aesthetics.

Following this, I shall discuss the link between Milner's seminal work on illusion (1952 [1987]) and Winnicott's account of the "transitional object" and the "potential space" (1953, 1971). Both thinkers were intensely preoccupied with the developmental importance of infantile illusion, together with the way that the child becomes able to recognize that there is a subjective and objective reality, negotiated by an "in-between" area that Winnicott called the "potential space". This area relates to play, as well as to religious and aesthetic experience in adult life—indeed, according to Winnicott, to the "whole cultural field".

The sagacity of the body: Milner's account of creativity

In Milner's early writings we find expressed in embryonic form ideas about the creative role of perception and the special kind of interplay between aesthetic experience and body awareness—themes that were to preoccupy her throughout her career. What makes Milner so interesting (and also quite difficult to categorize) is the interplay between her own creative experience, her meditations upon life and the problems of living, combined with many years of clinical experience. Many aspects of clinical work were, for her, elucidated by her own creative experiments, and this is why it is sometimes difficult to say where one begins and the other ends, for her work is an expression of her varied life experience and interests, including educational methods, concentration difficulties, religious experience and mysticism, creative experience, and aesthetics. In fact, the problem of boundaries—of merging and separation—is a major theme in her work, as well as providing a good image of the ways in which the many layers in Milner's thinking interpenetrate—and of how her work overlaps with that of Winnicott, particularly with reference to the study of illusion.

Milner's first book, *A Life of One's Own* (1934) first published under the pseudonym Joanna Field, was based on a diary she kept during the 1920s, where she would write about the event that had most affected her each day. Through these reflections she came to recognize what she called the "wide" focus—a quality of awareness that enabled her to perceive the world with greater enrichment and meaning, and was also found to be connected with an intensified body awareness and a correspondingly heightened perception of reality. This heightened awareness could be reached only through an "inner gesture" of letting go of the "narrow" focus (that is, everyday discursive thinking) and a deeper order would be revealed to her that sometimes had a very frightening quality, almost like a death itself, but when she submitted herself to it, it felt more like a liberation. This "deeper order" (cf. Ehrenzweig's "hidden order") was characterized by a sense of more fluid boundaries between self and the world—even to the point of subject–object union. This is a theme that was to play an important part in her writings, as in Winnicott's thinking, especially with regard to understanding aesthetic experience and the way in which creative perception is fostered by a negotiation of the "gap" between self and other, involving the active surrendering of conscious ego control.

It seems that from comparatively early on in her self-explorations, Milner was drawing attention to the poetic intuition of the ego state, which is a necessary phase in all creative experience: that is, the temporary and active surrender of conscious, discursive thought. Her second autobiographical book, *An Experiment in Leisure* (1937), explores more fully the nature of this special kind of awareness or attention, focusing especially on the process of surrender and the *phantasies* relating to it. In her effort to enhance her receptivity to the world, Milner searched her memory and her imagination for significant motifs, finding that the images that recurred all related to dying or tortured gods (for example, Jesus, Prometheus, Apollo, Osiris). Milner asks whether

> the still glow that surrounded some of these images in my mind, images of the burning god, of Adonis and Osiris, did it come because they satisfied surreptitiously some crude infantile desire that I ought to have left behind long ago? I could not believe that it was so, for I had enough psycho-analytical experience to recognise the feeling of disreputable desires ... the kind of thinking that

brought these other images was of a quite different quality, it had the feeling of greatest stillness and austerity. [1937, p. 151]

She believes that processes which seem sado-masochistic to the ego may actually open up *new* realities—ones that could not be fully explained by psychoanalytic interpretations in terms of id content. Such images seemed to reflect a crucial phase in psychic creativeness, inaccessible to direct language, enhancing the sense of self and the world.

Milner's *Experiment in Leisure* inspired Ehrenzweig to write a paper about its main ideas, and subsequently there was considerable interplay between them, each finding in one another's work clarification of their own ideas. He used the term "poemagogic" to denote these special images described by Milner, saying they embody a perception that can both *induce* and *symbolize* the ego's creativity: they "reflect the various phases and aspects of creativity . . . through the central theme of death and rebirth, of trapping and liberation". Such images mirror the ego's de-differentiation and re-differentiation, representing the interaction of the life and death principles working within the ego. (Ehrenzweig, 1957, p. 200). Correspondingly, Milner found Ehrenzweig's analysis of art and the creative perception helped her think more clearly about certain aspects of her work with patients, as well as her own painting activities. She mentions, for example, how his term "creative surrender" provided her with a conceptual tool for thinking about boundaries and their merging during the creative process. While writing the last chapters of *The Hands of The Living God*, Milner was reading the proofs of Ehrenzweig's *The Hidden Order of Art* (1967). In saying that the role of the art teacher is to teach students to overcome their fear of chaos, he parallels what the analyst Charles Rycroft (an analysand of Milner and a prominent member of the British School) was saying in "Beyond the reality principle" (1962) about the need to discard the idea that primary process thinking is archaic, unrealistic, maladaptive and chaotic. Also, Ehrenzweig's account of "unconscious scanning" compares with the analyst's need to learn "free-floating attention", and links with what Milner called the "wide stare" needed to make meaningful doodle drawings (Milner, 1988 [1969], p. 410n).

All Milner's writings, in fact, emphasize that the quality of perception itself—the empty, purpose-free hovering—is not simply a way of handling conflict and anxiety, but allows a reaching down deeper into the "depths of love and creativity". She also stresses throughout that what characterizes vivid perceptual experience is a particular quality of internal body awareness. With this bodily awareness, combined with relaxation, there is a kind of passive consciousness of one's breathing—of "being breathed" rather than breathing—and the giving up of any conscious striving or self-assertion. According to Milner, this is the key to making contact with that "inner something" that is both part of her and yet other than herself, a "non-symbolic awareness of the body" of significance for both a heightened sense of reality and for the production and enjoyment of art. In her third autobiographical book, *Eternity's Sunrise* (1987a), written some fifty years after *An Experiment in Leisure*, Milner repeated her diary-keeping exercise to see how far her psychoanalytic experience had influenced her perceptions. The book is written around a set of what she calls "beads"—a collection of resonant images, memories, moments of experience, objects she has bought, paintings, and dreams. What characterizes these images is a special feeling of significance and vividness. They are "organic images" whose impact is related to the state of awareness in which she had first experienced them, a particular state of bodily relaxation and, in particular, consciousness of her breathing. Although this gave her a profound sense of aliveness, it led also to a "darkness" where she felt that her life might be extinguished at any moment—indeed, it was the same fear of ceasing to exist that was described earlier in *A Life of One's Own*. With her clinical experience she can now link these somewhat disturbing elements more directly to "the very bread and butter of my daily psychoanalytic task with patients [. . .] the dread of loss and abandonment, the facing of anxiety and disillusionment, and the hope of true identity" (1987a, p. 36).

Thus, Milner sees as significant the connection between "the creation of a work of art and the growth of a vital emotional involvement in the world around one". The meeting of self and other is in fact the territory explored by the artist when he engages with his medium, and it is on the bedrock of his own body, its sensations and affects, that the artist bases his work. The reciprocating body rhythms are established in infancy through the care of a devoted mother; continued through the receptive role of toys in childhood, and appear in art in the reciprocating interplay with the particular qualities of a chosen medium. It is the inner observation of one's own bodily movements, including "the effects of deliberately directing one's attention to the whole internal body awareness" that dramatically enhances perception. In her paper "Painting and internal body awareness", she explains how it is the "nowness" of the perception of the body and thus the perception of oneself that she focuses on—indeed, this is true to Freud's (1923b) observation that the ego is first and foremost a body ego. Milner also emphasizes that it is not so much the act of perceiving itself, but rather the deliberate relating of ourselves to our own perceiving that makes our perceptions truly come alive.

I shall turn now to Milner's own artistic activities. She painted a great deal with fellow analysts Sylvia Payne and Margaret Little, and professionally exhibited her work. Her personal account of her struggles in learning how to paint, which grew out of some doodle drawings she did while training as an analyst, was published in *On Not Being Able To Paint* (1950), a book that appealed to clinicians and non-clinicians alike. According to art historian Michael Podro, the painter Robert Medley (head of the Camberwell School of Art in the early 1960s) recommended it to his art students. Although it might seem odd to recommend a book with such a title to aspiring artists, Podro believes that Medley was trying to counterbalance the kind of painting methods that had been instilled by his predecessor, William Coldstream, whose influence was still very apparent in the art school. Podro remarks that Coldstream's distinctive representational manner had become, in the hands of his followers, "a bloodless and rather mannered routine for registering appearances"; thus Medley was hoping that insights such as Milner's could help to overcome the "inhibiting, self-denying stance that had become school orthodoxy" (Podro, 1990, pp. 401–402). (Interestingly, in her response to Podro's paper, Milner reveals that her family had been acquainted with Coldstream and in fact his first portrait [of Mrs Burgher] was of her sister. Milner recalls that at the time it was painted, in the 1930s, it had taken seventy sittings, which she feels accounts for the fact that it is not a very good likeness! The portrait is now in the Tate Gallery, given by Adrian Stokes, and is also reproduced on the paperback edition of Virginia Woolf's *To the Lighthouse*.)

In her analysis of her own painting, Milner draws attention to the primitive oral aspect of artistic production. She points out (following Klein) that the phantasies accompanying creativity involve ingestion and incorporation, the phantasied envelopment of what one loves (and may also hate). Milner noticed that many of her free drawings demonstrated this theme of eating or engulfing, and one had a particularly cannibalistic quality. This made her aware of what she calls "sinister aspects of creation", for, as Klein made clear, the unconscious phantasy of taking part of the external world (incorporation) into oneself has sadistic and aggressive components; thus the act of painting and drawing, which involves taking part of the external world into oneself, can be perceived as a greedy, cannibalistic destruction of one's loved objects. Milner believed that this could partly explain the "unreasonable fears that a painting would be 'no good' which could so often make it impossible to begin". However, a more experienced painter will probably feel less anxiety in this act of spiritual envelopment in order to paint, for he knows that he can bring what he has taken inside himself back to life in the outside world as a work of art (1989 [1957], p. 63). This relates to what Kleinian aesthetics places at the centre of all art—that it strives to recreate externally what has been internally hurt or destroyed. However, although Milner believes that a large element of creating art relates to this need to preserve and restore one's objects, she feels that painting relates to much more primitive levels of functioning, suggesting that it goes "deeper in its roots than restoring to immortal life one's lost loves—it goes back to the stage *before one had found a love to lose*" (*ibid.*, p. 67, my italics).

She came to see the role of visual art as similar to that of the psychoanalyst—"facilitating the acceptance of both illusion and disillusion, and thus making possible a richer relation to the real world". This also links to the ideas presented in her two earlier books (1934, 1937), which examined the conditions that fostered a special kind of perception, one that made the world and the self come alive. However, through her drawing experiments, she was able to see certain "inescapable facts" that she had left out in her earlier studies: facts to do with "the primitive hating that results from the inescapable discrepancy between the unlimited possibilities of one's dream and the realities of the external world". Such tension can however acts a spur to find a creative solution to the "human predicament", and Milner contends that artistic and aesthetic experience, in allowing a temporary merge between dream and reality, lessens this primitive hate. In both artist and viewer, art can alleviate feelings of resentment and anger and the loss of a phantasized ideal world.

Milner's creative struggles in *On Not Being Able To Paint* also helped her to think about the challenges facing her schizophrenic patient Susan, who produced a great many drawings during her sixteen-year analysis. Although Milner saw these as expressions of a reparative activity for all her destructive intentions or actions (cf. Klein and Segal) she did not consider this their primary function. For not only did Susan's drawings take on a very important meaning in her gradual establishment of a relationship to her own body boundary and bodily experience, they also helped to establish a connection with Milner herself and the external world. The drawings reveal the effectiveness of artistic activity as a form of communication between patient and analyst, and also highlight the role of the medium (be it paper, paint, words, or even the analyst himself or herself) in the expression of fundamental psychic processes, facilitating the negotiation of the interface between inner and outer reality. The drawings functioned as "some sort of substitute mirror that her own mother had never been able to be for her"; in a primitive way they gave her back something of herself, as well as providing a substitute for Milner in the gap between sessions. The act of making and bringing Milner the drawings also served as a kind of bridge towards her acceptance of the "otherness" of the external world; they affirmed its real existence and at the same time the reality of her own experience by slowly building up (restoring) in symbolic form all kinds of denied aspects of her infantile bodily relation to her mother (1988 [1969], p. 240).

Milner had found aspects of Klein's theory useful in understanding what was going on with Susan. The theory of the paranoid–schizoid position illuminated what happened to parts of Susan's psyche, when the object and the self are split into good and bad, and the bad bits of the self are projected into the "not-me" world, so that the ego is left feeling good, but surrounded by enemies. This helped Milner to understand how her first picture of a face completely covered with eyes resulted from a fragmentation of her own inner eye—her capacity for painful self-awareness—and a projecting of the bits outwards into her mother, or into part of her. Milner also believed that the "whole tragedy" of Susan's ECT treatment could be seen as a kind of dramatizing of what Klein maintained was the girl child's deepest anxiety, comparable to a boy's castration fear: that is, the inside of her body will be destroyed by a persecuting and aggressive enemy-mother, in revenge for the little girl's wishes to get inside mother and to appropriate what she phantasies to be there (Klein, 1932). Milner points out that after Susan's ECT treatment she no longer felt emotional response to others; her capacity for sadness had been cut off, and she would cry piteously for Milner to "give me back my concern". She felt that after this episode she had become possessed by a devil and had "gone over to the wrong side". Milner saw in all this a retreat from the anguished doubt of her power to preserve what she loved both inside and outside from her own angry, cruel, revengeful feelings—a doubt about which was stronger, her love or her hate.

However, it was Susan's constant use of the circle symbol that drew Milner's attention to new aspects of Susan's problems and to wider problems of perception. What interested Milner was the way in which the circle had the quality of being a gap—one relating to the experience of not-knowing, or even a physical or emotional gap—the feeling of something missing, leaving a blank or an emptiness. With this image in mind, Milner became increasingly interested in trying to understand more about the whole process of fusion, merging, interpenetrating, not only of love and hate but also of subject and object. For she was slowly coming to the conclusion that the acceptance of a phase of some kind of fusion was necessary for all creative work, whether the work is within the psyche or in the outer world. Here we see that Milner was struggling with the growing idea that an illusion of unity that the psychoanalytic theory talked about as a manic state of fusion with the beloved is not just an attempted escape to the memory of being the satisfied infant at the mother's breast, but exists at one end of a constantly alternating polarity that is the basis of all psychic creativity, and therefore all symbol formation and psychic growth. Milner viewed Susan's constant use of the symbol of the alternation between two circles and one circle as a picture of her struggle to find "a fertile interplay between a state of two-ness and of one-ness". She saw the state of one-ness as one characterized by the indeterminacy of boundaries, akin to what Freud referred to as the "oceanic feeling". What interested Milner was the question of under what sort of conditions this "illusion of oneness", of no differentiation, might arise.

She found support for her own preoccupations in Stokes's paper "Form in art", published in *New Directions in Psycho-analysis* (1955b), an important collection of papers in honour of Klein's seventieth birthday. In "Form in art", Stokes wrote that

> As well as the vivid impress of self contained totalities we renew at the instance of aesthetic sensation the "oceanic feeling", upheld by some of the qualities of id "language", such as interchangeability, from which poetic identifications flow. [1973 (1955b), p. 110]

Indeed, after reading this, Milner was "to find all of Stokes's writings very stimulating" (1988 [1969], p. 249, n2). *New Directions* also included a revised version of a paper on symbolism that Milner first worked on in 1951–1952. The original version of her paper was "Aspects of symbolism in the comprehension of not-self" (1952), and in it she described moments in the play of an eleven-year-old boy that seemed to have a dramatic and aesthetic beauty, including in his own eyes, that she connected with "ecstasy" (the case of Simon, discussed below). She had begun by tracing his depression to insecure periods during his early childhood, times when it was not safe to be absent-minded because he had to keep a vigilant eye on the external world. In her work with Susan, she observed that "the state of fusion, of one-ness, which can also be seen from the observer's point of view, as a state of absent-mindedness ... does require a condition in the environment which ensures some kind of protection from intrusion, some kind of protective framework" (1988 [1969], p. 250). Milner then postulated the need for an illusion of unity that could be a necessary phase in the discovery of two-ness, of separateness, of differentiation between self and not-self. Through her own painting activities, in fact, she became convinced that "the 'other' has to be created before it can be perceived".

From watching Simon's play and Susan's use of the symbol of the circle as a framing device, marking off a "safe space" to play, and also through her own studies of painting, Milner had become very interested in the role of the *frame* of a picture—that which marks off a different kind of reality from that of everyday life, just as the frame of the room, its décor and arrangement, and the fixed period of time mark off an analytic session. She was also interested in how dreams are framed in sleep, and in how an inner frame forms around concentrated states of mind—a kind of inner space essential to all mental productivity, whether creating ideas or artworks. It was not until Susan brought her the drawing done after the ECT that Milner began to see the earliest roots of this relating back to the experience of being held in one's mother's arms. The impact of the post-ECT drawing had been so intense that Milner writes she "had been unable at first to concentrate upon its meaning. It produced such a complex state of feeling to do with anguish and tragedy that it seems I did not really know what to do with it" (1988 [1969], p. 251).

However, she recalls with horror her "cavalier treatment" of Susan's drawing, for, instead of making a traced copy, she had "inked it over". Milner remembers this action of hers as "a warning of how too great enthusiasm for the clarity of verbal interpretation can also, at times, disastrously distort what the patient is experiencing". When Milner did feel able to think about the picture, it seemed to illustrate the circle theme again: the arms were "womb-like", enclosing the baby/foetus. Yet despite the anguish, Milner sensed "a faint glimmer of hope" deep within the picture: the hope that she would somehow be able to find a psychic equivalent of the encircling arms, the enclosing "womb state" necessary to really to heal the splittings and for the "defusion" to become "fusion" again.

The circle motif also became for Milner a symbol of what she thought Susan needed from her: a capacity to achieve "a partially undifferentiated and indeterminate state", a "blankness, an empty circle, emptiness of ideas", rather than feeling the need to constantly fight against the muddle and produce an interpretation (1988 [1969], p. 253). To the conscious, purposive mind, the ego's surrender to fusion–undifferentiation feels like death itself (which concurs with Ehrenzweig's thesis that the de-differentiation of the ego under the sway of the death instinct is a prerequisite for creativity). Thus, Milner thinks that

> one aspect of the circle, when it was an empty one, could be to do with the urge to indeterminacy, a state which can be felt like being

both everything and nothing; and that this must be taken into account as the necessary counterpart of the urge to be something, the urge to differentiate oneself out from the whole. [1988 (1969), p. 253]

Milner links this with the idea of a "good" kind of self-loss that she had identified in her earlier autobiographical writings. During these "high moments of feeling", all ideas of one's "goodness" (in social or moral terms) disappeared, and with this came a sense of release and expansion of consciousness, combined with the feeling that "the world had been newly created".

Although this could be viewed in Kleinian terms as a manic state, Milner felt there was more to it than this. For this experience of self-loss, which seemed to lead to the refreshment of her perception of the world, was often preceded by a silencing of inner noise, a focusing on the background of her experience and in particular her body awareness. It related to a phenomenon she had noticed during in her painting efforts, when there were moments

when one seemed to have lost all the original inspiration and nothing good was emerging, a kind of despair that always came, if the picture was to be any good at all, and which included a giving-up of all idea of producing a good painting. [1988 (1969), p. 254]

This need to give up one's conscious strivings is reminiscent of Keats's "negative capability", or of Bion's (1970) stricture to analysts to escape from the bondage of memory and desire, including even the wish to cure the patient, and wait patiently for a "pattern to emerge". In both therapeutic change and artistic creation, therefore, Milner believes that there is de-differentiation not only of subject and object, but also between different levels of mental functioning—a view that concurs with Ehrenzweig's (1967) account of the creative rhythm. This fusion is a *vital* illusion: before there can be a perception of "two-ness" there has to be an initial sense of one-ness. Without adequate experience of infantile illusion, both the growth of the reality sense and the capacity for creative work are inhibited. This brings us into the realm of Winnicott's "potential space".

The dynamics of intrapsychic illusion

It is the belief in the irreducibility of the creative impulse that unites the work of Milner and Winnicott. Ego-psychological concepts of "drive reduction" and "adaptation" seemed to miss a vital dimension, as did the Kleinian account of art with its focus on the restoration of lost objects. Milner stressed that creativeness is not simply deployed for defensive purposes (as Freud and Klein had suggested); it is a condition of subjectivity itself. If a heightened sense of subject–object union is an illusion, then it is an essential one because it helps to give life meaning and is valued for its own sake. There was much reciprocity between the ideas of Milner and Winnicott; indeed the image of overlapping circles that was so important for Milner provides a good motif for the relationship between their thinking, and their convergence relates particularly to the nature of illusion. Milner was writing her paper on illusion at the same time that Winnicott was publishing his on transitional phenomena (1953), both of which explore the same territory that Kleinian and Freudian theory had largely ignored—the positive aspects of the "manic–oceanic" feeling and its role in establishing the reality sense.

The term "illusion" is used by a number of British School analysts and does not have the same kind of meaning as that attached to the Kleinian notion of "phantasy". Where most Kleinians would agree that "illusion" is a regression to a paranoid–schizoid position characterized by part-object relations and a sense of omnipotence and manic fusion, both Winnicott and Milner see illusion as a benign and necessary stage in the development of a reality sense. According to Milner (1952 [1955]) "phantasy" is not specific enough and the concept of illusion is needed because this word implies a relation to an "external object of feeling", even though it may be a phantasied one. The Kleinians' "phantasy" refers to the unconscious psychic representation of an instinct and is predominantly *internal*. Illusion, rather differently, is pointing to a phenomenon that is close to, even partly is, *both internal and external reality*. The term illusion refers to a "third area"—an area which is felt as within the self and yet is also part of the external world. Winnicott (1953) designated this area as the "transitional" or "potential" space, regarding it as the place where the child first begins to play and to use symbols. In her clinical work (especially as recounted with Susan and with Simon), Milner came to see the analyst (and also the drawings produced) functioning as a bridge, a "pliable medium" between inner and outer, and between patient and therapist. It is interesting that, towards the end of her therapy, Susan produced a vivid symbol of this meeting point for her self-created reality and the external world—the symbol of a communion cup into which she phantasied spitting (1988 [1969], pp. 370–372).

The cup thus functioned as both a *receptive* and a *transformative* container for her split-off parts, which could be fused and recombined to form something new. For Winnicott, such a bridge was the "transitional object", the child's first "not-me" possession, in the form of his teddy bear, rag, or piece of blanket. He saw this as the child's first use of a symbol, and the source from which all cultural activity arises.

Both Milner and Winnicott believed that the infant must *create* his own power to perceive the difference between inner and outer reality. In order for this to happen, there has to have been an initial experience of illusion (fostered by the mother's initial full adaptation to her child's needs) when the self and the environment–mother were felt to be mixed up together. Milner says this applies to all subsequent relationships with others: in order to fully understand/empathize with other people, we must temporarily undo the separateness of self and other, just as the artist must recreate the bodily tension of the model's pose in his imagination. During her training in the 1940s, Milner said some of her "biggest misgivings" about psychoanalytic theory concerned its approach to external reality. She felt that neither Freudian nor Kleinian theory fully addressed the interface between the "inner" and "outer", and "found it odd that psychoanalysis talked about [external reality] as if it was something out there, separate from oneself and one's seeing, so that one only had to open one's eyes and there it was" (Milner, 1987a, p. 119).

She describes how refreshing it was, "like coming from a stuffy room into the fresh air", when she came across the following words of the philosopher Santayana: "Perception is no primary phase of consciousness: it is an ulterior function acquired by a dream which has become *symbolic of its own external conditions* and therefore relevant to its own destiny" (*ibid.*, my italics).[2] This seems to be stating in philosophical terms what Winnicott meant when he talked of how the infant comes imaginatively to "create" the breast. Milner saw this recurrent phase of "feeling at one with what one sees" as part of the rhythm of oneness–twoness, unity–separation, which endows the world with significance and meaning, akin to the capacity which Blake called "each man's poetic genius". She felt that until the boundary between self and other was established in infancy, the mechanisms of projection and introjection could not begin; if these mechanisms are to be active, there must be an implicit sense of an ego-boundary. In her 1952 paper on symbol formation she had tried looking at Freud's "two principles of mental functioning" in terms of the "fusion" and "defusion" between subject and object: that is, in terms of two ways of being that differ according to whether one feels joined up, merged with what one looks at, or separate from it. It had become apparent to her that we seem to know a great deal about this "separated" state of mind, since our very speech depends upon it, but we know comparatively little about the "unseparated phase" of merged boundaries. This is very much defended against, she believes, from fear of the loss of identity and even loss of sanity. What followed from this was the idea that the illusion of no-separateness between subject and object, or between what Winnicott calls the "subjective object" and the "objective object", could possibly be a necessary phase in all creativity, even in our perception of the reality of the external world at all. Milner found confirmation in Santayana's words for the idea that perception itself is a creative process. (This could also be seen in terms of "aesthetic" criticism: not only does the aesthetic critic point out to the viewer certain visual attributes, but he also encourages us to think about these images in a different way—by association and metaphor, for example. These new thoughts must, in their turn, also *shape our perception* of the particular artwork. When the critic holds the artwork before us, he filters it through his own experience and re-evokes the artwork into a new symbolic form that we can think about. Like the good nursing mother, with her "reverie", the critic can help give meaning to our own perceptions by holding the dream for us, not by "explaining it away".)

As we can see, despite being active members of the Kleinian circle during the 1940s, neither Winnicott nor Milner accepted Klein's ideas uncritically. They both disagreed with a number of central Kleinian tenets: for example, the belief that object relations operate from birth; the literal acceptance of the death instinct; the concept of the paranoid–schizoid position; and Klein's view that envy is inborn. Although Winnicott praised Klein for her account of the infantile depressive position, he referred to the time when the infant becomes aware of the mother as whole and separate as "the stage of concern", a term with less melancholic and pathological associations. For both Winnicott and Milner, play is regarded as a largely benign and joyful affair, not fraught with the sadistic phantasies and conflicts emphasized by Klein. These differences came to a head in the years 1951–1955, focusing on Winnicott's concept of the "transitional object", which Klein found absolutely unacceptable, and which Winnicott detailed in his 1953 paper "Transitional objects and transitional phenomena". According to Grosskurth's biography of Klein, at an editorial meeting to discuss which papers should be included in the forthcoming collection, *New Directions in Psychoanalysis*, Winnicott had refused to alter his paper to fit in with Klein's ideas, and "with the manuscript tucked under his arm, he sadly left the room. As he later told his wife, 'Apparently Mrs Klein no longer considers me a Kleinian'" (Grosskurth, 1986, p. 398).

In that paper, Winnicott set out to examine what he later described as "the separation that is not a separation but a form of union", and explained how during the 1940s (an important phase during the development of his ideas about boundary and space) Milner had been able to convey to him through a visual image "the tremendous significance that there can be in the interplay of the edges of two curtains, or of the surface of a jug that is placed in front of another jug". This image refers to Milner's picture *Two Jugs*, which appeared on the cover of the first edition of *On Not Being Able to Paint* (1950). She, too, saw this as a powerful way of expressing in visual terms the nature of the interchange between objects, and how their separate identities are by no means fixed and straightforward.

Unlike Winnicott's, Milner's paper was included in *New Directions*, despite Klein's disagreement with her view of states of fusion as being part of healthy infancy. Grosskurth writes that "Klein was angry with Milner for having produced a very original idea on the capacity for symbol-making as the basis for creativity" (1986, p. 396). Milner in fact acknowledges the usefulness of Klein's theory of symbol formation, and cites Klein's (1930) belief that "symbolism is the basis of all talents". But her 1952 paper diverges from Klein in significant respects. She introduces here themes that will interweave throughout her work: the imagery connected with dying and rebirth involved in the creative process; the link between aesthetic value and creativity, together with the way that the body and instinctual processes are implicated in these experiences. (The theme of body experience, relaxation, and its relationship to creative living was also prominent in Winnicott's thinking.) She argues that Kleinian concepts such as splitting, projective identification, and introjection are not adequate to account for all the meanings of such experiences, for which the notion of a healthy return to a state of oceanic oneness is required.

In this paper, Milner describes how Simon, an eleven-year-old boy, had a lack of interest in hobbies and schoolwork that made him withdrawn and depressed. It is important to note that the case was, during the first part, supervised by Klein, and "Simon" was in fact Klein's own grandson, Michael Clyne. The case material centres around "a game of war between two villages". The child set up two rival villages and commanded Milner to "see his people as gods". With a dramatic, ritual quality, he would then close the curtains, light some candles, and throw matches over the "villages". Milner was very struck by the *aesthetic* dimension to these activities. She writes that

> there was a quality in his play which I can only describe as beautiful—occasions on which it was he who did the stage-managing and it was my imagination which caught fire. It was in fact a play with light and fire. He would close the shutters of the room and insist that it be lit only by candle light . . . And then he would make what he called furnaces, with a very careful choice of what ingredients should make the fire, including dried leaves from special plants in my garden [which] had to be put in a metal cup on the electric fire . . . And often there had to be a sacrifice, a lead soldier had to be added to the fire, and this figure was spoken of either as the victim or the sacrifice. In fact this type of play had a dramatic ritual quality comparable to the fertility rites described by Frazer in primitive societies. [1987b, p. 96]

This play recalls the "poemagogic" imagery connected with violent death and sacrifice that Ehrenzweig believed both induced and symbolized the creative process itself, and that Milner noticed in her earlier studies of visual imagery in *An Experiment in Leisure*. Simon's play expressed for Milner "the idea of integration" and the desire for a "passionate union with an external object". His game seemed to be telling her that the basic identifications that make it possible to find the "familiar in the unfamiliar" require an "ability to tolerate a temporary loss of self"—a giving up of the rational ego for a while (what Ehrenzweig termed the "creative surrender"). Indeed, Milner links it with what art historian Bernard Berenson (1948) describes as the "aesthetic moment":

> ... that fleeting instant, so brief as to be almost timeless, when the spectator is at one with the work of art he is looking at, or with actuality of any kind that the spectator himself sees in terms of art, as form and colour. He ceases to be his ordinary self, and the picture or building, statue, landscape, or aesthetic actuality is no longer outside himself. The two become one entity; time and space are abolished and the spectator is possessed by one awareness. When he recovers workaday consciousness it is as if he had been initiated into illuminating, formative mysteries. [Berenson, 1948, cited in Milner, 1987b, p. 97]

Stokes referred to this sense of feeling of fusion with the object as the "invitation in art", the pull exerted by the artwork—its tendency to draw us in so that we feel a sense of merging, becoming "lost" in the artwork. However, Stokes felt that this pole of the experience must be balanced by the depressive sense of "object otherness" if it is to be a truly full and mature aesthetic experience.

Milner saw Simon's struggles in terms of what poets and artists are also concerned with expressing. It is not that such "aesthetic moments" are confined to encounters with *specific* objects, but that art is a way, in adult life, of reproducing *states* that are part and parcel of healthy infancy. As is well known to those familiar with Wordsworth, he, like many of the Romantic poets, related such heightened states of awareness to infancy and childhood. In his "Immortality Ode", for example, he mourns the loss of childhood perception, that "visionary gleam" and "master light of all our seeing" which must inevitably fade as "Shades of the prison house begin to close / Upon the growing boy" (Wordsworth, 1958, p. 105). The receptive role of the toys that were the equivalent of an artist's medium alerted Milner to the process she had herself tried to observe introspectively when she was doing her "free drawings" in *On Not Being Able To Paint*. She (like Winnicott) believed that there was something important common to psychotherapy, artistic effort and playing, which distinguished them from day-dreaming. In play and aesthetic experience there is something of a half-way house between day-dreaming (the stuff of inner phantasy) and purposeful muscular activity—the reaching out and shaping the world according to one's inner phantasy. This was vividly illustrated when Milner noticed that as soon as Simon *moved* one of the toys, the play village was suddenly different and a whole new set of possibilities emerged—just as, in imaginative free drawing, the sight of a mark on paper provokes new associations, the line seems to answer back (reciprocate) and functions as a very primitive external object. In a similar spirit, in his analytical sessions with children, Winnicott developed the "squiggle game". Winnicott would start by drawing at random a squiggly line on a blank piece of paper, and the child would respond to this by joining it with a line of his own. Thus, a dialogue would emerge that enabled an interchange between the reality of the patient and therapist in the spirit of playful communication. Interestingly, this sense of a (psychic and bodily) reciprocity between the artist and his medium concurs with what the philosopher and art critic Richard Wollheim calls "thematisation"—an essentially *embodied* process by which the artist, after making an initial mark, starts to take account of its relationship to the surrounding space, the edge of the paper or canvas, and other material properties of the surface (Wollheim, 1987, pp. 19–25).

A few weeks after the war-of-the-villages game, something significant happened that gave Milner another clue as to the role of the toys. Simon's "bullying tone" had vanished when he was told that his form master had given him permission to work on his favourite hobby (photography) at school. The sudden disappearance of the bullying attitude led Milner to believe that it was his "spontaneously creative activity" (his play) being incorporated into the framework of the school that was fulfilling in real life the solution foreshadowed in the village war game. What he had felt to be the soulless, routine world of the school now appeared humanized—he could now take in a bit of himself that he had created for the outside world (the school). But what was important was that it was only *now* that he could "take in" what the school had to offer—for they had previously made a number of gestures that had largely been rejected. Milner thinks that these efforts had not been taken up by Simon because they had "not taken the particular form of the incorporation of, acceptance of, a bit of his own spontaneous creation" (1987b, p. 93). Because the school had now become receptive to his own personality (his love of photography), it demonstrated that, although a predominantly "male" environment, it was capable of good mothering. Indeed, this need was foreshadowed in his dreams when his mother had been present in his Latin class—the most problematic of his subjects. Milner interpreted that on an important level, the village play had to do with the "not-me-ness" of his school life. Milner also felt that, like the toys, *she became his medium*—a part of the external world that would accept his phantasy while remaining an independent object. (This concurs with Winnicott's account of the transitional object, which is "neither internal nor external but partakes of both".) Milner felt that Simon's use here "might not only be a defensive regression but an *essential recurrent phase of a creative relation to the world*" (1988 ([1937], p. 104, my italics). She believes that such moments are infused with an *aesthetic* sense; they are moments when "the original poet in each of us created the outside world for us, by finding the familiar in the unfamiliar" (*ibid.*, p. 88). These ideas were of great interest to Winnicott, who developed their implications in his account of play (1971, pp. 44–62).

In this context Milner also looked very closely at the question of boundaries and their significance, something linked with her interest in the "framing" of experience. For her own introspective study of the problems involved in painting had alerted her to the fact that "the variations in the feeling of the existence or non-existence of the body-boundary are themselves important". Both Winnicott and Milner felt uncomfortable that the Kleinian account of the paranoid–schizoid splitting of objects into good and bad "part-objects" *took for granted* the existence of a clear boundary between the self and the object from the start, and therefore did not reach the heart of what Simon's playing (and indeed all symbolic activity) was all about—for there was much in his play that involved burning and melting, suggesting the *obliteration* of boundaries. For Milner and Winnicott, the sense of a boundary between inner and outer reality is acquired gradually and is dependent on environmental factors. Milner contends that by "using art either as artist or audience, or by using psychoanalysis", we can keep our perception and aesthetic capacities fresh—for it is these worlds (the aesthetic and the psychoanalytic) that link subjective and objective, but without confusing them. Thus, the psychoanalytic frame promotes the "creative illusion" of the transference, a state of receptivity and tolerance where it is safe to fall apart and there is no need to worry about the practical business of living, and it is by means of this illusion that a better adaptation to the world is established.

Bion also saw the mother's capacity for reverie (her containing function) as essential for the infant's capacity for tolerating external reality and instinctual frustration; and Winnicott was pointing to a similar idea through his concept of "primary maternal preoccupation", which he regards a temporary kind of "madness" where the mother withdraws from the external world and becomes highly attuned to the needs of her infant. Without this capacity, she will be unable to give the infant the "holding" he needs in order to preserve his "vital illusion of oneness". Milner suggests that Simon was expressing with his metal fire cup the "inner fire of concentration" and, especially with the melted-down soldier, the *dissolution* of his ordinary common-sense ego (cf. Ehrenzweig's de-differentiation of ego-consciousness during the "unconscious scanning" process in creativity). This also implies that in the countertransference experience of herself catching fire, Milner was herself experiencing the dissolution or absence of boundaries in the infant–mother "reverie" with her patient. Thus, with both Milner and Winnicott, we can talk of "benign illusion" as a necessary stage or place not only in the establishment of both self and other but also as an essential to the repeated renewals and enrichments of self (particularly through "aesthetic moments") throughout life.

According to Winnicott's theory, everything that happens to a person is creative unless the individual is ill or is hampered by ongoing environmental factors that stifle the creative processes. He complained, in fact, that psychoanalytic aesthetics had directed too much focus on the art product and its content rather than on the creative impulse itself, and in *Playing and Reality* (1971) he explicitly separates the idea of creation from actual works of art. Winnicott believed that the *creative impulse* itself is the primary concern of all applications of psychoanalysis to the understanding of art. He is probably the first psychoanalyst to distinguish explicitly between creative activity and the actual production of artworks. Analytic writers who focus on specific artworks and/or questions of why a particular individual was a great artist miss the main point—the creative impulse itself. The actual art object is a secondary concern for Winnicott—in his view it obscures rather than illuminates, and "stands between the observer and the artist's creativity" (1988 [1971], p. 81). Primary creativity is the essential precondition for all meaningful experience. Although a creation can be a picture, a poem, a house, for example, he believes that it is better to say that these things *could* be creations: "the creativity that concerns him is a universal and belongs to being alive"(*ibid.*, p. 79). The creative impulse is a thing-in-itself involved in both artistic production and everyday creative living. Thus, there is no *qualitative* distinction between certain kinds of artworks, nor, indeed, what makes an object an artwork *per se*, as distinct from an ordinary object. Winnicott's theory sees no real difference between the creativity involved in humming a tune, baking a cake, creating a symphony, or everyday pleasure in one's bodily sensations, such as breathing, for instance.

So, although Winnicott praised Klein for her understanding of aggressive impulses in development, the importance of their fusion with the life impulse, and the role of guilt feeling in artistic experience, he believed that Klein's linking of creativity with reparation did not reach the subject of creativity itself. Both Freud and Klein, he argued, "took refuge in heredity", and thus avoided the implications of infantile dependence and the role of the environment. His concept of the transitional object and the potential space fulfil a crucial role here. The notion of an object that is neither internal nor external, but transcends both inner and outer reality and occupies a potential or transitional space, is very significant in the development of British School thinking. Not only does it introduce a whole new realm of experience into psychoanalysis, it also marks a new way of understanding symbol formation, creativity, and the aesthetic experience. It is this that distinguishes a "Kleinian" from a "Winnicottian" account of aesthetics. Unlike Klein, Winnicott did not believe that the mechanism of unconscious phantasy was operative at the start of life. Thus, the concept of the transitional object is the means by which the child learns to overcome the dramatic realization that he is not omnipotent. Where Klein's theory focuses on the drama of the inner world (the trajectory of psychological and emotional development from fragmentation to integration), Winnicott's focuses on the child's interactions with the external world via the transitional object. He stressed, however, that it is not the object itself but the use to which it is put that determines its "transitional" status. Similarly, the potential space is something that opens out when the child begins to recognize the gap between his needs and their fulfilment (at first, by the mother). It is within this space, somewhere between reality and phantasy, that a sense of a "me" and a "not-me" can be acquired gradually.

Winnicott would say that a human infant could not even develop fully, or at least not into an artist, unless he had actually experienced the transitional use of an object. The child's creativity is directly influenced by the mother's "good-enough" care. This is something most Kleinians would hesitate to allow because of the unnecessary burden it places on the *real* mother's maternal capacity. Winnicott believed that it is the child's environment that plays the decisive role in creative development: the mother must both allow her child illusion and facilitate its gradual abandonment. For

> The transitional object does not "go inside" nor does the feeling about it necessarily undergo repression. It is not forgotten and it is not mourned. It loses its meaning, and this is because the transitional phenomena have spread out over the whole intermediate territory between "inner psychic reality" and the "external world as perceived by two persons in common", that is to say, over the whole cultural field. [Winnicott, 1958, p. 255]

The transitional object is thus the foundation of Winnicott's account of cultural and aesthetic experience, upon which all subsequent cultural activity is based. The central feature of this approach to art and creativity is the focus on the creative *process* rather than on the art *product*. It is the relationship between playing and the formation of transitional objects that eventually leads to a shared art and culture, though no independent account of *aesthetic value* is provided. The emphasis is on the creativity of everyday living, rather than on specific artistic achievement and its value.

Interestingly, there are scholars who have observed a foreshadowing of Winnicott's concept of the transitional object and his ideas on creativity in the work of Otto Rank. Rank was Freud's closest disciple and colleague from 1906 to 1926. When, at the age of twenty-one, Rank presented Freud with a short manuscript on the artist, Freud was so impressed that he invited Rank to become secretary of the emerging Vienna Psychoanalytic Society. However, controversy over Rank's *The Trauma of Birth* (1929, first published in German in 1925) led to the final break with Freud, who first praised, then condemned, the book under pressure from Rank's rivals, especially Karl Abraham and Ernest Jones. Throughout his life, Rank wrote extensively on art and literature, and his *Art and Artist* (1932) marks a significant early contribution to the dilaogue between psychoanalysis and aesthetics. Indeed, the aesthetician Spitz argues the case for a reappraisal of Rank's work and his significant contribution to psychoanalytic aesthetics. Spitz points out that, despite a recent resurgence of interest in his work, his "fascinating contributions to the realm of the aesthetic continue to be underemphasised" (1989, p. 97). Spitz draws a parallel beween the work of Rank and Winnicott, and suggests that Rank's "notion of the neurotic as failed artist accords well" with Winnicott's emphasis on the "self-curative aspects of symptoms and their inherent creativity" (*ibid.*, p. 101).

In *The Psychoanalytic Vocation: Rank, Winnicott and the Legacy of Freud* (1991), Peter Rudnytsky explores this thesis further and makes a case for Rank as the unacknowleged precursor of contemporary object-relations theory, suggesting that Rank's most significant contribution "lies in [his] attention to art, play and creativity" (*ibid.*, p. 65). Rank dissented with the traditional Freudian view of art as sublimation or neurosis, suggesting that there is "something in the individual himself which is creative, which is impelling, which is not taken in from without, but which grows within". Rank discerned a continuity between the realm of play and the world of art, territory that Winnicott and Milner were to explore some twenty years later. Rank also speaks of "the intermediate character of the work of art . . . links the world of subjective reality with that of objective reality—harmoniously fusing the edges of each without confusing them" (*ibid.*, p. 65). This is an uncanny foreshadowing of Winnicott's concept of the transitional object, although Winnicott makes no reference to Rank. Rudnytsky notes that Milner, however, does acknowledge Rank's work as lending support to her notion of how "art provides a method, in adult life, for producing states that are part of everyday experience in healthy infancy" (Milner, 1987b, p. 65).

Let us now turn to explore the work of Independent British psychoanalyst Christopher Bollas, who has been much influenced by Winnicott, and whose ideas have been usefully deployed by a number of aestheticians and cultural historians. (Scalia [2002] collects a number of essays from a variety of eminent clinicians and aestheticians in both the social sciences and humanities, exploring Bollas's contribution to aesthetics and cultural studies.) In *The Shadow of the Object: Psychoanalysis of the Unthought Known* (1987) Bollas emphasizes the essential, formative role played by the primary care-taker in the psychological development of the infant, which, he argues, can also be viewed as the basis for adult creative and aesthetic experience. Bollas speaks of "the transformational object", a memory from early object relations, when the mother "continually transforms the infant's internal and external environment". In later life, we may "*search for an object that is identified with the metamorphosis of the self*" (*ibid.*, p. 17, my italics). In aesthetic experiences, for example, we may feel "an uncanny fusion with the object". The uncanny feeling derives from the return of something strangely familiar, "something never cognitively apprehended but existentially known" (*ibid.*, pp. 16–17). Bollas claims this is a recollection of fusion with the maternal "transformational object". The "aesthetic moment" is an evocative resurrection of this early experience, an instant when we are perhaps "captured" by an object and enjoy the sensation of being engaged in a meaningful, and perhaps even reverential, experience. He writes,

> In the aesthetic moment, when a person engages in deep subjective rapport with an object, the culture embodies in the arts varied symbolic equivalents to this search for transformation. In the quest for deep subjective experience of an object, the artist both remembers for us and provides us with occasions for the experience of ego memories of transformation. In a way, the experience of the aesthetic moment is neither social nor moral; it is curiously interpersonal and even *ruthless*, as the object is sought out only as deliverer of an experience. [*ibid.*, pp. 28–29, my italic]

According to Bollas, the pursuit of such moments is an endless search for something in the future that actually resides in the past. In reality, we are always looking for "transformational objects" that promise to change us, to bring us into harmony with the non-self—at least within the limited confines of a cultural framework. Although Bollas's general emphasis is on the positive nature of aesthetic experience he adds that "a person may seek a negative aesthetic experience, for such occasion 'prints' his early ego experiences and registers the structure of the unthought known". He suggests that "some borderline patients . . . repeat traumatic situations because through the latter they remember their origins existentially" (*ibid.*, p. 17).

At this point, we may recall our earlier discussion of Meltzer and Harris Williams' (1988) notion of "aesthetic conflict". At first glance, their thesis appears to plough a furrow similar to Bollas's account of psychological development, in that both frameworks highlight the central role of the mother's *aesthetic impact* on the baby. However, Meltzer and Harris Williams' framework (deep-rooted in poetry and informed by Kleinian thinking) suggests that it is the *conflict* aroused in the baby by the mother's presence, and specifically by the perception of the match between her known exterior features and her mysterious hidden "interior", that gives rise to the creative imagination. If the baby can tolerate the "burden of the mystery" (Wordsworth, 1958, p. 53) this bodes well for his or her psychological well-being. Bollas's account of psychological development, of course, is not intended as an exploration of aesthetics *per se*. His work suggests that healthy psychological development and well-being arise through the mother's "total idiom of care" (1987, p. 13). The mother negotiates the outside world for the baby and provides an "aesthetic of being that becomes a feature of the infant's self".

Bollas's notion on the "transformational object" thus builds upon and develops further Winnicott's theme of the "creativity of everyday life" and his account of the transitional object and its relevance for cultural experience. As well as inspiring clinicians such as Bollas, Winnicott's ideas have also been of great interest to a number of writers in the academic domain. For example, the philosopher Richard Kuhns (1983) developed an account of culture based on insights from Winnicott's theory of child development, and as we shall see in the next chapter, the art critic Peter Fuller deployed Winnicott's ideas in his analysis of American "colour field" painting.

Notes

1. "The body is a big sagacity, a plurality with one sense, a war and a peace, a flock and a shepherd. . . . There is more sagacity in thy body than in thy best wisdom" (Nietzsche, 1883–1885).
2. The quotation is from Santayana's 1920 essay entitled "The suppressed madness of sane men", which Milner borrowed as the title for her book of collected papers. According to Santayana, "suppressed madness" relates to certain people or states of mind that are cut off from what he calls the "instincts", and Milner takes this to mean to be "cut off from the body". She notes that Winnicott describes similar kinds of states when he refers to a "lack of indwelling" and also to a "lack of psychosomatic collusion", both of which describe an aspect of madness when the psyche and soma (head and the heart) are not working together.

CHAPTER SEVEN

Painting as the body: the aesthetics of Fuller and Wollheim

> "There is a sense in which all art is of the body, particularly so in the eyes of those who accept that the painted surface and other media of art represent as a general form, which their employment particularises, the actualities of the hidden psychic structures made up of evaluations and phantasies with corporeal content"
>
> (Stokes, 1978, *III*, p. 328)

This chapter will consider how a number of important British psychoanalytical concepts, discussed above, have been deployed in the aesthetic theory and art criticism of two significant contributors to contemporary aesthetics. I shall be focusing on the writings of art critic Peter Fuller, and philosopher and aesthetician Richard Wollheim, with a view to exploring their respective contributions to a British psychoanalytic aesthetic: one that is essentially grounded on a *corporeal* theory of pictorial meaning and aesthetic value.

Fuller's account of the "colour field" painters, Robert Natkin and Mark Rothko, provides an interesting example of how

Winnicott's "potential space" and Bion's account of mental space illuminate both the affective meaning of pictorial space and the dynamics of the aesthetic encounter, while Wollheim's concern with the corporeal basis of visual art demonstrates his allegiance to the aesthetic criticism of Adrian Stokes and, through this, to the psychoanalytical insights of Kleinian theory. It must be emphasized that there was no collaboration between the two writers, and that there are fundamental differences between them in terms of age, profession, and commitment to psychoanalytic thinking, which should be appreciated from the start. Wollheim, being some twenty-four years Fuller's senior, enriches his understanding and love of painting with some fifty years of philosophical experience, and nearly forty years of involvement with British psychoanalytic thinking. Fuller, on the other hand, was primarily a journalist and popular art critic, and his involvement with psychoanalsis, albeit intense, was somewhat transient, and seems to have been related more to the vicissitudes of his own psychoanalytic therapy than with any long-standing commitment to psychoanalysis. None the less, a comparison of the respective theoretical positions of these two writers can help to prepare us for a wider consideration of some of the themes and implications of what can be identified as a "British psychoanalytic aesthetic".

Evocative space: the work of Natkin and Rothko

Fuller's *Art and Psychoanalysis* (1980) arose out of a dissatisfaction with Marxist and ideological approaches to art and culture, and was also shaped significantly by his own analytic experience. Indeed, it was in many ways an "autobiographical journey", and the four chapters parallel the course of Fuller's own "self-discovery through psychoanalysis": the book begins with a critique of the mechanistic world-view of Freud and Marx, moves on to Klein's account of the mother–child relationship, and eventually breaks through into "the warmth and light of Winnicott's 'potential space'" (Fuller, 1988 [1980], p. x). The details of this autobiographical "journey" are explored more fully in his autobiographical *Marches Past* (1986). This makes clear the role that both Freud and Marx played his own oedipal drama; it seems that he felt he had to "overthrow" them in order to move on, intellectually and emotionally. As his analysis progressed, he became aware of the importance of the mother–child relationship and its vicissitudes; this marked a growth period in his own personal life, and also made him change his approach to art and aesthetics. Fuller felt that because psychoanalysis is devoted to exploring certain biologically constant, unchanging aspects of human nature (such as the mother–child relationship and the oedipal drama), it could therefore help to ground his search for a material (biological) basis for aesthetics that would reduce art neither to ideology nor to a product of historical circumstance. (It should be noted that, while coming from the political left, Fuller in the 1970s became increasingly dissatisfied with the kinds of theory that reduced art to being the products of ideology or of social conditions and circumstance, or theories that treated artworks merely as historical documents, or analysed them in terms of linguistic structures, leaving "art-shaped holes" (1988 [1980], p. x). He is especially critical of Terry Eagleton's aesthetics—see his preface to *Images of God* (1991), which expresses a rather personalized attack on Eagleton's ideas.)

Fuller's discomfort with ideological approaches was not entirely academic, as his preface to the 1988 edition of *Art and Psychoanalysis* makes clear. For it was largely through his acquaintance with the work of Robert Natkin that he was forced into rethinking his own aesthetic beliefs. It seems that the work of this artist profoundly disrupted his preconceptions about the nature of the aesthetic encounter, and this compelled him to focus on his growing dissatisfaction with much orthodox left-wing aesthetics—and to write *Art and Psychoanalysis*. He grants that Natkin's style belongs within the "colour field" convention. But at the same time it "tears through" its own ideology or convention:

> not by a flight into a supra-historical domain of "timeless" spiritual essences, but rather a penetration metaphorically downwards, into the region of psycho-biological being, into that great reservoir of *potentiality* upon which our hopes of a better personal and social future ultimately rest. [1988 (1980), p. 208]

The overwhelming feeling of "goodness" evoked by Natkin's work could not be explained by appealing to formalist and socialist explanations of artistic practice; rather, it was concepts such as Winnicott's "potential space" that enabled Fuller to make sense of his aesthetic experience. Not only this, but at the same time as Natkin's impact, Fuller's personal analysis was "moving backwards ... from preoccupations surrounding my relationship with the father on towards an analysis of feelings involved in the prior relationship with the mother" (*ibid.*). Winnicott's theories must have featured prominently in his analysis, and perhaps helps to explain why Fuller found Natkin's work so profoundly moving. (It is significant that *Art and Psychoanalysis* is dedicated to his own analyst, Kenneth Wright, and to the analyst Charles Rycroft, with whom he corresponded.) The paintings evidently resonated with aspects of his own inner life, for apparently he would often refer to them in his analytic sessions.

The profound influence of Winnicottian ideas on the understanding of his aesthetic experiences appears in the following extract from his introduction to a catalogue for an exhibition of Natkin's work in 1974:

> ... the dynamic of our interaction with [Natkin's] canvases took the form of a seduction into an experience where the distinction between the *"outside"* and the *"inside"* of the picture became ambiguous. The realisation of this simultaneously involved a sense of fear, of horror, and *tragedy*. It may be possible to interpret these events by saying that Natkin evokes a stage in our development when it was difficult to differentiate between "self" and "not-self"; when the skin of our bodies did not provide an absolute, concrete limitation to our sense of our physical being; a stage in which we also lacked the sense of time. The reconstruction of that phase turns out to be fascinating, alluring and satisfying—though simultaneously frightening and tragic. By now it should be self-evident that the stage to which I am referring is that before separation from the mother and her breast. Natkin's painting may, in part, be seen as an act of reparation for that universally experienced tragedy, an interpretation which is supported by its paradoxically "epic" and "intimate" aspirations. Thus it may be true to say that Natkin's painting *recaptures aspects of infantile experience* about the nature of time, space, and ourselves which, in adult life, we have been compelled to renounce, defensively, and sometimes to the impoverishment of our perceptions. [1974, pp. 3–5, my italics]

It is clear here how Winnicott's concept of the potential space helped Fuller to identify powerful aspects of the aesthetic encounter: to clarify what this "aesthetic" emotion might be; its material grounding; and why it can often seem relatively unrelated to most other kinds of adult emotions about the world.

The "goodness" of Natkin's work seemed to be related specifically to its capacity to re-evoke the *oscillating relationship between inner and outer reality*; the formal mechanics of the painting seemed to be rooted in the immediate emotions and paradoxes of the potential space. It is as if

> Natkin began by enticing you with an illusion. . . . But no sooner have you recognised the facticity[1] of the materials than you become aware of yet another way of reading the painting . . . the uniform skin of light evaporates in part because its tenuous existence came about only through the mixing of colours and the organisation of forms into a shimmering, illusory film on the retina. But as this film disintegrates, it gives way to billowing and boundless hazes of colour, to seemingly limitless vistas of illusionary space. . . . The eye is compelled to penetrate deeper and deeper *inside* the painting. You may even experience anxiety as you realise that there is no fixed viewpoint which you can continue to adopt outside the work which will allow you to perpetuate a detached observation of its skin. . . . Only by denying the illusion, by moving reassuringly back one step . . . can you find an anchored raft. [Fuller, 1988 (1980), p. 179]

Fuller argues that the only way to describe this "illusionary space" is to say that "it is *contained within the painting*" itself. Far from being an external viewpoint, it becomes a "deep plummeting illusion" evoked through the building up of many thin layers of paint on the canvas surface. This contradiction between the "skin of paint, as a limiting membrane" (one which effectively defines the boundary between the self and other) and that "plummeting illusory space" that "sucks you into itself" can be explained (so Fuller suggests) by the interplay between separateness and fusion, as similarly described by both Winnicott and Milner. We can also see that Fuller's experience here concurs with the dynamics of Ehrenzweig's "enveloping pictorial space", in which, Fuller argues, we may feel trapped and lost in the infinite at the same time. (Although he does not specifically refer to Milner, Winnicott, and Ehrenzweig, Fuller is using their terms in a parallel way.) For, as we have explored in Chapter Five, according to Ehrenzweig, these contradictory yet compatible experiences of pictorial space mirror "the undifferentiated substructure of art [where there] is a womb being prepared to receive, nurse, and ultimately return the artist's projections, an inner space that both contains and repels the spectator" (Ehrenzweig, 1967, p. 94).

However, as the above quotations reveal, Natkin's work evoked in Fuller not only a powerful sense of "goodness", but also fear, unease, even a sense of "tragedy". So how does Fuller explain this complex blend of feeling in Winnicottian terms? We should recall Winnicott's view that, in order for the infant to acquire a sense of an external reality, the mother first has to "disillusion" her child. In practical terms, this may mean that she (for example) no longer satisfies his hunger immediately on demand, so he experiences a temporary *gap* between his needs and their satisfaction. This is all quite normal and necessary, but if the length of this gap is unduly prolonged, then the infant may feel persecuted by what Winnicott termed an disruption of "going on being"—a threat of chaos and displacement. Winnicott adds that this can be exacerbated by congenital defects such as acute astigmatism—a condition from which Natkin apparently suffered. Fuller contends that the disturbing feelings aroused by the (seemingly benign) paintings are akin to these primitive anxieties, the disruption of existence itself felt when the separation from the mother once posed an overwhelming threat to the infant's fragile ego. But how exactly do the paintings evoke this response? Fuller believes it is to do with how they question the viewer's sense of autonomy, setting the viewer "loose and drifting in a boundless, unstructured illusion of space" because they challenge one's sense of being separate from the painting itself (1988 [1980], p. 208). Interestingly, Milner talks about something very similar, for, as we have seen above, she saw painting as intimately concerned with the negotiation of boundaries between the self and the world of other bodies occupying different bits of space.

Fuller believes that an interesting correspondence can be traced between Natkin's "struggle to give his paintings form and aesthetic integrity, and his personal struggle to structure his psychic space" (1988 [1980], pp. 209–210). Once again he draws on Winnicott's theory of the mother–child relation in order to understand the way in which Natkin's emotional need for containment and integration is implicated in the material transformation of the canvas. The activity of painting could be seen as partly a search to find a "container" in which to integrate the split-off aspects of his psyche. (In Ehrenzweig's terms, the painting functioned for Natkin as a "containing womb".) In the 1950s, Natkin's work was "characterised by a search for a limiting membrane, a skin that can contain the fragmented elements out of which the painting was made" (*ibid.*, p. 210). After he moved to New York in the early 1960s, he started painting the *Apollo* series, where the paintings are all marked by a strong vertical organization representing—in Winnicottian terms—the "split-off male" parts of Natkin's psyche. In the 1970s, however, these were superseded by the distinctly more feminine *Intimate Lighting* and *Colour Bath* series, with their alluring seductiveness. Yet another characteristic in many of the paintings is Natkin's frequent use of a *grid* structure, which could be seen as the equivalent of the integrated and organized ego, binding parts of the self in what would otherwise be (*vide* Bion) the self-annihilating limitlessness of infinite internal space. And in his best works of the 1970s we see Natkin "constructing artificially, through visual forms, that potential space which [he] was largely ... denied". The space of these new images (inspired by his encounter with post-Impressionism in the 1950s) promised the possibility of "becoming something other than that which he was—a fractured and dissociated individual, in his own self-estimation, monstrous" (*ibid.*).

Natkin remarked that everything he painted from the time of his early portraits onwards represented for him a *face*. When he moved to Redding, Connecticut, in the mid-1970s, the first place he felt he could truly call home (he was born into an immigrant family), he began a series of *Face* paintings that Fuller considers are his best. This theme of "the face" in Natkin's work is highly significant, and Fuller relates it to yet another central idea of Winnicott: the highly important *mirroring* process that takes place between mother and child. Winnicott suggests that "when the baby in his mother's arms gazes into her face, he sees himself or herself". In other words, "the mother is looking at the baby and what she looks like is related to what she sees there" (1971, p. 131).[2] Thus the mother acts like a mirror through which the baby comes to integrate himself. But if she fails (through depression, or too many defences), the baby cannot see himself. Instead,

> perception takes the place of apperception, perception takes the place of that which might have been the beginning of a significant exchange with the world, a two-way process in which self-enrichment alternates with the discovery of meaning in the world of seen things. [Winnicott, 1971, p. 132]

Fuller notes that, in his early portraits, Natkin depicts "the masked, maternal grimace", usually accompanied by "acute pictorial disorganisation". Indeed, a photograph of Natkin's mother shows her "locked artificiality of expression"—inimical to "good-enough" mirroring—and one that Natkin seems to have been recreating in his paintings. Then later, when he turned to more expressive portraits, the artist found that he had to *release* the fixed facial features altogether. According to Fuller, these *Face* paintings (of 1975) "touch intimately, directly, and convincingly upon, and also . . . transform these earliest pre-verbal experiences" (1988 [1980], p. 212).

Thus, for Natkin, the paint surface facilitated a reciprocal exchange, taking on the role of the responsive mother's face. The paint sur-*face* was able to respond to his movements and gestures, so that he could begin to constitute his own reality, while at the same time retaining its autonomy. It constituted "a face which can transform itself infinitely in response to our gaze, which certainly has a skin which separates it from us but which, in the next moment, can engulf and enfold us into itself" (*ibid.*, p. 231). Through this reciprocal exchange with the medium, Natkin was able to explore his own identity, or face, and gradually discover his artistic style. In addition, Fuller claims that the spectator, too, experiences the same kind of self-enhancing mirroring through the experience of looking at the painting. Thus we, as viewers, experience through our own bodily experience a similar constellation of affects to that of the artist as expressed through his physical encounter with the paint medium. This account of Natkin's bodily relationship to his materials, and the mirroring role his canvases provided for him, finds an echo in Milner's patient, Susan, and her use of paper and pencil to explore not only the sense of her own body boundary, but also her growing sense of *self*. These materials became "a substitute for the responsive, ideal mother . . . on a primitive, non-verbal level", writes Milner: enabling a "bridge" that "provided some sort of substitute for the mirror that her mother had never been able to be to her . . . they gave her back to herself" (Milner, 1988 [1969], pp. 240–241).

Continuing with his exploration of the affective dynamics of pictorial space, Fuller turns to consider the work of Rothko. This time he draws on Wilfred Bion's post-Kleinian account of the vicissitudes of mental space to explore the relation between the spatial dynamics of Rothko's haunting works of the late 1960s and his increasing psychic turbulence. He argues that Rothko's mental and artistic development followed a very different trajectory to that of Natkin. Where the latter travelled back into, and found a way of recreating, the "potential space" of "going on being", Rothko encountered the "absolute primary narcissism" of non-being.[3] In *Attention and Interpretation* (1970) Bion's hypothesis of a persecutory, pathological inner space was, we recall from Chapter Four, an expanse that is felt to be so infinite, so vast, that it threatens to completely engulf the individual. No visual images can be found to represent and therefore contain this unfathomable expanse, and the person concerned is in a state akin to that of "surgical shock": his capillaries dilate to the extent that the patient literally bleeds to death in his own tissues (*ibid.*, p. 12). Drawing on these insights, Fuller constructs a narrative that links Rothko's troubled personal history to a corresponding change in the spatial dynamics of his paintings: the struggle to negotiate a space which "appears empty at first" and then becomes "limitless, infinite, flat and without depth". As Rothko's psychotic breakdown encroaches, the pictures "lose their capacity to move us . . . they speak of only the grey, monochromatic silence of an impending grave" (1988 [1980], p. 22).

Rothko's paintings indeed evoke awe, reverence, tranquillity, rapture, sadness—with a hint of something sinister there, too. It is not unusual to see people sit and gaze for a long while at these paintings, with their compelling and mesmerizing undulating clouds of colour beckoning like gateways to another world. According to Fuller, we are witnessing in these paintings nothing less than Rothko's "struggle against a state beyond even depression and despair". The boundaries of his canvasses contain "deep black spaces of beckoning nothingness which seems to invite you, the viewer, to annihilate yourself in them"; they are "sinister clouds of emptiness" that are the artist's attempt to "construct a viable ground to his being over the imminent terror of empty, black space, through a realisation of sensuous, affirmative planes of colour" (*ibid.*, p. 222). In *Two Openings In Black over Wine*, Fuller sees "the night encroaching":

> ... you cannot be certain whether the blackness or the "wine" constitutes the ground or the figure. Although the title suggests that you are looking at two gateways or windows into a vanishing vista which is rapidly being dissolved into the void, you could also read the "openings" as flimsy sentinels, or vestiges of the affirmatively real, holding you back from being swallowed up within that nothingness. But either way, there is no escape. [*ibid.*]

This is worth comparing with the case of the painter Ruth Kjär (referred to by Melanie Klein). Unlike Rothko, Ruth was able, through the act of painting, to fill her own inner emptiness, depression, and despair (symbolized by the blank space on her wall) by symbolically recreating (making reparation to) the mirror–mother she needed in order to establish a sense of self and wholeness. However, as the above analysis implies, Rothko's trajectory takes almost the *reverse* direction. In his confrontation with the void, via his painting, the infinity of inner space finally overwhelms and engulfs him. We are told by Fuller that the artist was found dead in a pool of blood on his studio floor, having cut his wrists. This is a chilling image of Bion's analogy between the fear of being annihilated and lost in such infinite spaces, and the patient bleeding to death in his own tissues.

Painting and corporeality: Wollheim's account of pictorial meaning

Painting as an Art (1987), by the philosopher and aesthetician Richard Wollheim, is an eloquent and profound contribution to a material (body-founded) account of art, enriched by some forty years' involvement with British psychoanalytic thinking. Where

Fuller focuses on theories of intrapsychic space (especially Winnicott's "potential space"), Wollheim emphasizes the efficacy of Kleinian theory, and, in particular, the role of *unconscious phantasy* in the grounding of pictorial metaphor. He draws much on the writings of Adrian Stokes in looking more closely at the specific ways in which certain paintings acquire corporeality: that is, the *formal* means by which the artist transfers his unconscious phantasies to the *surface* of the actual painting itself. For, as we have already noted, Kleinians conceive unconscious phantasy as the link between bodily experience and its mental (symbolic) representation; this concept has thus proved to be a highly productive conceptual tool in the study of the visual arts. It enabled (for example) Adrian Stokes to link the formal, aesthetic elements of artistic production (carving and modelling) with specific psychic mechanisms (the depressive and paranoid–schizoid positions), and it also allowed clinicians such as Hanna Segal to develop an account of aesthetic value that correlates with a specific kind of unconscious phantasy—that of *reparation*.

It was largely through his acquaintance with Adrian Stokes, who became a close friend and mentor, that Wollheim's involvement with British psychoanalysis flourished into a deep and personal commitment: an interest which remained an important influence on his theoretical writings and also on his appreciation of the arts. (My account of Wollheim's friendship with Stokes is drawn from "Memories of Adrian Stokes" [Wollheim, 1973]; his article "Adrian Stokes: critic, painter, poet" [1980]; *Adrian Stokes: A Retrospective* [Arts Council of Great Britain, 1982]; the Preface to Wollheim [1973], and also Wollheim [1987].) It was at about the time he had been asked to review *Greek Culture and the Ego* (1958) that Wollheim first met Stokes, and was also introduced to Klein. It was not until 1962 that he got to know Stokes really well, and this was also around the time that Wollheim began his own analysis with the Kleinian, Leslie Sohn. It is interesting to note some of Wollheim's observations regarding Stokes's relationship with painting, for it is apparent that he shares much of the Stokesian sensibility. For instance, he recalls that "Adrian saw a great deal of art", and

> did not take the dispute between abstraction and figuration seriously ... all he required was that the work should have ... "visual

relevance", by which he meant the power to *support some image of the human body* and therefore of the human psyche. [Wollheim, 1980, p. 36]

This is particularly relevant, for this view is certainly echoed in "Painting, metaphor and the body"—the last chapter of Wollheim's *Painting as an Art* (1987), which will be our main concern here. Like Stokes, Wollheim hesitates to make too much of the so-called distinction between the "abstract" and the "figurative", arguing that (in de Kooning's work, for example) this distinction is not a fundamental one, and actually "obscures more than it reveals". What Wollheim considers important is the extent to which figuration mattered to the artist (1987, p. 352). One of the reasons why Wollheim mistrusts this distinction is owing to the view of pictorial meaning he develops. He firmly believes that the most fundamental thing that a picture metaphorizes is the body—and the body can be *metaphorized* (he argues) without actually being represented figuratively at all. Indeed, Wollheim's affinity with Stokes is most profoundly expressed through his valuation of the *corporeal* in art (for example, see Wollheim [1987], pp. 62, 101, 348, 350–352).

Wollheim was also involved in psychoanalysis through the Imago Group (which Stokes founded). At these meetings, Wollheim would have encountered psychoanalysts such as Wilfred Bion, Hannah Segal, Marion Milner, Roger Money-Kyrle, Eric Rhode, and Donald Meltzer, as well as non-practitioners such as the philosophers Stuart Hampshire and John Wisdom; he was thus in close touch with British psychoanalytic ideas and the ongoing debates at a time when the dialogue between the analytic community and the wider community of thinkers was flourishing. In his review of Stokes's *Greek Culture and the Ego* (1958), a work which emphasizes the deep connections between the body and art, Wollheim suggests that what makes Kleinian theory a particularly valuable contribution to aesthetics and criticism is that it "seeks to interpret works of human creativity in a new and original way", improving greatly on more orthodox Freudian approaches to art. (A more detailed critique of Freudian aesthetics can be found in "Freud and the understanding of art", in Wollheim, 1974.) However, although Wollheim finds orthodox Freudian aesthetics and criticism unsatisfactory, his debt to certain aspects of Freudian thinking is very apparent, particularly in the chapter on "Ingres, the Wolf-Man, Picasso". Wollheim's achievement here is praised by the cultural historian Stephen Bann, who suggests that he has "added one more example to the genre which began with Freud's essay on Leonardo, and has only rarely produced work which so faithfully reproduces the insight and taste of the founder of the psychoanalytical movement" (Bann, 1989, p. 10). Yet Wollheim does not intend to subject paintings to the kind of "pathographical" interpretation that gave Freudian aesthetics a bad name. He explores, for example, the psychological implications of Ingres's persistent distortions and contortions of *pictorial space*.

As Bann also points out, this theme brings his work in line with that of Norman Bryson's study of Ingres in his *Tradition and Desire, from David to Delacroix* (1984). Yet, where Bryson is more concerned with Ingres's revolt against the traditional canons of the Renaissance, Wollheim looks specifically at how the painter's oedipal anxieties are implicated and negotiated through the idiosyncrasies of the material aspect of his relationship to painting. By focusing on the artist's relationship to his medium and the kinds of phantasies he projects into his work and his materials, Wollheim's deployment of traditional Freudian themes (the family romance, oedipal anxieties, rivalry, for example) acquires a distinctly *Kleinian* perspective. Indeed, when Wollheim suggests that for Ingres the act of painting was an attempt at the "restitution of the father" who "must melt" (with the suggestion of not only a yielding but also of his destruction) he adds a new dimension to the Kleinian emphasis on art as reparation to the destroyed mother.

There are a number of interlinked Kleinian themes that Wollheim draws upon throughout *Painting as an Art*: the "manic defence", "projective identification", "unconscious phantasy", together with Klein's theory of envy and gratitude, idealization and creativity. (For his understanding of the relationship between idealization, envy, and creativity, Wollheim has drawn upon Klein, "Some theoretical conclusions regarding the emotional life of the infant" [1988b]; Segal [1974, 1984]; and Stokes (1961, 1963). In "Painting, textuality and borrowing" [Chapter IV of his *Painting as an Art*], he draws upon Harold Bloom's 1975 classic study *The Anxiety of Influence* to examine the theme of "borrowing" and artistic rivalry and the anxieties attendant on such activities.) Many of these themes are integral to Wollheim's general philosophical account of, for example, "twofoldedness", "expressive perception", and his fascinating account of the "embodied spectator"—also referred to as the "spectator in the picture". His preoccupation with the link between corporeality, mental states, and symbolic activity is long-standing. In an earlier essay, "The mind and the mind's image of itself" (1968), he wove the insights of Klein, Segal, and Bion into a subtle philosophical argument stressing that our notions and reports of mental states *themselves presuppose* a conception of the mind that is itself "tinged with spatiality". He adds further that

> all such conceptions derive ultimately from an assumption of the mind to the body, of *mental* activity to *bodily* functioning, of mental contents to *parts of the body*. So the mysterious union of mind and body occurs also at a stage further back than the traditional philosophers apprehended. It is not merely that we are at home in our body: we are at home in our mind somewhat as in a body. This, we may say, is the mind's image of itself. But if it is, if this is the image that the mind sees when it sees itself, this is, in part at least, because it is this image that the mind *draws* when it *draws* itself. [Wollheim, 1974, p. 53]

This illustrates the extent to which Kleinian theory informs his philosophical position, and also prepares us for the important theme of "painting as the body", which he develops in the closing chapter of *Painting as an Art* (1987). We note how Wollheim uses the verb "to draw" to mean something that includes not only the activity of "describing", but also the metaphorical relationship between painting and the body. Wollheim's paper reinforced Stokes's own belief in the "strong corporeality-cum-spatiality . . . associated with art as a reflection of mental states and their communication" (Stokes, 1973, p. 127). Thus, he did not simply absorb Stokes's ideas and thereby deploy Kleinian theory; rather, he modified them in terms of his own philosophical views, which in turn enabled Stokes himself to think more deeply about the theme of art and the body.

In Wollheim's aesthetics, pictorial metaphor is held to be one of the most fundamental ways in which a painting acquires content and (primary) meaning. He distinguishes between the "primary" meaning of a picture (which refers to its representational, textual, and historical meaning) and its "secondary" meaning, which refers to what the act of making it meant to the artist (1987, pp. 249, 304). When the *full* resources of pictorial metaphor are deployed, "the painting becomes a metaphor for the body, or . . . some part of the body, or for something assimilated to the body" (p. 305). It should be stressed that he is not concerned with paintings that have metaphors as their *textual* content (for example, Blake's *The River of Life* or Chardin's *House of Cards*); he is concerned with paintings that in some way stand for or metaphorize the body, and not only through their representational content. Wollheim does not believe that pictorial metaphor can be reduced to linguistic metaphor, although there are a number of similarities. The similarities are: first, neither kind of metaphor requires that the elements involved lose their normal sense; second, there need be no special or pre-existent link between these elements (for instance, in "Juliet is the sun" there does not have to be a symbolic link between Juliet and the sun; nor does there have to be an iconographical link between what a picture expresses and what it metaphorizes). Third, both kinds of metaphor aim to show the subject in a new light.

The important *difference* between the two kinds of metaphor is that where linguistic metaphor links with something other than itself, pictorial metaphor makes a link to *the painting itself*. It is not a link to what the picture portrays, although it does have to portray *something* in order to be a metaphor. Wollheim concludes that pictorial meaning is grounded in "some mental condition" of the artist that is somehow able to induce in the spectator an "appropriately related" mental condition, dependent not on knowing about the picture's rules and conventions (as with language) but on having a shared sensibility (*ibid.*, p. 357) founded on a common human nature and the relative constancy of the human body. When the painting metaphorizes the body (which, for Wollheim, is the "most fundamental case of pictorial metaphor"), we assign to the picture the global property of *corporeality*, and "when the way of metaphor works, what is paired with the object metaphorised is the picture as a *whole*". The metaphorical content of the painting is "given by what the emotions, sentiments, phantasies, which the response mobilises, are normally directed on to" (*ibid.*, p. 306), and the psychic mechanism that is responsible for the transmission of meaning is that of unconscious phantasy, as in the Kleinian concept.

For, as Susan Isaacs emphasized, "phantasies are primarily about bodily aims, pains and pleasures, directed to objects of some kind" (1948, p. 90). We can appreciate how, through the concept of unconscious phantasy, Wollheim is able to forge a link between "metaphorizing" and the kind of affective experience that is set in motion by perception. In addition, it is through this corporeal response to the painting (grounded in the rich reservoir of unconscious phantasy life) that our attitudes to the body are themselves modified, deepened, and intensified. This concurs very closely with Stokes's view, expressed in his essay on "Art and embodiment", that

> we learn to see the spirit, the animation, in terms of art's inoffensive material. That material *stands for the body whether or not it has been used to represent the body*. Art, truly seen ... does not so much educate us about animation, about the mind or spirit, about the intentions of others good or bad in which we find a source of persecutory feeling or of trust, as about the resulting body-person, about the embodiment that is much more than an embodiment because *bodily attributes have always been identified with those intentions*. [Stokes, 1978, *III*, p. 328, my italics]

Stokes, we recall, following Vasari, believed that a painting of the "carving" mode should be apprehended in "una sola occhiata" (1978, *II*, p. 45). Wollheim's similar emphasis on a global or total, as opposed to a piecemeal, response also appears to have affinities with Ehrenzweig's account of unconscious "depth" perception.[4] But, because Ehrenzweig presents a depth response as being *prior* to other kinds of perception, specifically to that of representational seeing, Wollheim argues that it is "irrelevant to our understanding of pictorial metaphor". The nature of the experience that underlies metaphor cannot be like this, for it is one that comes *after*, and can therefore benefit from, other modes of perception; metaphor capitalizes on this other (unconscious) mode of perception, using it as part of the "cognitive stock" that infuses greater meaning into representational seeing (1987, p. 306). In fact, one could take issue with this and argue that Ehrenzweig's "depth" perception is not necessarily prior to representational seeing, as Wollheim claims it is. In Ehrenzweig's account of creative perception, "unconscious scanning" works in conjunction with "surface" (conscious, representational) seeing. As we have noted, Ehrenzweig's view is supported by revised accounts of the relationship between the primary and secondary processes that have been developed by a number of British School analysts (Rycroft, 1962; Milner, 1956 [1987]) who see them as more homogenous, working together, rather than one supervening on the other.

I will now turn to some of Wollheim's examples of how pictorial metaphor operates in practice. In "Painting, metaphor and the body", Wollheim studies the work of painters from different traditions to consider the ways in which they come to achieve a sense of corporeality. He shows how a variety of conceptions (phantasies) about the body are metaphorized by the artist through the way he uses the medium, whether or not the body is made the central object of representation. He is especially indebted to Stokes in his consideration of how a painting can suggest the body without actually *representing* it—that is, when it is not depicted as the central feature of representation. He believes that specific kinds of pictures *can* do this, particularly those that incorporate architecture or depict building scapes. The Stokesian vision was grounded in architecture as a representation of the mother's body; consequently, Stokes was highly sensitive to the connections between architecture, painting, and the body, and, in one of his later writings, he observes that

> Viewed as an image of mind and body the painting shows the flesh, with the forces that animate and those to which it is subject, as divided, as mingled in new combinations. . . . Building has figured in nearly all our landscape painting up to the middle of the last century when architecture for the first time ceased to epitomise the co-ordination of the body and thereby the integration of the ego, of the person or the mind. Yet the old theme was notably exploited by Corot at times, he and those who accompanied and followed him have continued to provide through the *texture of their paint*, or through *other insistence on the picture plane*, many of those *surface values* that an *environment of architecture* once had lavished. [Stokes, 1978, III, p. 341, my italics]

He says it is "through the texture of the paint"—the artist's engagement with the medium—that corporeality is infused into the painting. Wollheim, in his studies of two-dimensional works, pursued Stokes's insights about these "surface values" that inhere in both painting and buildings. He describes how, in becoming a surface, the paint takes on the metaphorical value of being a skin, "not in its localised character, but in its overall effect" (Wollheim, 1987, p. 341). He also looks more closely at what this "other insistence on the picture plane" (alluded to by Stokes) might involve as far as the theme of painting as the body is concerned.

I will first consider Wollheim's examination of two lesser-known artists whose work features architecture to a prominent degree: Bernardo Bellotto (a follower of Canaletto), and the Welsh eighteenth-century artist, Thomas Jones. In Bellotto's *View of Schloss Königstein*, Wollheim suggests that the buildings seem to "swell under our eyes . . . they promise to take over the total picture" (1987, p. 340). This is accomplished in three ways: the first of these is the affective and spatial differences evoked by the sense of *mass* and *massiveness* in architecture—something first described by Stokes in *The Quattro Cento* (1932). Bellotto's buildings, suggests Wollheim,

> strike us as solid. They are not gimcrack. But they do not just lie on the grass in the way we would expect their constituents, or the building materials out of which they are constructed, to do so if they were taken apart: that would be massiveness. They reach upwards: reach, not soar. They seem capable of upward gentle movement. [1987, p. 340]

Next, Wollheim makes another Stokesian point when he refers to Bellotto's "carving" of the wall surface depicted by the painting, which he suggests performs the same role as "the block of marble does for the carved sculpture when the sculpture gives the impression of having been retrieved from the stone by the chisel" (*ibid.*). Thus, Bellotto achieves corporeal effects by way of the *correspondence* that he establishes between the paint surface and the wall surface, between the texture of what he represents with, and the texture of what it is he represents (1978, III, pp. 217, 313, 318). This is a function of a "carving" or reparative (Kleinian) phantasy such as that Stokes would say "draws upon the origin of all sense of wholeness" (*ibid.*, I, p. 230; II, pp. 241, 244). What is so special about them, according to Wollheim, is that these apertures appear *integral* to the wall surface, which gives the impression that the wall has not been perpetrated or damaged. And finally, Wollheim suggests that there is something special about the way that *apertures* are represented in Bellotto's pictures: his windows and doors are not treated as mere modifications upon the wall surface: black patches upon lighter ground. Nor are they represented as places where the wall surface has been cut into, a part of it excised and thrown away, and something else behind it revealed to exist. [1987, p. 340]

Rather, they appear *integral* to the wall surface, which gives the impression that the wall has not been perpetrated or damaged. Yet they seem to allow us imaginative "access to, and exit from, and above all, knowledge of, what lies beyond the wall".

Wollheim's descriptive language here is clearly deeply influenced by Stokes's Kleinian account of the reparative phantasy inherent in "fine architecture", such as that in *Smooth and Rough*, where he writes of how we come to realize that "we partake of an inexhaustible feeding mother" despite our phantasies of attacking and destroying through working the stone materials (Stokes, 1978, II, p. 240). The same reparative aspect features in the building scapes of a comparatively unknown eighteenth-century artist, Thomas Jones, whose "simple, unaffected pictures", according to Wollheim, radiate primitive feeling with "an immediacy that is absent from the statelier, more grown up pictures of Bellotto". Jones gets "timeless discoloured buildings of great dignity and humble materials to revive the infant's perception of the body . . . stretched out, close-up, palpable, taken in through the eyes of desire and destruction" (1987, p. 345). This is achieved primarily through his use of perspective. The buildings are greatly elevated by a wide-angled vision, encouraged by the horizontal format together with a slippage from linear to orthogonal perspective in which the orthogonals are drawn as parallel lines, giving the optical effect of a series of close-up views on to the object, up and down its length. Thus, the buildings appear "near and prone", reviving the infant's earliest vision of the mother's body. Another device relates to the paint surface itself, which "allows the shadow to convert itself into texture: it smooths the stone, or it roughens the plaster, on which it is cast" (*ibid.*, p. 346). Wollheim finds in Jones' work both Stokes's "smooth and rough" dichotomy (the basis of all architectural value) and the Kleinian phantasy of evoking the mother's body and its capacity to survive the infant's greedy and envious attacks. As Wollheim succinctly puts it, in the context of the "visual ambiguity" of these paintings of southern Mediterranean townscapes, "These buildings, having come down, or once destroyed, are now restored: they go up again" (*ibid.*, p. 347).

In the work of Titian, Wollheim seeks beyond the depiction of architecture itself for architectural and carving values in the body of a painting. Titian evokes (for him) very powerful feelings about the body—its vitality, yet also its vulnerability and mortality. Titian's central device at achieving corporeality exploits what Wollheim calls "twofoldedness", a property that allows us to "see [things] in" the painted surface.[5] This concept avoids the gross dichotomy between "illusion" and "realism" characteristic of certain accounts of representation, such as that of Gombrich in *Art and Illusion*. It also allows Wollheim to make the crucial point that representation is by no means to be equated with figuration (1987, p. 360, note 6). There are, he argues, two distinct yet inseparable aspects to this experience. There is the recognition of something absent (the body) and also an awareness of the marked surface. We sense in Titian's paintings "a body poised for action", and we are also aware of "the coloured expanse in which we see the body as something spreading or pushing outwards" (p. 310). Although he first conceived of twofoldedness as two distinct experiences occurring simultaneously, he came to see them as "two aspects of a single experience". This could perhaps be seen in terms of Stokes's view that the aesthetic encounter combines "the sense of fusion with the sense of object-otherness" (1973, p. 110).

Corporeality is also achieved by connecting the represented body with action, and this "action" must be understood in its broadest sense. Not only does it concern muscular energy and movement, it also concerns "the relaxation of the body, the sudden sagging of limbs, in which the body also reveals its vitality", evident in both *Concert Champêtre* and the *Three Ages of Man*. In these paintings it is apparent that the *gaze* is yet another active element: seeking knowledge, expressing adoration, arousing desire. (However, it is not the "secret weapon" deployed by Ingres and Picasso [as Wollheim argues in Chapter V] but more the "outpouring of the mind . . . a second, naïve, voice" [1987, p. 312].) Another way that Titian establishes the sense of the body in these two paintings is by setting up a number of pictorial equivalences: for example, between body and nature, flesh and stone, young skin and sky.

This is enhanced by the use of near-complementaries, which has a "special binding effect". Here, Wollheim is indebted to the insights of Stokes's *Colour and Form* (1937 [1978]), where he emphasizes that "a picture should be like an open concertina capable of being packed in harmoniously". It is interesting to note that he, too, uses the *Concert Champêtre* as an example of this "colour-binding" effect, suggesting that "by far the most striking colour ... is a segment of crimson hat belonging to the central seated musician [. . .] the colour and form of the rest of the picture could be folded up in that hat" (Stokes, 1978 (1937)).

Stokes also insisted that this use of near-complementary colour is an expression of the *carving* mode in painting, for the artist creates (quite literally) a "family tree" of resemblance using colour combinations that are related more as "brothers" than as "rivals" (1978, II, pp. 47, 40). In addition to this, the painting acquires corporeality through the production of "what demands to be thought of as a paint skin" (Wollheim, 1987, p. 312). In the *Three Ages of Man*, for example, there are many deliberate alterations of texture that produce the effect of swelling and mass; the brushstrokes suggest the abundance of foliage in the meadow. Another device operates through Titian's ordering of the picture plane, and in particular, his "benign neglect of perspective". This, like the effect of colour-binding, encourages a global response to the picture—it is taken in at a glance.

The artist's special use of his medium, therefore, can encourage us to think of the painting in terms of a container. Wollheim draws attention to an element that features in other paintings of the same period—one that is a characteristic of the great High Renaissance structures of Leonardo and Raphael—but in Titian, he says, is "self-consciously torn out of its context". Wollheim points out the "diminutive profiles cut totally in conformity with linear perspective by figures in the middle distance or the background". In a High Renaissance painting these figures "would add to the monumental effect", but apparently this is not the case here. Titian gives us no orthogonals, with no vanishing point and no indicated point of origin. This lack of projection makes the delicate profiles appear as "tiny decorative fragments which have been scattered across the picture" (*ibid.*, p. 314). How does this create the sense of corporeality? Wollheim suggests it does so not immediately, but *mediately*.

The picture endowed with corporeality can also get itself thought of as something that the body also is—a container. He is, of course, drawing on a fundamental Kleinian theme here, for the mother's body is the primary container into which the infant projects his phantasies. In the case of Titian these tiny profiles, like delicate "odds and ends", are assimilated into the picture, which acts like a container, gathering the fragments together as if they were trinkets in a jewellery box.

For yet another way in which the painting can get itself thought of as a body, Wollheim draws on the beautiful passage by Walter Pater that dwells on the significance of *listening* in the paintings of Giorgione and his school. This highlights a painting's potential capacity to evoke imagined *sound*, and such a picture is the *Concert Champêtre*. Pater thought that "all art constantly aspires to the condition of music", especially early Cinquecento Venetian painting, where

> music or musical intervals in our existence, life itself, is conceived as a sort of listening—listening to music, to the reading of Bandello's novels, to the sound of water, to time as it flies. . . . The presence of water—the well, or marble-rimmed pool, the drawing or pouring of water, as the woman pours it from a pitcher with her jewelled hand in the *Fête Champêter* [sic] listening, perhaps to the cool sound as it falls, blent with the music of the pipes—is characteristic, and almost as suggestive, as that of music itself. [Pater, 1986 (1873), pp. 86; 96–97]

However, Wollheim adds a distinctly Kleinian perspective to Pater's analysis by suggesting that the sound "in" the picture encourages us to engage with the painting as if it were a container (and therefore a body). But we might ask, in what sense does a painting "contain" sound? Wollheim admits that he cannot appeal to any systematic theory of representation or expression to adequately explain this property, but he does suggests that the picture gives rise to the thought that sound is "in" the painting in the same way that we might imagine "the notes lie around inside the music box when the tune has stopped . . . or that the hum lies around inside the fridge" (1978, p. 315).

Wollheim then takes a large leap (art historically speaking) into the genre of American abstract expressionism, and explores the work of Willem de Kooning. For, just as Stokes's "spatial" history of art enabled him to connect artists from a wide variety of traditions and genres, so Wollheim's "corporeal" account of art allows him to make the surprising (if somewhat controversial) link between the style of de Kooning's work and that of early Cinquecento Venice. What is common to both (he argues) is a tendency to create a sense in which the picture space as a container filled with a variety of objects, and not just those of sight. But where Titian and other Venetians filled their picture space with sounds, Wollheim suggests that de Kooning collects sensations of *movement*, but "all experienced in a heavily regressive mode": the paintings are containers crammed with "infantile experiences of sucking, touching, biting, excreting, retaining, smearing, sniffing, swallowing, gurgling, stroking, wetting". According to Wollheim, we can identify *two* elements working in dynamic conjunction in the pictures: the sensations themselves (whose archaic character appears in the "lusciousness of the paint"), and the presence of an *experiencer* (whose fragile, rudimentary ego corresponds to the near-squareness of the "box-like support") (*ibid.*, p. 349). These paintings are "enormous shallow saucers in which a great deal of primitive glory is held in delicate suspense: it slops around, but is kept back by the rim". The regulatory, "containing" role of the rim is an important aspect, and recalls Milner's observations concerning the containing and directive role of the frame (see Chapter Six). A drama is established between the movement of the massive, furrowed paint marks as they swerve to avoid, or actually collide with, the edge. This creates a tension that sensitizes the viewer to the way in which the edge "holds" the turbulence of sensations conveyed by the paint surface itself. It is this that evokes the sense of control exercised by the infantile self, as it struggles to make sense of the chaotic experiences that threaten to engulf the delicate barriers of the mind. Although as adults we may look with disdain upon such experiences, it must be remembered that they have great significance for the infant, for it is largely through these activities that the child explores the world, gains knowledge, and experiences its pleasures. But not only pleasure, for (as Fuller's account of Natkin and Rothko also emphasized) these pictures also remind us of the fragility of the early ego; and that the threat of being engulfed and submerged by such a plethora of primitive sensation was very real.

It needs to be said that Wollheim's analysis of pictorial meaning and the general thesis put forward in *Painting as an Art* received a mixed reception at the time. One particularly hostile reaction came from the art historian, Nicholas Penny; and it is worth examining his objections, for they do provide an insightful illustration of the perennial clash between traditional art history and the "shock of the new". Wollheim says he rejects "traditional" art history because it is "deeply infected with positivism, and central to positivism are the overestimation of fact, the rejection of cause, and the failure to grasp the centrality of explanation" (1987, p. 9). In short, his approach suggests that we can do without art history—or at least, we should question its privileged status as the art discourse *par excellence*. He writes that

> Standardly we do not call the objective study of an art the history of that art. We call it criticism. We talk of literary criticism, of musical criticism, of dance criticism. What then is a special feature of the visual arts, something which must be over and above the general way in which all the arts are connected with a tradition, and which has allegedly, the consequence that, if we are to understand painting, or sculpture, or graphic art, we must teach an historical understanding of them? I do not know, and, given the small progress that art-history has made in explaining the visual arts, I am inclined to think that the belief that there is such a feature is itself something that needs historical explanation: it is an historical accident. [*ibid.*]

In the light of these remarks, it is not surprising that Wollheim has come under fire from traditional art historians such as Penny, although the latter does make some valid criticisms. He points out certain inaccuracies in Wollheim's picture of the artist at work: for example, his contention that "it has been the practice for the painter to position himself in front of the support, on that side of it which he marks, facing it, with his eye open and fixed upon it" (*ibid.*, p. 43) is not actually corroborated by visual evidence. In all but one of the illustrations the artist seems not to look at his own painting but at his *subject*; the exception is a photo of Pollock working, and he had no "subject" in this sense. So Penny qualifies Wollheim by saying that "in their paintings of painting, artists did not, then, always bother to make it clear that they looked at the marks they were making". It is also true that Wollheim's book is written in that "jerky, tightly self-observant prose favoured by philosophers" (Penny, 1988, p. 19), making it hard to follow at times, and that Wollheim's methodology for looking at paintings is idiosyncratic, seeking for a personal encounter with the object on a deep, almost meditative level:

> I evolved a way of looking at paintings which is massively time-consuming but also deeply rewarding, For I came to recognise that it often took the first hour or so in front of a painting for stray associations or motivated misperceptions to settle down, and it was then, and only then, with the same amount of time or more to spend looking at it, that the picture could be relied upon to disclose itself as it was. [Wollheim, 1987, p. 8]

It is clearly a response that does not require other kinds of "evidence" in order to grasp art's essential value, or "message", and, like Stokes, Wollheim values the quality of *otherness* in art, the capacity of the painting to reveal itself slowly, to speak for itself, as if it were a person, with a rich inner life. And Penny is certainly not impressed by Wollheim's deployment of Kleinian psychoanalytic ideas. Wollheim's description of those "infantile sensations of sucking, touching, biting, excreting, retaining, smearing, sniffing, swallowing, gurgling, stroking, wetting" renders him speechless, and he leaves with a rhetorical flourish of tailing-off into silence.

The dismissiveness of traditional art historians to such an approach should not unduly surprise, for most of us are perhaps reluctant to admit that infantile experiences could be implicated in the "respectable" world of art and culture, realms which apparently transcend this realm of primitive psychic functioning. Precisely how far these experiences are truly "regressive" will be considered in the conclusion. Suffice it to say, at this point, that Penny's remarks do hint at what Bann describes as "the constraining force of a kind of art-historical norm, which asserts itself whenever certain boundaries are transgressed" (Bann, 1989, p. 12). However, there are difficulties with Wollheim's approach. As Bann points out, it is not enough to ground a theory of art and pictorial meaning on the psychoanalytic supposition that we share a common human nature that our personal response can universalize. Psychoanalytic aestheticians need to bear in mind that the "subjective" stance needs balancing with "objective" analyses that take into account the wider historical and structural dimensions that an intrapsychic approach cannot accommodate.

I would like to conclude with an overview of the way in which Wollheim and Fuller, whose work is otherwise unrelated, each testify to the productivity of British psychoanalytic theory for aesthetics and criticism. Both critics share a radical dissatisfaction with the traditional canons of art history, as well as with other more recent approaches: structuralism, iconography, hermeneutics, and semiotics. Such approaches fail because they cannot address the specifically *aesthetic* aspects of art. Fuller speaks of "art-shaped holes" and Wollheim of the "pernicious disease of positivism".[6] Like Fuller's distaste for the Lacanian–Althusserian approach, Wollheim passes over the poststructuralist tradition, though adherents included many of his esteemed friends. One of the most problematic features of such accounts, he said, was their assimilation of *pictorial* meaning to *linguistic* meaning, and their "seeming indifference to the particularity of the works they engage with". The "blurring of perception" by "theory" was the result of a failure to respect the distinction between *description* and *explanation* (Wollheim, 1987, p. 10). Linguistic meaning cannot exhaust all the possibilities regarding the meaning of a picture; neither does it fully explain why works of art exert such a profound impact on us affectively as well as intellectually. As we have seen, corporeality lies at the heart of his account of pictorial meaning: it is a meaning that operates independently of narrative and linguistic structures, and is grounded in unconscious phantasy.

Wollheim combines his theory of pictorial meaning with a defence of intentionalism. Like Fuller, he believes that there is a crucial link between what the artist intends (that is, his "fulfilled" intention) and the affective experience (and phantasies) of the viewer. It is largely through the artist's *bodily* relationship to the canvas (and the viewer's visceral, kinaesthetic response) and the phantasies surrounding these, that the painting acquires corporeality. In such cases, the painting will have greater richness and depth of meaning, and thus can most deservedly be thought of as an art. Fuller, too, was interested in the relationship between aesthetic value and the artist's *physical* relationship to his medium. To illustrate this, he compares the work of Natkin and of Olitski, another colour field painter. Fuller argues that although both artists evoke the sense of "a skin, or an illusory suffusing depth", the *affective* experience of Olitski's spray paintings is of a very different kind. With the latter, there is a sense of "inauthenticity . . . something like milk-shakes, of faked and plastic flavours". Fuller claims that the difference largely resides in the artist's respective *bodily* relationship to their paintings, as the observation of Natkin's painting method seems to show, for he

> paints like a dancer . . . the rhythms of his body inform the way in which he gradually builds up the image. This is both controlled and seemingly instinctive: watching him, it is possible to observe both his informing *energy* and his technical mastery of the medium working together. There is a real sense in which every painting he makes is imprinted with his touch and movement: it cannot but stand in an intimate close relation to his body, and be expressive of the emotions and sensations which he experiences through his body [. . .] we feel, and are moved by, the artist's *touch* pervading every part of the canvas. [Fuller, 1988, p. 233]

Thus, both Fuller and Wollheim concur with the view that the "authenticity" of a painting, its aesthetic value, is partly determined by the extent to which the affects of the artist have undergone material transformation (or, in psychoanalytic terms, have been *cathected*) via the medium: "we feel, and are moved by, the artist's touch pervading every part of the surface". This is not so with Olitski's sprayed canvases, for "the spray gun is *mechanical*". It can *evoke* a sense of space but it cannot itself *constitute* it—the area of negotiation between inner and outer, subjective and objective, can be alluded to through such a technique, but it cannot be materially expressed by it.

However, there are some important distinctions to be made between the two writers regarding their respective allegiance to traditions within the British School. Fuller essentially moves away from Freud and Klein, and aligns himself with the post-Kleinian insights of Bion, Milner, and Winnicott, who are "much more interesting heirs of Freud than France or America have produced". In particular, he regarded their ideas concerning the creative role of illusion in human development and cultural life as being "among the most significant of any post Second World War insights into human nature" (Fuller, 1988, p. xiv). His *Art and Psychoanalysis* was, he admits, largely motivated by the vicissitudes of his own analysis. Indeed, judging by the shift in direction his thinking took thereafter, it would seem that, in part, the book was also a "working through" of his relationship to psychoanalysis, for he has progressively distanced himself from a psychoanalytic approach, returning to an aesthetic grounded in a theological framework. His *Theoria, Art and the Absence of Grace* (1988) and *Images of God* (1991) show the unmistakable influence of Ruskin on his thinking. This later work argues that we should search once again for the "objective" basis of beauty in the patterns of nature—ostensibly a return to a Ruskinian aesthetic. Indeed, that Fuller called his art journal *Modern Painters* suggests a close identification with the great Victorian thinker. The young Stokes certainly experienced much "anxiety of influence" regarding his precursors, and particularly Pater and Ruskin. With Stokes, however, one feels that, partly through his analysis and the progressive refining of a career, he is responsive to nuances of associations and feelings within himself—and his readers—and that these insights inform his evocative prose, often shaping the very subject matter he is concerned with at the time. Perhaps one could say that where Fuller writes *about* psychoanalysis, Stokes writes *psychoanalytically.*

Wollheim's allegiance, on the other hand, is firmly with the Kleinian wing of the British School, as the last section of his book makes clear, for his account of "Painting, metaphor, and the body" is profoundly indebted to the insights of Klein and the aesthetic criticism of Adrian Stokes. Writing both as a philosopher and a lover of painting, Wollheim's account is a tightly-woven, highly theoretical argument, which he effectively combines with the detailed scrutiny of a wide range of individual paintings—thus making *Painting as an Art* both challenging and absorbing to read. Fuller acknowledges that Wollheim's *Painting as an Art* is "a magisterial summary of a lifetime's thinking . . . truly a great book", adding that it made his own "fumbling sorties into this area look feeble and redundant" (1988, p. x). Perhaps Fuller is being overly humble and self-deprecating, but it is fair to say that, in terms of its style and sensibility, Wollheim's contribution is by far the most profound and certainly has more to offer both in terms of breadth and depth. Psychoanalytically speaking, one might say that the trajectory of Fuller's theoretical development manifests the paranoid–schizoid defences of *splitting* (from psychoanalysis) and idealization (of Ruskin). Wollheim, however, has succeeded in integrating a variety of his long-standing interests: philosophy, the love of painting, the insights of psychoanalysis, and a commitment to socialism. By the lights of Kleinian theory, he has come closer to a "depressive integration" of these varied (and no doubt sometimes competing) elements in his oeuvre. Perhaps this is why his work leaves the impression of integrity and hard-won insight—a reciprocity between art, psychoanalysis, and philosophy that has been nourished over many years.

Viewed together, the combined contributions of Fuller and Wollheim demonstrate that British School thinking has a great deal to offer the study of aesthetics and criticism. It is an approach that could be identified as a uniquely *British* psychoanalytic aesthetic—one that grounds our response to art in corporeality, forges a *material* link between the formal elements of art, the intrapsychic dynamics of the creative process, and also aesthetic response. Thus, it fleshes-out the "art-shaped holes" left by (for example) Marxist, structuralist, post-structuralist, and postmodern accounts of art. It offers a humanistic account of meaning and value, one that is grounded in the reciprocity between inner and outer worlds (Klein), the interchange between mother and baby (Bion, Meltzer, and Winnicott). It goes further than any other psychoanalytic theory of art to explain why the activity of painting itself is meaningful and valuable to us, partly by appealing to our shared humanity and a common cultural base. Most importantly, it is an approach informed by a commitment to the love of truth combined with "negative capability"—the capacity to tolerate mystery and doubt and the burden of "not knowing".

Notes

1. The term is first used by the philosopher Fichte, and has a variety of meanings. It can refer to facts and factuality, as in nineteenth-century positivism, but comes to mean that which resists explanation and interpretation in Dilthey and Neo-Kantianism. The Neo-Kantians contrasted facticity with ideality, as does Jürgen Habermas in *Between Facts and Norms* (*Faktizität und Geltung*). It is a term that takes on a

more specialized meaning in twentieth-century continental philosophy, especially in phenomenology and existentialism, including Edmund Husserl, Martin Heidegger, Jean-Paul Sartre, and Maurice Merleau-Ponty. (http://en.wikipedia.org/wiki/Facticity, accessed 4 July 2007).

2. Although Winnicott acknowledges the influence of Lacan's paper, "Le stade du miroir" (1949) on his thinking, particularly Lacan's reference to the use of the mirror in each individual's ego development, Winnicott stresses that "Lacan does not think of the mirror in terms of the mother's face in the way that I wish to do here" (1971, p. 130). It is interesting to compare their respective positions, for they are based on very different conceptions of the human imagination and, therefore, their notions of creativity. Their differences also represent an index of fundamental differences between the British and French traditions of psychoanalysis. Lacan considers the whole concept of the creative imagination as fundamentally bound up with humanist anthropology. The notion of imagination is deemed synonymous with the idea of a point of origin from which the self produces or reproduces its ideals. Hence Lacan's negative definition of the *imaginary* (as opposed to the "symbolic" and the "real") as an idealized ego formation that it is the business of psychoanalysis to dissolve. Lacan traces the genesis of the imaginary ego back to the "mirror phase". The human infant first experiences itself as a "fragmented" body. To overcome its feeling of dispersion it constructs an *imago* of unified selfhood—essentially a delusion. The imaginary "double" takes the form of a mirror reflection. For it is in response to the desire of the other—expressed, for example, in the mother's look—that the infant seeks to become a self-possessed identity. Lacan describes the imaginary accordingly in terms of a "specular ego", which imitates the look of the other and constructs its imago "like another". Thus, from the outset, the imago is not an autonomous creation of the child's own desire, as the self would subsequently like to believe, but a simulation of what the mother desires the child to become. This idealized ego is also regarded as the basis of narcissism. For a Winnicottian account of the main differences between their respective positions regarding the concept of the mirror, see Phillips (1988, pp. 128–130).

3. Within the object-relations tradition of the British School, some psychoanalysts, such as André Green (1975), posit that the first state is one of "primary absolute narcissism", which is to be distinguished from that derived by instinctual auto-eroticism as Freud conceived it.

This "absolute narcissism" is the "non-existence" from which the existence of consciousness starts, the void or blankness that is the ground of our psychological being. Bion (1970) as we have mentioned above, advised the psychoanalyst to purge himself from the "bondage of memory and desire" in order to approach this state of the unknowable, but yet which is the starting point for all knowledge, designated by the symbol "O". Particularly with the work of Milner, the later work of Bion, and more recently Meltzer (Meltzer & Harris Williams, 1988), there are interesting connections to be traced between psychoanalysis and mysticism. Ehrenzweig also makes some interesting remarks about mysticism, the potential space, and the enveloping tendency of modern art (1971, pp. 118–119). See also Milner (1987b, Chapter Eighteen) for an interesting insight into the possible direction research into this overlap between psychoanalytic and mystical experience might take.

4. Other examples of such "global" or "gestalt" accounts are Wörringer's *Abstraction and Empathy* (1908), and Bell's *Art* (1914). Bell claimed that there is a certain uniquely "aesthetic emotion", and that aesthetic qualites are the qualities in an object that evoke this emotion. In the visual arts, what arouses this emotion is certain "forms and relations of forms" (including line and colour), which Bell called "significant form". Aesthetic response to significant form is not to be identified, according to Bell, with other emotional responses. For example, a photograph of a loved one might evoke fond memories and feelings of love; a War Memorial might evoke feelings of grief or lament (my examples). While these are all perfectly appropriate responses, according to Bell, they are not *aesthetic* responses. Rather, the aesthetic response is a response to the forms and relations of forms themselves, *regardless of what other meanings, associations or uses they may have*. It is a strong emotion, often a kind of ecstasy, akin to the ecstasy felt in religious contemplation. The emotion, and the kinds of significant form that evoke it, are the same for cave art, Polynesian carvings, a Vermeer painting, or a Cezanne. Bell's theory has obvious philosophical connections to the aesthetics of Immanuel Kant, who also stressed the detachment of aesthetic appreciation from other sorts of interest we might have in an object. See www.rowan.edu/philosop/clowney/ Aesthetics/philos_artists_onart/bell.htm (accessed 3 July 2007).

5. In the light of comments from Martin Budd and Michael Podro, he later argued that they are "neither two separate experiences, which I sometimes hold in the mind at once, nor two separate alternating

experiences, between which I oscillate". They are "two aspects of a single experience, and these aspects are distinguishable but are also inseparable." (For the earlier account see his "Reflections on *Art and Illusion*" and "On drawing an object", in Wollheim [1974]; for the revised version, see Wollheim [1987, pp. 46–47, and especially p. 360, n. 6].). It is also interesting to compare Wollheim's concept of twofoldedness with Winnicott's account of paradoxical, or "potential space"— the interface between two (related) aspects of experience (reality–fantasy, subjective–objective, inner–outer) where neither is reduced to the other, and yet (we must trust the paradox) they cannot be separated, for the experience "partakes of both" (see p. 00, above).

6. Indeed, Bann argues that, objectively speaking, Wollheim is "a revolutionary". For, although he declares his allegiance to the tradition of *connoisseurship* and greatly values the practice of *criticism*, his way of proceeding is, at the same time, intimately related to those of the New Art Historians (Bryson and Kristeva, for example), and that his ideas gain "considerable enrichment" from an interchange with theirs (Bann, 1989, p. 3). Yet neither is he drawn to the kind of sociological explanation of the arts, championed by those such as Timothy Clark or Francis Haskell, for, although he is very much devoted to the spirit of socialism, he does not believe that an allegiance to social explanation is a necessary concomitant of this. What is fundamentally wrong with such accounts, he argues, is their tendency to reduce art to a set of social and historical functions and conditions.

Conclusion

This study has traced one particular trajectory of psychoanalytic theory: the progression from the Freudian paradigm, to the work of Klein and "post-Kleinians" such as Wilfred Bion, Marion Milner and Donald Winnicott. This account has also emphasized how their clinical and metapsychological contributions have had important consequences for the development of psychoanalytic aesthetics, particularly through the writings of those such as Adrian Stokes, Anton Ehrenzweig, Peter Fuller, and Richard Wollheim.

In the first chapter, the shortcomings of Freud's "neurotic model" of art were considered, together with his failure to develop his account of the joke mechanism in terms of aesthetic experience and the structural aspects of art—this, however, was explored further by Kris (1952) and Ehrenzweig (1967). This model was too reliant on biographical material; it construed the artwork as a container for the artist's desires, repressions, and aggressions, making the critic more like a detective. The formal, aesthetic qualities of this "container" were left unaddressed by this approach; it did not yield insight into the structure of the artwork itself—its purely formal qualities *qua* object. Indeed, Freud himself noted that psychoanalysis was unable to tackle the problem of aesthetic value, but he was optimistic that eventually it would provide a coherent account. Although Wollheim (1974) was no doubt right to point out that Freud was implicitly aware that the artwork was the outcome of a *process* (quite literally, art *work*) the implications of this were not fully developed into an explicit theoretical position. Freud's approach to art, we concluded, was limited by his own artistic preferences, his cultural milieu, and his personality. Much of the art that he selected for scrutiny perhaps tells us more about his own desire to elucidate clinical theory (for instance, his *Leonardo* essay, 1910c), and his personal struggles with fellow analysts (for example, the *Moses of Michelangelo* essay, 1914c).

In Chapter Two, we outlined the major theoretical contributions of Melanie Klein that have had import for the study of art: her account of the inner world; unconscious phantasy; the theory of "positions"; the theory of innate envy; and also the focus on the *structure* of symbols and the mechanisms underling their formation, rather than purely their *content*. In essence, she transformed the Freudian paradigm, giving it a decidedly Platonic orientation by discovering that the inner world has its own type of geographic concreteness, and that it was in the transactions of the inner world (manifest in dreams and unconscious phantasy) that the meaning of the outer world derived its origins (Meltzer, 1978). Although Klein never formulated a systematic aesthetic theory of her own, and, like Freud, looked at art mainly in terms of clarifying her clinical work, her contributions enabled new developments in psychoanalytic aesthetics. Chapter Three described how Hanna Segal and the art critic Adrian Stokes developed the fuller implications of Klein's insights into a distinctive and coherent Kleinian aesthetic— a tremendous improvement on the classical Freudian practice of "pathography".

Broadly speaking, traditional Kleinian accounts emphasize the role of depression and mourning in creativity, and derive aesthetics from the nature of the object. This means that a Kleinian approach addresses the *formal* qualities of specific artworks, and their relationship to the psychic mechanisms (unconscious phantasies) that are implicated in its production. According to Segal, "authentic" creativity demands the artist's actual engagement with a medium— and the aesthetic value of an art object is inextricably linked to the kinds of unconscious phantasies projected during the encounter with this medium. Kleinians emphasize that creativity and the aesthetic sense are linked via the developmental achievement of the depressive position. As Wollheim emphasizes, unlike orthodox theory, Kleinian criticism does not demand information about the artist's mind and experience "on the same extravagant and impossible scale as Freudian criticism" (1959a, p. 43). For the classical Freudian approach, which interprets works of art in terms of instinctual impulse (closely resembling dream interpretation), raises a serious methodological problem: one needs to know a great deal about the associations and circumstances of its creator, which may or may not be available—or even desirable—to know. There are "obvious economic advantages" in dispensing with this, as Wollheim points out (*ibid.*). And, in addition, it becomes possible to address the specifically *aesthetic* aspect of art, not merely its content. For, as Wollheim rightly points out, "if products of identical content are treated identically, how do we distinguish between, say, a Leonardo and a day dream or a child's game with the same motivation?" (Note that for Winnicott, there is no essential difference. Winnicott explicitly separates the idea of creativity and aesthetic experience from the formal qualities, the art product itself. He argues that "it would perhaps be better to say that these things could be creations". The creativity that "is a universal [and] belongs to being alive" is what concerns him, not "the finished creation [which] never heals the underlying lack of sense of self" [Winnicott, 1971, pp. 64, 79]. See Chapter Six.) Kleinian aesthetics redress the balance by defining an artwork in terms of its possession of certain formal characteristics—being the natural correlates or products of certain processes within the ego.

Chapter Three of this history explored the developments that have taken place in psychoanalytic aesthetics since Segal and Stokes first put forward a "traditional" Kleinian account of art. Segal and Stokes were followed by Bion's enlargement of the Kleinian paradigm through his placing of Freudian and Kleinian theories in the context of much wider, literary and philosophical dimensions. His (1970) account of "O", or "Ultimate Reality" (the "thoughts that exist without a thinker") resonates with Plato's theory of the Ideal Forms that await their sensuous realization. But where aesthetic experience is thrice removed from reality in the Platonic schema, it occupies central stage for Bion. (For a full account of the philosophical background to Bion's thought, see James Grotstein [1981, pp. 10–31].) Bion regarded both the aesthetic and the psychoanalytic encounter as occupying the same space: both are an engagement with "O", an experience which cannot be directly "known about", although we can *be* it. Thus, rather than viewing art and aesthetic experience as an outcome of repression and instinctual renunciation (Freud) or mourning and reparation (Klein), the Bionian schema views art in terms of a Kantian *thing-in-itself*, which is itself *responsible* for growth: Bion regards it as being as necessary to psychic health as food is to the body. Indeed, Meltzer's (1988) development of this view suggests that, rather than applying psychoanalytic insights to aesthetics, aesthetics is shown to shed light on early infantile experience and extends psychoanalytic theory. Rycroft concurs with this view when he says that "psychoanalysts have more to learn from historians, literary critics and philosophers than they have to teach them" (1957, p. 276).

The fundamentality of aesthetic experience is also integral to Winnicott's account of human nature, though he prefers to talk of an innate and fundamental *creativity*. He believed that it is through creative apperception, essentially grounded in bodily aliveness, that life becomes truly meaningful (1971). Christopher Bollas further develops the implications of Winnicott's insights when he suggests that the first aesthetic is grounded in the *maternal idiom*, the mother's handling of her child and her total system of care (Bollas, 1978, 1979, 1987, 1989).

However, despite these resonances between Bion and Winnicott, there is an important shift in emphasis with the clinical contributions of the latter, and with the work of Ehrenzweig from the non-clinical domain. These differences were polarized in the Klein–Winnicott debate of 1952, with important consequences for their respective views concerning art and creativity (recounted here in Chapter Six). Winnicott and Milner both disagreed with the fundamental Kleinian view that there was a rudimentary ego from birth and that it is the interplay of the life and death instincts that structure mental life (via the unconscious phantasies of projection and introjection) from the start. They took the view that the newborn child is essentially a *tabula rasa*: the basis of all thinking and knowledge being derived from the child's interaction with the mother and especially her "mirroring" role. (This follows the empiricist philosophical tradition of Hume and Locke, as opposed to the distinctly Platonic and Kantian idealism implicit in Bionian and Kleinian thinking.) Unlike Klein and Segal, Winnicott and Milner did not regard the essence of art as being reparative and (as we saw in Chapter Five) Ehrenzweig concurred with this view, arguing that the production of specific objects is not the central feature of creativity—neither does he assign a central role to depression in creative experience. He emphasizes the "manic–oceanic" fusion of the infant, the role of illusion, and the need to recreate within the creative unconscious a sense of infantile omnipotence and oneness with the mother—an experience which the Kleinians regard as a regressive feature, inimical to creativity and emotional creative development. Indeed, Kleinians would argue that, with this account, no distinction is made between "authentic" creativity grounded in the specific phantasy of recreation (*reparation*), and omnipotent (inauthentic) phantasies of *creation* (see Segal, 1986, pp. 207–216, for she explores this distinction through a reading of William Golding's *The Spire*).

While Bion (1970, 1990) and Meltzer and Harris Williams (1988) regard the aesthetic capacity as being fundamental, Winnicott (1971) argues that it is the capacity for creative living that grounds our being. What is clear in both traditions, however, is the increasing focus on Truth as being at the heart of the post-Kleinian approach to human behaviour and meaning. Where Winnicott (1958) postulates a spontaneous, non-compliant "True Self" arising from the partnership of psyche and soma (to be distinguished from the adaptive compliance of the "False Self"), Bion talks in terms of a transcendental, Kantian self that cannot itself be known, but which is the filter through which we perceive ourselves and the world as they truly are. This is akin to what could be described as the Neo-Platonic view, which conceives art as being one of the most profound ways by which we apprehend the true nature of the world, and also our place within it—ostensibly a return to the idea that art and aesthetic experience are essentially concerned with the "True, the Good and the Beautiful".

Taken as a whole, the post-Kleinian contributions of Bion on the one hand, and Milner and Winnicott on the other, have come a far distance from the normative, adaptive account of art propounded by Freud and the ego psychologists on the one hand, and "traditional" Kleinians such as Segal, on the other. What seems to be one of the most interesting developments in post-Kleinian psychoanalytic theory is the centrality that is increasingly being given to the role of aesthetic and creative experience in the analytic encounter itself—a theme considered in Chapter Four of this book.

Perhaps one of the most significant developments in both psychoanalytic aesthetics and clinical theory, which has in part been spurred by this "dialogue" between art and psychoanalysis, is the reappraisal of the classical distinction between the primary and secondary processes. Ehrenzweig's (1967) account of art drew attention to the need for this revision, and much of his thinking was informed by developments in British school thinking that were beginning to question the classical view that the conscious and the unconscious were two quite distinct, antithetical systems (Milner, 1956, 1967; Rycroft, 1956, 1962). Ehrenzweig says that we do wrong to assume that art's structure is exclusively shaped by secondary processes and believes that the questioning of the primary/secondary process distinction is an example of the "applied" psycho-analysis of art actually modifying original clinical theory (1971, p. 3). Indeed, Milner pointed out in her Freud Centenary Lecture (1956), that such a revision has been partly stimulated by the problems raised by the nature of art (1987, p. 211). More recently, Meira Likierman has noted that because of a too clear distinction between primitive and higher levels of mentality in psychoanalytic theory, aesthetic experience and creativity have unfortunately been assigned to "purgatory"—to a "developmental limbo which places them neither in the underworld of primitive mental life, nor in the 'higher' realm of civilised functioning" (1989, p. 133).

This brings us to the objection that a "British psychoanalytic aesthetic" is problematic because it conceives the origin of aesthetics and creativity almost entirely in terms of infantile psychic functioning. It is certainly true that in these chapters we have encountered a number of theorists who do claim that aesthetic experience and creativity evoke earliest infantile experiences—as, for instance, Fuller's analysis of Natkin and the "potential space". So, the question must be addressed as to how far we "regress" into more "primitive" modes of functioning during the aesthetic encounter and during creative experience. Perhaps part of the problem is to do with our modern tendency to value scientific, "rational" thinking over and above intuition and iconic, non-verbal ways of thinking. Not only do we privilege words over images, but also our scientific world-view tends to isolate the two modes of functioning. (For a useful account of the ideological, political, and cultural vicissitudes underlying this distinction between the visual and the verbal, between discursive and non-discursive ways of thinking, see William Mitchell's *Iconology: Image, Text, Ideology*, 1986.) As Rycroft observes, it is

> not surprising that this idea that the primary processes are unconscious, primitive, neurotic, archaic, etc., and are normally subject to repression, was to cause psychoanalysis considerable trouble, both in its theorising and its public relations, since it soon became evident that there was some similarity between the imaginative activity displayed by artists and writers and the primary processes described by Freud as characteristic of dreaming and symptom-formation. Given the clinical origins and bias of psychoanalysis, the easiest and most tempting way of explaining this similarity was to assert that artists and writers are neurotic and that works of art are analogous, or homologous to, dreams and neurotic symptoms; and that the techniques of psychoanalytical interpretation can be transferred without modification to artists and their works. [1957, p. 265]

Rycroft reminds us that Freud lived in a cultural milieu very different from our own; he was born in 1856, which meant that during his formative years he would not have encountered revolutionary figures such as Picasso, Pound, and Joyce, who challenged the superiority of words over images, and questioned the so-called "rational" structure of linguistic syntax. Thus, it would have been natural for Freud to have assumed a much closer relationship between verbal discourse and rationalism on the one hand, and the non-verbal, the irrational, and the imaginary on the other. However, despite developments in art, our culture still tends to be suspicious of the artist; we still tend to regard the creative individual as possibly unstable, possessed of a little "divine madness", perhaps (Storr, 1972). Maybe this is also motivated in part by an envy of creative people. It is certainly true that most of us would like to think that we could create an enduring work of art. Rycroft suggests a much healthier alternative to this view. He believes that the primary and secondary processes coexist from the beginning of life and under favourable conditions they may continue to function in harmony with one another, one providing the imaginative, the other the rational basis of living. [1957, p. 266]

So, rather than assuming that creativity is grounded in more than just a little craziness, Rycroft suggests that we should regard as creative those individuals who "retain in adult life something of that imaginative freedom which healthy children display" (*ibid.*). However, this is a freedom that, sadly, we tend to lose when we enter the adult world of our present rationalist, bourgeois culture.

For those such as Kris and Hartmann, the primary process is still relegated to an archaic and primitive form of functioning, one that is supposed to be antithetical to constructive, conscious thought. They asserted that creativity controls the "regression towards the primary process", but not the work of the primary process itself. But, as we saw in Chapter Five, the *constructive* role of the primary process is central to Ehrenzweig's account of art. He criticized the ego psychologists for viewing art and creativity as a controlled "regression at the service of the ego" (Kris, 1952), a view which essentially construes art as an *adaptive* achievement—autonomous of the id and libidinal impulses. It is the Kleinian concept of unconscious phantasy that is highly significant here, and played a key role in the development of Ehrenzweig's account of artistic perception. It is a concept that cuts across the primary/secondary process distinction, and caused much controversy in the "Controversial Discussions" that divided the British Psychoanalytical Society during the early 1940s (King & Steiner, 1992, pp. 330–331, 373–377).

Isaacs's (1948) account of the mechanism suggested that, although it was "unconscious", phantasy includes activities of so-called "secondary process" functioning: it has cognizance of space and time and recognizes opposites. It is the Kleinian view that unconscious phantasy structures *all* mental activity and perception—including both conscious and unconscious modes of functioning. Indeed, by virtue of these qualities, the notion of unconscious phantasy corroborated Ehrenzweig's (1967) thesis concerning the positive, constructive role of the id, and provided him with a structural and dynamic concept that gave considerable substance to his belief that conscious and unconscious mental life are not merely linked: "surface thought is wholly immersed in the matrix of the primary process" (1948, p. 262). He admits that "this constructive role of the unconscious is difficult to accept" from the point of view of our conscious, "surface" thinking, yet it is the *facts of art* that suggest that the undifferentiated matrix is technically far superior to the narrowly focused conscious processes, if only because of its wider focus that can comprehend serial structures irrespective of their order in time and space. Indeed, most of us would agree that there is certainly nothing that could be described as primitive or regressive about Riley's handling of pictorial space, or Schoenberg's ability to handle a theme without regard to its sequence in time. For, according to Ehrenzweig's account of "dedifferentiation", the kind of syncretistic, wide-sweeping vision that is needed to perceive these hidden structures cannot be described as a regression to pre-existing infantile or primitive percepts and concepts. He prefers to describe it as "the creation of an entirely new matrix, the undifferentiated structure of which is made to fit precisely a particular task"; creative work infuses "new and controlled stimulation into an utterly flexible unconscious phantasy" (*ibid.*, p. 261).

In these various ways, therefore, it can be seen how clinical theory and applied psychoanalysis have significantly developed and modified one another in the ongoing conversation between clinicians and non-clinicians. It would seem that this openness to change and insight is a sign of health, and augurs well for future dialogue between the two domains. As noted in the Introduction, the British School comprises a variety of psychoanalytic approaches: Freudian, Kleinian, Bionian, Winnicottian. What I hope has become apparent through this study is the extent to which the thinkers explored above share a common understanding—the commitment to a view of human nature that is broadly humanistic in conception, yet not in any sentimental sense of this term. For their account of human nature is one that emphasizes the importance of a *truthful* relationship to the world, where the forces of cynicism, perversity, and violence (Bion's "minus L, H, K" links) are mitigated by an openness to change and growth (which is often painful) nourished by the non-omnipotent, aesthetic apprehension of psychic reality.

A British psychoanalytic approach to art and creativity (indeed, to human behaviour in general) teaches us humility: that "creativity is for the self, impossible" (Meltzer & Harris Williams, 1988, p. xiii). Essentially, it is a function of what Bion called the unknowable self, the filter through which we perceive inner and outer reality veridically, asserting the Kantian belief in the existence of a transcendental noumenal reality. Similarly, Winnicott (1958) developed his account of the "True Self" as being the basis of a creative relationship to the world, through which arises a sense of meaning and value. This "True Self" (in contrast to the "False Self") is spontaneous and arises from the partnership of psyche and soma—when the head and the heart are working together. There is, then, in both the Bionian and Winnicottian conception of human nature, an emphasis on the necessity of *truth*—which the mind needs for growth just as the body craves food for its nourishment. This truthfulness is essentially an aesthetic and creative phenomenon (Meltzer & Harris Williams, 1988; Winnicott, 1971). Indeed, this emphasis on the love of truth (what Bion calls the "K" link) as a factor basic to all creative human relationships would seem a fruitful approach to the dynamics of aesthetic encounter. Such a conception provides an approach to criticism which is not grounded in positivism on the one hand, or the barrenness of structural–linguistic approaches on the other— approaches that do not distinguish between explanation and description or between symbols and signs, or have any conception of psychic change and growth. The humanistic conception of human nature characteristic of the British School can be viewed as a welcome counterbalance to the nihilism characteristic of much poststructuralist, postmodern thinking—a stance that has been dominant in much current academic debate for the past three decades. However, one notable exception has been Colin Falck's *Myth, Truth, and Literature* (1989). This is an attempt to re-work the somewhat unfashionable notions of "inspiration", "truth" and "intuition" towards what he calls "a true post-modernism". Although he focuses on literary theory, his insights have relevance to aesthetics and criticism in general. He argues that Saussurean and post-Saussurean linguistics have "abolished reality". Such linguistic theories effectively eliminate any notion of "incarnation, transcendence, a concept of the self, intuition, creativity, apprehended extra-linguistic meaning, poetry, historical context and truth". Falck stresses that its "crucial weakness" is that the fact that it "undermines our belief in—and must therefore indirectly help to bring about an actual withering of—our capacity for particular insights into the real meanings of particular life situations". Such theories are thus incapacitated to be any kind of value-establishing branch of aesthetics and criticism. Falck suggests that all meaning and value originate in a shared *corporeality*, which is reflected by, and structured within, language. This view resonates with much British School thinking, especially Isaacs's (1948) account of the link between language and the body—structured through unconscious phantasy.

Many academic approaches to art, in addition, tend to conceive of the critic as one who imposes some "secondary process" on art's "primary process" in order to keep it within the bounds of the explainable and the known. Such criticism shows no awareness of a distinction between sign systems and symbolic forms; it is based on the unconscious phantasy of uncovering the secrets of the unconscious, thereby making no distinction between "secrecy" and "mystery" (Meltzer & Harris Williams, 1988). It talks about the art-symbol as if it were the merely the outcome or manifestation of ideological forces, the "basic assumptions" of society (Bion). Yet, as Herbert Read argued, "art is art as symbol, not as sign" (1951, p. 73). According to the British School, what makes an artwork of aesthetic (symbolic) significance is the very fact that it is the outcome of psychic work, a *process* that involves the negotiation between self and other, inner and outer reality. Art is not purely imagery and "content"; it concerns an activity that is itself symbolic, and therefore more than merely the deployment of learnt skills and techniques (Podro, 1990; Wollheim, 1987). (This could be seen in terms of preparing a special meal for one's guests. It is not so much the *meal* itself that is overridingly important [although it is by no means insignificant], but more a case of what the *actual activity* of preparing the food and sharing it means to the cook and the guests.) Indeed, the question of how the activity of painting has developed in such a way as to be an *art*—that is, why it is more than just the rendering of a mundane copy of the world—is one that the British Psychoanalytic tradition has been able to address perhaps more effectively than many other approaches to the visual arts.[7]

The aesthetic critic, according to the British psychoanalytic view, is aware of these distinctions: he or she respects the difference between symbol and sign, secrecy and mystery; evocation and explanation—between "knowing" and "knowing about". The sensitive critic will have a grasp of the aesthetic quality of the material he is handling, and will try to approach it in an aesthetic manner (we may think, perhaps, of those such as Stokes and Wollheim). Seen in this perspective, the task of the critic is analogous to that of the artist, for both are trying to conceive a language that is capable of containing the implications and resonances of emotional experience. Thus, in the practice of aesthetic criticism, the critic's sensibility is grounded in the faculty of a receptive congruence to the formal structures evolved by the artist for containing of "meaning" (Bion, 1970) or the "artistic import" (Langer, 1942). As Harris Williams argues, he is "dealing with the same mysterious phenomena, the life of the mind in process" (Meltzer & Harris Williams, 1988, p. 180). Indeed, this theme of "creative criticism" takes us right back to the Introduction to this book, where the overlapping areas of creativity, criticism and the aesthetic encounter were identified. What much of the work of British School thinking has done is to forge a link between these areas in such a way as to give an account of the mind which is in itself based on a conception of aesthetic experience, from out of which grows the human individual—one who is capable of growth and reciprocity—even in the face of uncertainty, anxiety and "catastrophic change". In Bion's (1970) view, the creative individual is one who can bear the "cloud of unknowing" (Meister Eckhart), one who respects "the burden of the mystery" (Wordsworth) and can tolerate frustration: that is, he has what Keats called "Negative Capability".

The Victorian critic Walter Pater believed that the aim of all true criticism is "to see the object as in itself it really is" and that the task of aesthetic critic is to "know one's impression as it really is" (1986 [1873], p. xxix). One could regard these as analogous to the tasks of the psychoanalytic encounter itself (especially in the light of Bion's insights). Indeed, Harris Williams has expressed very clearly what, for me, is the *raison d'être* informing a British psychoanalytic aesthetic, and one which this study has undertaken to explore. For under the aegis of its broadly humanistic approach, both art and psychoanalysis

> may be seen as different media for exploring the world of the mind, related through congruence and a common drive towards

self-knowledge, rather than reductively in terms of a literary phantasy content and psychoanalytic interpretation. [1991, p. 1, my italics]

What British psychoanalysis teaches us is that this "self-knowledge" is not an abstract, mystical, or transcendental awareness, but one that is grounded in the "sagacity of the body"—the partnership of body and mind, when the head and the heart are in dialogue.

Note

1. Since I started researching this text in 1991, I am aware that there are an increasing number of scholarly texts that recognize the significance of the British School's contribution to the refinement of a broadly humanistic psychoanalytic aesthetic. These writers emphasize a philosophical approach to art that gives due cognizance to the intersubjectivity of our emotional experience and its central role in aesthetics and creatvity. Gosso (2004) brings together a collection of classic essays on the relationship between psychoanalysis and art, with contributions from Klein, Segal, Riviere, Milner, Stokes, Meltzer, Harris Williams, and Waddell. Gosso introduces the collection by way of a comprehensive overview of the development of psychoanalytic approaches to art from Freud to the developments of Klein and the post-Kleinian movement. In her preface, Gosso highlights how aesthetic criticism derived from post-Kleinian models has congruence with those elements of "contemporary thought that make an appeal to the imagination, to wonder, to the gratuitous the gift of the moment" (*ibid.*, p. xxi). Gosso argues that the "evocative quality of [this] poetic communication" fosters a reciprocity and a "close rapport" between the work of art and its interpreter and between interpreter and reader, comparing it to the "intimacy of mother-baby" (*ibid.*).

    Jacobus (2005) explores the *literary* aspects Kleinian psychoanalysis, focusing on Melanie Klein's legacy and the contribution of psychoanalysts such as Ella Sharpe, Joan Riviere, Susan Isaacs, Winnicott, Milner, and Bion. Jacobus gives a central place to the literary and aesthetic concerns of the British School of Psychoanalysis, arguing against the "misplaced separation" of British and Continental traditions and making a case for the continuing links between psychoanalysis and aesthetics (p. vii). Rather than applying psychoanalytic ideas to literature and aesthetics, Jacobus explores what she calls the "poetics" of the British Psychoanalytic tradition as a form of discourse in its own right. Such a discourse, Jacobus asserts, not only derserves "the attention of literary and cultural historians" but it "also forms the basis for a living, changing and contestatory body of clinical ideas ... that are constantly evolving in reation to contemporary clinical practice, theory and intellectual exchange" (*ibid.*).

A further a noteworthy contribution to the dialogue between art and psychoanalysis is Sayers (2007), where Sayers innovatively "retells" the story of psychoanalysis by way of exploring its contribution to art and aesthetics. The book charts a wide territory, beginning with the pioneering work of Freud and Jung and then moves on to explore the Kleinian, post-Kleinian, and Continental Schools of Psychoanalysis, with chapters devoted to Stokes, Milner, Ehrenzweig, Winnicott, and Bion, as well as the French psychoalaysts Julia Kristeva, Jean Laplanche, and Jacques Lacan.

REFERENCES

Abraham, K. (1927). *Selected Papers on Psychoanalysis*. London: Hogarth.
Abrams, M. H. (1971). *The Mirror and the Lamp: Romantic Theory and the Critical Tradition*. London: Oxford University Press.
Adams, L. S. (1994). *Art and Psychoanalysis*. London: Basic Books.
Adams, T., & Duncan, A. (2003) (Eds.), *The Feminine Case: Jung, Aesthetics & the Creative Process*. London: Karnac.
Alford, C. F. (1989). *Melanie Klein and Critical Social Theory: An Account of Politics, Art and Reason Based on Her Psychoanalytic Theory*. New Haven, CT: Yale University Press.
Alvarez, A. (1992). *Live Company: Psychoanalytic Psychotherapy with Autistic, Borderline, Deprived and Abused Children*. New York: Brunner-Routledge.
Anderson, D. R. (1987). *Creativity and the Philosophy of C. S. Peirce*. Dordrecht: Kluwer Academic.
Arnheim, R. (1943). Gestalt and art. *Journal of Aesthetics and Art Criticism*, 2: 71–5. Reprinted in J. Hogg (Ed.), *Psychology and the Visual Arts* (p. 258). New York: Penguin, 1969.
Arnheim, R. (1949). The Gestalt theory of expression. *Psychological Review*, 56: 156–71. Reprinted in J. Hogg (Ed.), *Psychology and the Visual Arts* (pp. 263–287). New York: Penguin, 1969.

Arnheim, R. (1954). *Art and Visual Perception*. Berkeley, CA: University of California Press.
Arts Council of Great Britain (1982). *Adrian Stokes 1902–72: a Retrospective*. London: Serpentine Gallery, exhibition catalogue.
Astor, J. (2002). Analytical psychology and its relation to psychoanalysis: a personal view. *Journal of Analytical Psychology*, 47: 599–612.
Bann, S. (1978). The case for Stokes (and Pater). *PN Review*, 6: 6–9.
Bann, S. (Ed.) (1980). Adrian Stokes 1902–1972: a supplement: with contributions from Richard Wollheim, Ben Nicholson, Richard Read, Eric Rhode, Andrew Forge, Eric W. White, Colin St. John Wilson, Peter Leech, David Carrier, Paul Smith, and Peter Robinson. *PN Review*, 15: 30–54.
Bann, S. (1988). Adrian Stokes: English aesthetic criticism under the impact of psychoanalysis. In: E. Timms & N. Segal (Eds.), *Freud in Exile: Psychoanalysis and its Vicissitudes* (pp. 134–144). New Haven, CT: Yale University Press.
Bann, S. (1989). Art history in perspective. *History of the Human Sciences*, 2(i): 1–18.
Bann, S. (Ed.) (2007). *The Coral Mind: Adrian Stokes's Engagement with Art History, Criticism, Architecture and Psychoanalysis*. Pittsburgh, PA: Penn State Press.
Barthes, R. (1973). *Mythologies*. London: Paladin.
Bell, C. (1914). *Art*. J. B. Bullen (Ed.). Oxford: Oxford University Press [reprinted London: Oxford University Press, 1987].
Benvenuto, B., & Kennedy, R. (1986). *The Works of Jacques Lacan: An Introduction*. London: Free Association.
Berenson, B. (1948). *Aesthetics and History*. London: Constable.
Bion, F. (Ed.) (1980). *Bion in New York and São Paulo*. Strathtay: Clunie Press.
Bion, F. (Ed.) (1992). *Cogitations*. London: Karnac.
Bion, W. R. (1955). Language and the schizophrenic. In: M. Klein, P. Heimann, & R. Money-Kyrle (Eds.), *New Directions in Psycho-Analysis* (pp. 220–239). London: Tavistock.
Bion, W. R. (1961). *Experiences in Groups*. London: Heinemann.
Bion, W. R. (1962). *Learning From Experience*. London: Heinemann.
Bion, W. R. (1963). *Elements of Psycho-Analysis*. London: Heinemann.
Bion, W. R. (1965). *Transformations*. London: Heinemann.
Bion, W. R. (1967). *Second Thoughts*. London: Heinemann [reprinted London: Maresfield & Karnac, 1987].
Bion, W. R. (1970). *Attention and Interpretation*. London: Tavistock.

Bion, W. R. (1978). *Four Discussions with W. R. Bion*. Strathtay: Clunie Press.

Bion, W. R. (1985). *All My Sins Remembered: Another Part of a Life*. Abingdon: Fleetwood Press.

Bion, W. R. (1982). *The Long Weekend: 1897–1919*. London: Free Association.

Bion, W. R. (1990). *A Memoir of the Future*. London: Karnac.

Bishop, P. (2007). *Analytical Psychology and German Classical Aesthetics: Goethe, Schiller and Jung*. London: Routledge.

Bleandonu, G. (1994). *Wilfred Bion: His Life and Works*. London: Free Association.

Bloom, H. (1975). *The Anxiety of Influence: A Theory of Poetry*. London: Oxford University Press.

Bollas, C. (1978). The aesthetic moment and the search for transformation. *Annual of Psycho-Analysis*, 6: 385–94.

Bollas, C. (1979). The transformational object. *International Journal of Psycho-Analysis*, 60: 97–107.

Bollas, C. (1987). *The Shadow of the Object: Psychoanalysis of the Unthought Known*. London: Free Association.

Bollas, C. (1989). *Forces of Destiny*. London: Free Association.

Bryson, N. (1984). *Tradition and Desire, from David to Delacroix*. Cambridge: Cambridge University Press.

Carrier, D. (1973). Adrian Stokes and the theory of painting. *British Journal of Aesthetics*, 13: 133–145.

Carrier, D. (1997). *England and Its Aesthetes: Biography and Taste*. London: Routledge.

Coleridge, S. T. (1960). *Shakespearean Criticism. Volume 1*. London: Dent.

de Sausmarez, M. (1970). *Bridget Riley*. London: Studio Vista.

Dewey, J. (1934). *Art as Experience*. New York: Minton.

Ehrenzweig, A. (1948). Unconscious form-creation in art: parts 1 & 2. *British Journal of Medical Psychology*, 21: 88–109.

Ehrenzweig, A. (1949a). Unconscious form-creation in art: parts 3 & 4. *British Journal of Medical Psychology*, 22: 185–214.

Ehrenzweig, A. (1949b). The origin of the scientific and the heroic urge. *International Journal of Psycho-Analysis*, 30: 32.

Ehrenzweig, A. (1953). *The Psychoanalysis of Artistic Vision and Hearing*. London: Routledge & Kegan Paul.

Ehrenzweig, A. (1957). The creative surrender. *American Imago*, 14: 193–210.

Ehrenzweig, A. (1961). The hidden order of art. *British Journal of Aesthetics*, 1: 121–133.

Ehrenzweig, A. (1962). A new psychoanalytic approach to aesthetics. *British Journal of Aesthetics*, 2: 301–317.

Ehrenzweig, A. (1965). The pictorial space of Bridget Riley. *Art International*, 9(i): 20–24.

Ehrenzweig, A. (1967). *The Hidden Order of Art*. Berkeley, CA: University of California Press [reprinted 1971].

Eigen, M. (1981). The area of faith in Winnicott, Lacan and Bion. *International Journal of Psycho-Analysis*, 62: 413–433.

Eliot, G. (1871) [1994]. *Middlemarch*. London: Penguin.

Eliot, T. S. (1936). *Collected Poems 1909–1962*. London: Faber & Faber [reprinted 1985].

Fairbairn, R. (1937). A prolegomena to a psychology of art. *British Journal of Psychology*, 28: 288–303.

Fairbairn, R. (1952). *Psychoanalytic Studies of the Personality*. London: Tavistock.

Falck, C. (1989). *Myth, Truth and Literature*. Cambridge: Cambridge University Press.

Fordham, M. (1998). *Freud, Klein & Jung: The Fenceless Field*. London: Routledge.

Freud, S., (1895). *A Project for a Scientific Psychology. S.E.*, 1: 283–398. London: Hogarth.

Freud, S. (1895d) (with J. Breuer), *Studies on Hysteria S.E.*, 2 . London: Hogarth.

Freud, S. (1900a). *The Interpretation of Dreams. S.E.*, 4,5. London: Hogarth.

Freud, S. (1901b). *The Psychopathology of Everyday Life. S.E.*, 6. London: Hogarth.

Freud, S. (1905c). *Jokes and their Relation to the Unconscious. S.E.*, 8. London: Hogarth.

Freud, S. (1905d). *Three Essays on the Theory of Sexuality. S.E.*, 7: 125–230. London: Hogarth.

Freud, S. (1905e). *Fragment of an Analysis of a Case of Hysteria. S.E.*, 7: 3–124. London: Hogarth.

Freud, S. (1907a). Delusions and dreams in Jensen's Gradiva. *S.E.*, 9: 3–96, London: Hogarth.

Freud, S. (1908e). Creative writers and day-dreaming. *S.E.*, 9: 143–153. London: Hogarth.

Freud, S. (1910c). *Leonardo da Vinci and a Memory of his Childhood. S.E.*, 11: 59–138. London: Hogarth.

Freud, S. (1911b). Formulations on the two principles of mental functioning. *S.E.*, 12: 218–226. London: Hogarth.

Freud, S. (1913f). The theme of the three caskets. *S.E., 13*: 289–302. London: Hogarth.
Freud, S. (1913j). The claims of psychoanalysis to scientific interest. *S.E., 13*: 165–200. London: Hogarth.
Freud, S. (1914b). *The Moses of Michelangelo. S.E., 13*: 211–240. London: Hogarth.
Freud, S. (1914d). On the history of the psycho-analytic movement. *S.E., 14*: 3–66. London: Hogarth.
Freud, S. (1915–1917). *Introductory Lectures on Psycho-analysis. S.E., 16*: 243–463. London: Hogarth.
Freud, S. (1917e). Mourning and melancholia. *S.E., 14*. London: Hogarth.
Freud, S. (1918b). *From the History of an Infantile Neurosis. S.E., 17*: 3–122. London: Hogarth.
Freud, S. (1920g). *Beyond the Pleasure Principle. S.E., 18*. London: Hogarth.
Freud, S. (1923b). *The Ego and the Id. S.E., 19*. London: Hogarth.
Freud, S. (1925d). An autobiographical study. *S.E., 20*: 3–76. London: Hogarth.
Freud, S. (1927c). *The Future of an Illusion. S.E., 21*: 3–58. London: Hogarth.
Freud, S. (1928b). Dostoevsky and parricide. *S.E., 21*: 175–198. London: Hogarth.
Freud, S. (1930a). *Civilization and its Discontents. S.E., 21*: 59–148. London: Hogarth.
Freud, S. (1933a). *New Introductory Lectures on Psycho-Analysis. S.E., 22*. London: Hogarth.
Freud, S. (1939a). *Moses and Monotheism. S.E., 23*. London: Hogarth.
Friedman, L. (1958). Toward an integration of psychoanalytic and philosophic aesthetics. *American Imago, 15*: 371–88.
Fuller, P. (1974). *Robert Natkin*. New York: Abrams.
Fuller, P. (1980). *Art and Psychoanalysis*. London: Hogarth, reprinted 1988.
Fuller, P. (1986). *Marches Past*. London: Chatto & Windus.
Fuller, P. (1988). *Theoria: Art and the Absence of Grace*. London: Chatto & Windus.
Fuller, P. (1991). *Images of God*. London: Chatto & Windus.
Gedo, M. (Ed.) (1985). *Pyschoanalytic Perspectives on Art*. Hillsdale, NJ: The Analytic Press.
Gervais, D. (1981). Adrian Stokes and the benignity of form: part one. *Cambridge Quarterly, 10*(i): 40–64.

Gervais, D. (1982). Adrian Stokes and the benignity of form: part two. *Cambridge Quarterly*, 11(i):224–251.
Glover, N. (1989). Wilfred Bion: his Kleinian heritage and post-Kleinian legacy. Unpublished MA dissertation, University of Kent.
Gombrich, E. (1954). Psychoanalysis and the history of art. Reprinted in B. Nelson (Ed.), *Freud and the Twentieth Century* (pp. 182–293). London: Allen & Unwin, 1958. Also reprinted in E. Gombrich, *Meditations on a Hobby Horse*. London: Phaidon, 1963.
Gombrich, E. (1960). *Art and Illusion*. London: Phaidon [Reprinted 1987].
Gombrich, E. (1966). Freud's aesthetics. *Encounter*, 26: 30–40.
Gosso, S. (Ed.) (2004). *Psychoanalysis and Art: The Aesthetic Conflict*. London: Karnac.
Gowing, L. (1973). Memories of Adrian Stokes. *The Listener*, 90(2313): 821–815.
Green, A. (1975). The analyst, symbolization and absence in the analytic setting. *International Journal of Psycho-Analysis*, 56: 1–22.
Grosskurth, P. (1986). *Melanie Klein, her World and her Work*. London: Maresfield.
Grotstein, J. (Ed.) (1981). *Do I Dare Disturb The Universe? A Memorial to W. R. Bion*. London: Karnac.
Harris Williams, M. (1999). Psychoanalysis: an art or a science? *British Journal of Psychotherapy*, 16(2):127–35.
Hartmann, H. (1958). *Ego Psychology and the Problem of Adaptation*. New York: International Universities Press.
Hazlitt, W. (1891). *Table Talk*. London: Bell and Daldy.
Heimann, P. (1942). A contribution to the problem of sublimation. *International Journal of Psycho-Analysis*, 23: 8–17.
Hindle, D. (2000). L'enfant et les sortileges revisited. *International Journal of Psycho-Analysis*, 81: 1185–1196.
Hinshelwood, R. (1989). *A Dictionary of Kleinian Thought*. London: Free Association.
Hughes, J. (1990). *The Reshaping of the Psychoanalytic Domain*. London: Oxford University Press.
Hulks, D. (2001). Painting, atom bombs and nudes: symbolism in the later psychoanalytic writings of Adrian Stokes. *Journal of Psychoanalytic Studies*, 3: 95–109.
Hulks, D. (2006). The dark chaos of subjectivisms. In: B. Taylor (Ed.), *Sculpture and Psychoanalysis* (pp. 95–116). Aldershot: Ashgate.
Isaacs, S. (1948). The nature and function of phantasy. *International Journal of Psycho-Analysis*, 29: 73–97.

Jacobus, M. (2005). *The Poetics of Psychoanalysis: In the Wake of Klein*. London: Oxford University Press.

Jaques, E. (1965). Death and the mid-life crisis. *International Journal of Psycho-Analysis, 46*: 502–514.

Jones, E. (1914). The Madonna's conception through the ear. In: *Essays in Applied Psycho-Analysis* (pp. 312–317). London: The International Psycho-Analytical Press, 1923.

Jones, E. (1916). The theory of symbolism. *British Journal of Psychology, 9*: 181–229.

Jung, C. (1971). *The Spirit in Man, Art and Literature, Collected Works of Jung, Volume 15*. Princeton, NJ: Princeton University Press.

Keats, J. (1958). *The Letters of John Keats: 1814–1821* (H. E. Rollins, Ed.). Cambridge: Cambridge University Press.

King, P., & Steiner, R. (1992). *The Freud–Klein Controversies*. London: Routledge.

Klein, M. (1923). Early analysis. *Imago, 9*: 222–259). Reprinted in *Love, Guilt and Reparation and other works 1921–1945* (pp. 77–105). London: Virago, 1988.

Klein, M. (1929). Infantile anxiety situations reflected in a work of art and the creative impulse. *International Journal of Psycho-Analysis, 10*: 436–43. Reprinted in *Love, Guilt and Reparation and other works 1921–1945* (pp. 210–218). London: Virago, 1988.

Klein, M. (1930). The importance of symbol-formation in the development of the ego. *International Journal of Psycho-Analysis, 11*: 24–39. Reprinted in *Love, Guilt and Reparation and other works 1921–1945* (pp. 219–232). London: Virago, 1988.

Klein, M. (1932). *The Psycho-Analysis of Children*. London: Hogarth [reprinted London: Virago, 1989].

Klein, M. (1935). A contribution to the psychogenesis of manic-depressive states. *International Journal of Psycho-Analysis, 16*: 145–74. Reprinted in *Love, Guilt and Reparation and other works 1921–1945* (pp. 262–289). London: Virago, 1988.

Klein, M. (1940). Mourning and its relation to manic-depressive states. *International Journal of Psycho-Analysis, 21*: 125–53. Reprinted in *Love, Guilt and Reparation and other works 1921–1945* (pp. 344–369). London: Virago, 1988.

Klein, M. (1946). Notes on some schizoid mechanisms. *International Journal of Psycho-Analysis, 27*: 99–102. Reprinted in *Envy and Gratitude and other works 1946–1963* (pp. 1–24). London: Virago, 1988.

Klein, M. (1955). On identification. In: P. Heimann, M. Klein, & R. Money-Kyrle (Eds.), *New Directions in Psychoanalysis*. London:

Tavistock. Reprinted in *Envy and Gratitude and Other Works 1946–1963* (pp. 141–175). London: Virago, 1988.

Klein, M. (1959). Our adult world and its roots in infancy. Reprinted in *Envy and Gratitude and Other Works 1946–1963* (pp. 247–263). London: Virago, 1988.

Klein, M. (1963). Some reflections on the Oresteia. Reprinted in *Envy and Gratitude and Other Works 1946–1963* (pp.275–299). London: Virago, 1988.

Klein, M. (1988a). *Love, Guilt and Reparation and Other Works 1921–1945*. London: Virago.

Klein, M. (1988b). *Envy and Gratitude and Other Works, 1946–1963*. London: Virago.

Kofman, S. (1988). *The Childhood of Art: An Interpretation of Freud's Aesthetics*. New York: Columbia University Press.

Kohon, G. (1986). *The British School of Psychoanalysis: The Independent Tradition*. London: Free Association.

Kris, E. (1952). *Psychoanalytic Explorations in Art*. New York: International Universities Press.

Kristeva, J. (1980). *Desire in Language: A Semiotic Approach to Literature and Art*. New York: Columbia University Press.

Kuhns, R. (1983). *A Psychoanalytic Theory of Art*. New York: Columbia University Press.

Lacan, J. (1949). Le stade du miroir. Reprinted in *Écrits*. London: Norton, 2005.

Langer, S. (1942). *Philosophy in A New Key*. Cambridge, MA: Harvard University Press.

Langer, S. (1953). *Feeling and Form*. New York: Schribner.

Langer, S. (1967). *Mind: An Essay in Human Feeling*. Baltimore, MD: Johns Hopkins University Press.

Lewin, B. D. (1946). Sleep, the mouth and the dream screen. *Psychoanalytic Quarterly*, 15(iv): 419–34.

Lewin, B. D. (1948). Inferences from the dream screen. *International Journal of Psycho-Analysis*, 29:224–231.

Likierman, M. (1989). The clinical significance of aesthetic experience. *International Review of Psycho-Analysis*, 16:133–150.

Little, M. (1985). Winnicott working in areas where psychotic anxieties predominate: a personal record. *Free Associations*, 3: 9–42.

Lyotard, J.-F. (1974). Beyond representation: preface to *L'Order Caché de l'Art* by Anton Ehrenzweig. Reprinted in A. Bejamin (Ed.), *The Lyotard Reader* (pp. 154–168). Oxford: Blackwell, 1989.

Meltzer, D. (1973). *Sexual States of Mind*. Strathtay, Perthshire: Clunie.
Meltzer, D. (1978). *The Kleinian Development*. Strathtay, Perthshire: Clunie.
Meltzer, D. (1981). The Kleinian expansion of Freud's metapsychology. *International Journal of Psycho-Analysis, 62*:177–184.
Meltzer, D., & Harris Williams, M. (1988). *The Apprehension of Beauty*. Strathtay, Perthshire: Clunie.
Milner, M. (1934). *A Life of One's Own*. London: Chatto & Windus [republished London: Virago, 1986].
Milner, M. (1937). *An Experiment in Leisure*. London: Chatto & Windus [reprinted London: Virago, 1988].
Milner, M. (1950). *On Not Being Able To Paint*. London: Heinemann [reprinted London: Heinemann, 1989].
Milner, M. (1952). Aspects of symbolism in the comprehension of the not-self. *International Journal of Psycho-Analysis, 33*: 181–195). Reprinted as: The role of illusion in symbol-formation, in: P. Heimann, M. Klein, & R. Money-Kyrle (Eds.), *New Directions in Psychoanalysis*. London: Tavistock, 1955. Reprinted in M. Milner, *The Suppressed Madness of Sane Men* (pp. 83–113). London: Routledge, 1987.
Milner, M. (1956). Psychoanalysis and art. Reprinted in *The Suppressed Madness of Sane Men* (pp. 83–113). London: Routledge, 1987.
Milner, M. (1957) [1950]. *On Not Being Able to Paint* (2nd edn with new Appendix). London: Heinemann, reprinted 1989.
Milner, M. (1960). The concentration of the body. Reprinted in *The Suppressed Madness of Sane Men* (pp. 234–240). London: Routledge, 1987.
Milner, M. (1967). The hidden order of art. Reprinted in *The Suppressed Madness of Sane Men* (pp. 241–245). London: Routledge, 1987.
Milner, M. (1969). *In The Hands of The Living God*. Reprinted London: Virago, 1988.
Milner, M. (1987a). *Eternity's Sunrise*. London: Virago.
Milner, M. (1987b). *The Suppressed Madness of Sane Men: Collected Papers, 1942–1986*. London: Routledge.
Mitchell, W. (1986). *Iconology: Image, Text, Ideology*. Chicago, IL: University of Chicago Press.
Money-Kyrle, R. (1961). *Man's Picture of His World*. London: Duckworth.
Nietzsche, F. (1883–1885). *Thus Spake Zarathustra: First Part: Zarathustra's Prologue, Zarathustra's Discourses. IV: The Despisers of the Body.* www.literaturepage.com/read/thusspakezarathustra-38.html accessed 2 March 2008).

O'Shaughnessy, E. (1981b). A clinical study of a defence organization. *International Journal of. Psycho-Anaysis, 62*: 359–369.
Pater, W. (1873). Leonardo da Vinci. In: *The Renaissance: Studies in Art and Poetry* (pp. 68–79). Oxford: Oxford University Press, 1986.
Pater, W. (1878). The child in the house. Reprinted in *Miscellaneous Studies* (pp. 147–169). London: Macmillan, 1898.
Pater, W. (1895). *Appreciations*. London: Macmillan.
Pater, W. (1898). *Miscellaneous Studies*. London: Macmillan.
Penny, N. (1988). Meltings: a review of *Painting as an Art*, by R. Wollheim. *London Review of Books, 10*(iv): 19–20.
Philipson, M. (1994). *An Outline of Jungian Aesthetics*. Boston, MA: Sigo.
Phillips, A. (1988). *Winnicott*. London: Fontana Modern Masters.
Plaut, F. (1974). Part-object relations and Jung's "luminosities", *Journal of Analytical Psychology, 19*: 2.
Podro, M. (1990). The landscape thinks itself in me: the comments and procedures of Cezanne. *International Review of Psychoanalysis, 17*: 401–409.
Rank, O. (1929). *The Trauma of Birth*. New York: Harcourt Brace.
Rank, O. (1932). *Art and Artist*. New York: Knopf.
Rayner, E. (1990). *The Independent Mind in British Psychoanalysis*. London: Free Association.
Read, H. (1951). Psychoanalysis and the problem of aesthetic value. *International Journal of Psycho-Analysis, 32*: 73–82.
Read, R. (1999). The unpublished correspondence of Adrian Stokes and Ezra Pound: modernist myth-making in sculpture, literature, aesthetics and psychoanalysis. *Comparative Criticism, 21*: 79–127.
Read, R. (2003). *Art and its Discontents*. Pittsburgh, PA: Penn State Press.
Read, R. Biography of Adrian Stokes. http://www.pstokes.demon.co.uk/ads5/biowbib.htm (accessed 2 September 2007).
Rhode, E. (1973). Memories of Adrian Stokes. *The Listener, 90*(2313): 812–815.
Rickman, J. (1940). The nature of ugliness. *International Journal of Psycho-Analysis, 21*: 297–298.
Rudnytsky, P. (1991). *The Psychoanalytic Vocation: Rank, Winnicott and the Legacy of Freud*. New Haven, CT: Yale University Press.
Ruskin, J., (1885–1889). *Praeterita*. Oxford: Oxford University Press.
Rycroft, C. (1956). Symbolisation and its relationship to the primary and secondary processes. *International Journal of Psycho-Analysis, 37*: 137–146.
Rycroft, C. (1957). Psychoanalysis and the literary imagination. In: W. Phillips (Ed.), *Art and Psychoanalysis* (pp. 250–279). New York: Criterion.

Rycroft, C. (1962). Beyond the reality principle. *International Journal of Psycho-Analysis*, 43: 388–394.
Rycroft, C. (Ed.) (1966). *Psychoanalysis Observed*. London: Constable.
Rycroft, C. (1968a). *Imagination and Reality*. London: Hogarth Press.
Rycroft, C. (Ed.) (1968b). *A Critical Dictionary of Psychoanalysis*. London: Penguin.
Sachs, H. (1940). Beauty, life and death. *American Imago*, 1: 81–133.
Sachs, H. (1942). *The Creative Unconscious*. Cambridge, MA: Sci-Art.
Sandler, P. C. (2005). *The Language of Bion: A Dictionary of Concepts*. London: Karnac.
Sarup, M. (1988). *An Introductory Guide to Post-Structuralism and Postmodernism*. Athens, GA: University of Georgia Press.
Sayers, J. (2007). *Freud's Art: Psychoanalysis Retold*. London: Routledge.
Scalia, J. (Ed.) (2002). *The Vitality of Objects, Exploring the work of Christopher Bollas*. Middletown, CT: Wesleyan University Press.
Segal, H. (1950). Some aspects of the analysis of a schizophrenic. *International Journal of Psycho-Analysis*, 31: 268–278.
Segal, H. (1952). A psychoanalytic approach to aesthetics. *International Journal of Psycho-Analysis*, 33: 196–207. Reprinted in *The Work of Hannah Segal* (pp. 185–205). London, Free Association, 1986).
Segal, H. (1957). Notes on symbol formation. *International Journal of Psycho-Analysis*, 38: 391–397.
Segal, H. (1973). *An Introduction to the Work of Melanie Klein*. London: Karnac.
Segal, H. (1974). Delusion and artistic creativity: some reflections on reading *The Spire* by William Golding. *International Review of Psycho-Analysis*, 1: 135–142. Reprinted in *The Work of Hannah Segal* (pp. 207–216). London: Free Association, 1986.
Segal, H. (1981). *Melanie Klein*. Harmondsworth: Penguin.
Segal, H. (1984). Joseph Conrad and the mid-life crisis. *International Review of Psychoanalysis*, 11: 3–9.
Segal, H. (1986). *The Work of Hannah Segal*. London: Free Association.
Segal, H. (1991). *Dream, Phantasy and Art*. London:Routledge.
Shakespeare, W. (1982). *Arden Shakespeare Second Series*. London: Methuen.
Sharpe, E. (1930). Certain aspects of sublimation and delusion. *International Journal of Psycho-Analysis*, 11: 12–23.
Sharpe, E. (1935). Similar and divergent unconscious determinants underlying the sublimation of pure art and pure science. *International Journal of Psycho-Analysis*, 16: 186–202.

Silver, A. (1981). A psycho-semiotic model: an interdisciplinary search for a common structural basis for psychoanalytic symbol-formation and the semiotic of C. S. Peirce. In: J. Grotstein (Ed.), *Do I Dare Disturb The Universe?* (pp. 269–316). London: Karnac.

Smith, P. (1980). Adrian Stokes and Ezra Pound. In: Adrian Stokes 1902–1972: a supplement. *PN Review, 15*: 51.

Spector, J. J. (1972). *The Aesthetics of Freud: A Study in Psychoanalysis and Art.* New York: Praeger.

Spitz, E. H. (1985). *Art and Psyche.* New Haven, CT: Yale University Press.

Spitz, E. H. (1989). Conflict and creativity: reflections on Otto Rank's theory of art. *Journal of Aesthetic Education, 23*(iii): 97–109. Reprinted in *Image and Insight: Essays in Psychoanalysis and the Arts.* New York: Columbia University Press, 1991.

Stokes, A. (1930). Painting, Giorgione and Barbaro. *Criterion 9*: 491. Revised in 1945 as Giorgione's "Tempesta" and reprinted in L. Gowing (Ed.), *The Critical Writings of Adrian Stokes: Vol. II.* New York: Thames & Hudson, 1978.

Stokes, A. (1932). *The Quattro Cento.* London: Faber. Reprinted in L. Gowing (Ed.), *The Critical Writings of Adrian Stokes, Volume I* (pp. 29–180). New York: Thames & Hudson, 1978.

Stokes, A. (1933). Review of *The Psycho-Analysis of Children*, by M. Klein. *Criterion, 12*(April): 44–46.

Stokes, A. (1934). *Stones of Rimini.* London: Faber. Reprinted in L. Gowing (Ed.), *The Critical Writings of Adrian Stokes, Volume I* (pp. 181–302). New York: Thames & Hudson, 1978.

Stokes, A. (1937). *Colour and Form.* London: Faber. Reprinted in L. Gowing (Ed.), *The Critical Writings of Adrian Stokes, Volume II* (pp. 7–84). New York: Thames & Hudson, 1978.

Stokes, A. (1945a). *Venice: an Aspect of Art.* London: Faber. Reprinted in L. Gowing (Ed.), *The Critical Writings of Adrian Stokes, Volume II* (pp. 85–138). New York: Thames & Hudson, 1978.

Stokes, A. (1947). *Inside Out.* London: Faber. Reprinted in L. Gowing (Ed.), *The Critical Writings of Adrian Stokes, Volume II* (pp. 139–182). New York: Thames & Hudson, 1978.

Stokes, A. (1951). *Smooth and Rough.* London: Faber. Reprinted in L. Gowing (Ed.), *The Critical Writings of Adrian Stokes, Volume II* (pp. 213–256). New York: Thames & Hudson, 1978.

Stokes, A. (1955b). Form in art: a psycho-analytic interpretation. In: P. Heimann, M. Klein, & R. Money-Kyrle (Eds.), *New Directions in*

Psycho-analysis. London: Tavistock [reprinted in A. Stokes, *A Game That Must Be Lost: Collected Papers* (109–115). Cheadle: Carcanet, 1973].

Stokes, A. (1958). *Greek Culture and the Ego*. London: Tavistock. Reprinted in L. Gowing (Ed.), *The Critical Writings of Adrian Stokes, Volume III* (pp. 77–142). New York: Thames & Hudson, 1978.

Stokes, A. (1961). *Three Essays on the Painting of Our Time*. London: Tavistock. Reprinted in L. Gowing (Ed.), *The Critical Writings of Adrian Stokes, Volume III* (pp. 143–184). New York: Thames & Hudson, 1978.

Stokes, A. (1963). *Painting and the Inner World*. London: Tavistock. Reprinted in L. Gowing (Ed.), *The Critical Writings of Adrian Stokes, Volume III* (pp. 207–260). New York: Thames & Hudson, 1978.

Stokes, A. (1964). Living in Ticino, 1947–50. *Art and Literature*, 1(March): 232–238.

Stokes, A. (1965). *The Invitation in Art*. London: Tavistock. Reprinted in L. Gowing (Ed.), *The Critical Writings of Adrian Stokes, Volume III* (pp. 261–300). New York: Thames & Hudson, 1978.

Stokes, A. (1966). The image in form. *British Journal of Aesthetics*, 4 (July). Reprinted and revised in A. Stokes, *Reflections on the Nude*. London: Tavistock, 1967. Reprinted in L. Gowing (Ed.), *The Critical Writings of Adrian Stokes, Volume III* (pp. 331–342). New York: Thames & Hudson, 1978.

Stokes, A. (1973). *A Game That Must Be Lost: Collected Papers*. Cheadle: Carcanet.

Stokes, A. (1978). *The Critical Writings of Adrian Stokes* (3 volumes). L. Gowing (Ed.). London: Thames and Hudson.

Stokes, A. (1981). *With All The Views: the Collected Poems of Adrian Stokes* (Edited by P. Robinson). Manchester: Carcanet.

Storr, A. (1972). *The Dynamics of Creation*. London: Pelican.

Sylvester, D. (1961). All at once: a review of Stokes's *Three Essays on the Painting of Our Time*. *Statesman* (11 August).

Symington, J., & Symington, N. (1996). *The Clinical Thinking of Wilfred Bion*. London: Routledge.

Trilling, L. (1955). Freud: within and beyond culture. In: L. Trilling, *Beyond Culture*. New York: Viking.

Turkle, S. (1986). *Psychoanalytic Politics*. New York, Basic Books.

Tustin, F. (1972). *Autism and Childhood Psychosis*. London: Hogarth.

Tustin, F. (1981). *Autistic States in Children*. London: Routledge & Kegan Paul.

Winnicott, D. W. W. (1953). Transitional objects and transitional phenomena. *International Journal of Psycho-Analysis, 34*: 89–97.
Winnicott, D. W. W. (1958). *Collected Papers: Through Paediatrics to Psychoanalysis*. New York: Basic Books.
Winnicott, D. W. W. (1966). The location of cultural experience. *International Journal of PsychoAnalysis, 48*: 368–372.
Winnicott, D. W. W. (1971). *Playing and Reality*. London: Routledge [reprinted London: Pelican, 1988].
Winnicott, D. W. W. (1987). *The Spontaneous Gesture: Selected Letters of D. W .W. Winnicott* (F. Rodman, Ed.). Cambridge, MA: Harvard University Press.
Winnicott, D. W. W. (1988). *Human Nature*. London: Free Association.
Wölfflin, (1915). *The Principles of Art History: The Problem of the Development of Style in Later Art*. M. D. Hottinger (Trans.). Reprinted New York, 1950.
Wollheim, R. (1959a). A critic of our time: a review of *Greek Culture and the Ego*, by Adrian Stokes. *Encounter, 12*(3): 41–44.
Wollheim, R. (1959b). *F. H. Bradley*. London: Penguin.
Wollheim, R. (1968). The mind and the mind's image of itself. In *On Art and the Mind*. Cambridge, MA: Harvard University Press, 1974.
Wollheim, R. (1973). Memories of Adrian Stokes. *The Listener, 90(2313)*: 821–815.
Wollheim, R. (1974). *On Art and the Mind: Essays and Lectures*. Cambridge, MA: Harvard University Press.
Wollheim, R. (1980). Adrian Stokes: critic, painter, poet. *PN Review, 15*: 31–37.
Wollheim, R. (1987). *Painting as an Art*. London: Thames and Hudson.
Wordsworth, W. (1958). *Selected Poems of William Wordsworth*. R. Sharrock (Ed.). London: Heinemann.
Wörringer, W. (1908). *Abstraction and Empathy: A Contribution to the Psychology of Style*. New York: International Universities Press, 1967.
Wright, E. (1984). *Psychoanalytic Criticism*. London: Methuen.

INDEX

Abraham, K., xvi, 30, 53, 120–121, 182, 233
Abrams, M. H., 6, 233
Adams, L. S., xv, 233
Adams, T., xxiv, 233
aggression/aggressive, xvi, 13, 17, 33, 40, 49–50, 52–54, 56–58, 60, 73–74, 77, 144, 150, 165, 167, 180, 219
Agostino, 87, 91, 94–95
Alford, C. F., 63, 233
alpha
　elements, 114, 117
　function, 114, 116, 133
Alvarez, A., 133, 233
ambivalence, 7, 33, 54, 132
Anderson, D. R., 37, 233
anxiety, xxi, 7, 32–34, 38–42, 45, 48, 51–52, 54, 56–58, 67–68, 72, 74, 82, 113–116, 120, 133, 148–149, 153, 155, 163, 165, 167, 191–192, 199, 214, 230

castration, 51, 167
depressive, 33, 53–55, 69–70, 73, 109, 153
paranoiac/persecutory, 33, 53–54, 56, 61
psychotic, 107–108
repressed, 4, 40
Arnheim, R., xviii, 233–234
Arts Council of Great Britain, 80, 84, 197, 234
Astor, J., xxv, 234

Bann, S., 80–81, 85, 98–99, 199, 211, 218, 234
Barthes, R., xxiv, 125, 234
basic assumption(s), 107–108, 229
Bell, C., 217, 234
Bellotto, B., 204–205
Benvenuto, B., xxiv, 234
Berenson, B., 176, 234
beta elements, 110, 114, 117, 133
Bion, F., 129–130, 234

INDEX

Bion, W. R., xi, xxi, xxv, xxvii–xxx, 20, 36–37, 57, 61, 63–64, 67, 70, 72, 76, 86, 95, 97–98, 103–135, 138, 141, 144, 146–147, 151–153, 156, 159, 170, 179, 188, 193, 195–196, 198, 200, 213, 215, 217, 219, 221–223, 227–232, 234–235
Bionic school *see* school, Bionic
Bishop, P., xxiv, 235
Blake, W., 134, 173, 201
Bleandonu, G., 103, 235
Bloom, H., 74, 80, 199, 235
Bollas, C., xxvi, 183–184, 222, 235
breast, 39, 44, 58–60, 116, 119, 122, 156, 167, 173, 190
  "bad", 57, 59, 63
  "good", 57–58, 63
  "thinking", 116
British
  psychoanalysis, xi, xiv, xxiii–xxv, xxx–xxxi, 14, 33, 152, 187–188, 196–198, 212, 215, 224, 227, 229–232
  school *see* school, British
British Psychoanalytic Institute, 120
British Psychoanalytical Society, xxv, 30, 81, 106, 226
Bruegel, P., 87
Brunelleschi, F., 88
Bryson, N., 199, 218, 235
Budd, M., 217
Butler, R., 134–135

Canaletto, 204
Carrier, D., 79, 98–99, 235
carving, 78, 80, 86–87, 90–97, 197, 202, 204, 206–207 *see also*: modelling
Cezanne, P., 87, 94, 217
Chadwick, L., 134
Chardin, J.-B. S., 87, 94, 201
Clark, K. (Sir), 84
Clark, T., 218
Coldstream, W., 164
Coleridge, S. T., xxviii, 78, 134, 235

complex(es), 4, 6
  Oedipus, 8, 30–32, 48, 59, 74, 80, 106–107, 110, 144, 154, 188–189, 199
conscious(ness), xvi, xix, 15–16, 18–21, 44–47, 62, 81, 83, 85, 108, 113, 117, 138–140, 142–143, 145–149, 153, 155, 157, 161, 163, 169–170, 172, 176, 202, 217, 224, 226–227 *see also*: ego, unconscious
containment, xxx, 97, 110–113, 115–119, 124, 172, 193, 207–209, 219
"Controversial Discussions", xxv–xxvi, 32, 35, 45, 226,
countertransference, 5, 11, 134, 179 *see also*: transference

de Kooning, W., 198, 209
de la Tour, G., 94
de Sausmarez, M., 150, 235
depression, xi, 33, 50, 52–56, 63, 69–71, 73, 75, 77–78, 81, 96, 109, 111, 114, 116, 123, 147, 153–154, 156–158, 168, 174–176, 194–197, 215, 220–221, 223 *see also*: anxiety, melancholy
  manic, 30, 34
  position, xi, 29–30, 33–34, 41–43, 46, 52–56, 58, 60, 63, 65–68, 70, 73–74, 76–78, 94, 96, 98, 107, 111–112, 115, 121, 123, 151, 153, 158, 174
Descartes, R., 113
Dewey, J., xvi, 235
Donatello, 90–91
Dostoevsky, F. M., xx, 8
dream(s), 8–9, 17–19, 25, 36–37, 41–42, 47, 62–63, 70–71, 75, 117, 122, 126, 139, 141
  day, xviii, 8–10, 31, 44, 68, 97, 146 *see also* mother, reverie
  interpretation, 25
  work, 14–15, 17, 36
Duncan, A., xxiv, 233

INDEX 249

Eagleton, T., 189
Eckhart, M., 104, 230
ego, xvii, xix–xx, xxiii–xxiv, xxviii, 8, 10, 13–17, 20–24, 36–40, 42–43, 46–48, 54–57, 59–60, 63, 66, 68–69, 109–110, 121, 133, 138–142, 144, 146–148, 153–157, 161–162, 164, 166, 169, 171, 173, 176, 179, 183–184, 192–193, 203, 209, 216, 221–222, 224, 226 *see also*: id, instinct
conscious, xi, 13, 138, 146, 148, 157, 161, 179
infantile, 56–57
super, 15, 21–22, 30, 48, 60, 109, 121, 144, 148, 155
Ehrenzweig, A., x, xiv, xvii–xx, xxvii, xxix, 12, 16–25, 41, 47, 69–71, 76, 78, 89, 112, 116, 137–158, 161–162, 169–170, 175–176, 179, 191–193, 202, 217, 219, 222–224, 226–227, 232, 235–236,
Eigen, M., 147, 236
Eliot, G., 130, 236
Eliot, T. S., 65, 129, 131, 236
Elstir, 70
empty space", xxi, 50–52
envy, 34, 58–61, 63–64, 110, 124, 126, 131, 199, 225
innate, 30, 58, 64, 174, 220
Eros *see* instinct, life

Faber, G. (Sir), 84
Fairbairn, R., xxvi, 56, 66, 236
Falck, C., 228–229, 236
fantasy, xiv, 31, 43, 83, 140, 218
Fichte, J. G., 215
Fordham, M., xxv, 236
Forge, A., 98
Frazer, 138, 154, 175
free association, xxiii, 31–32, 36, 41, 130
Freud, A., xxiii, xxv, 32, 35–36, 47
Freud, S., x–xi, xiv–xvii, xix–xx, xxiii, xxv–xxvii, xxix, 3–34, 36–37, 42–45, 47–49, 53, 55–56, 62, 65–68, 71–72, 75–77, 80–82, 85, 103, 107, 110, 113, 120–121, 132, 138–139, 141, 143–145, 147, 153–154, 164, 168, 171, 173, 180, 182, 188, 198–199, 213, 216, 219–220, 222, 224–225, 231–232, 236–237
Freudian school *see* school, Freudian
Friedman, L., xv, 237
Fuller, P., xxi, xxx, 6, 77, 85, 105, 116, 118, 120, 156, 185, 187–197, 209, 212–215, 219, 224, 237

Gedo, M., 237
Gervais, D., 237–238
Gestalt, xvii–xix, 20, 24, 137, 140, 142–143, 146–148, 150, 217
Giorgione, 81, 87, 94, 208
Glover, N., ix–xii, 118, 238
Golding, W., 223
Gombrich, E., xiv, xvi, xviii, xx, 12, 14–16, 79, 206, 238
Goodman, N., 79
Gosso, S., 231, 238
Gowing, L., 83, 84, 98, 238
gratitude, 34, 55, 61, 63–64, 128, 199
Graves, R., 138, 155
Green, A., 216, 238
grief, 34, 55, 217
Grosskurth, P., 55, 64, 174, 238
Grotstein, J., 104, 113, 222, 238
group mentality, 108
guilt, 54, 60, 73, 137, 143–144, 155, 180

Habermas, J., 215
Hamlet, 124
Hampshire, S., 86, 198
Harris Williams, M., xi, xiv, xxi, xxix, 78, 86, 98, 103–105, 120, 122–126, 133–134, 184, 217, 223, 228–231, 238, 241
Harris, M., 86, 104

Hartmann, H., xxiii, 139–140, 226, 238
Haskell, F., 218
Hazlitt, W., 83, 85, 238
Heidegger, M., 216
Heimann, P., 66–67, 238
Hepworth, B., 87
Hindle, D., 49, 238
Hinshelwood, R., xxviii, 32, 40, 53, 92, 111, 118, 238
Hobbes, T., 77
Hughes, J., xiii, xxvi, 64, 238
Hulks, D., 99, 134–135, 238
Hume, D., 106, 223
Husserl, E., 216
Huxley, A., 119

id, xvii, xix, 138, 140, 142, 148, 154–156, 162, 168, 226 *see also*: ego
idealization, 4, 54, 56, 58, 69, 74, 76, 78, 85–86, 126, 156, 199, 215–216, 223
Imago Group/Society, 86, 152, 198
  New, 86
infantile experience, 29, 32, 83, 190, 209, 211, 222, 224
infantile sexuality *see* sexuality, infantile
Ingres, J. A. D., 199, 206
inner world, xxvi, 3, 11–12, 15, 29–31, 36, 39, 43–44, 47–50, 53, 55, 62–63, 71, 73, 77, 90, 115, 118–119, 122, 124, 141, 181, 220
instinct
  death, 20–23, 33–34, 56–58, 66, 75–76, 109, 144, 153, 169, 174, 222
  ego-, 22
  life, 20–22, 66, 75, 222
  sexual, 22
  survival, 22
introjection, 44, 46, 48, 57–59, 68, 114, 116–117, 121, 134, 153, 173, 175, 222

Isaacs, S., 31, 35, 45, 47, 140, 202, 226, 229, 231, 238

Jacobus, M., 103, 132, 231–232, 239
Jaques, E., 157, 239
jealousy, 58–59
joke mechanism/theory, xvii, xix–xx, xxvii, 3, 12–19, 24–25, 138–139, 141, 219
Jones, E., 8, 24, 30, 34–35, 38, 41–42, 67, 81, 182, 239
Jones, T., 204–205
Joyce, J., 225
Jung, C., xxiv–xxv, 76, 138, 232, 239

Kant, I., 104–106, 111, 113, 119, 215, 217, 222–223, 228
Keats, J., xxviii, 70, 72, 104, 112, 117, 128, 134, 156, 170, 230, 239
Kennedy, R., xxiv, 234
Kent, A., 93
King, P., xxvi, 32, 45, 226, 239
Kjär, R., 50–52, 75, 196
Klein, M., x–xi, xiv, xxi, xxv, xxvii, xxix–xxx, 9, 20, 22–25, 29–42, 44–45, 47–69, 73, 75, 77, 79, 81–82, 86, 91–92, 96–97, 103–104, 106–109, 111–112, 115–116, 118–121, 123, 132, 135, 138, 144, 152–153, 155, 165–168, 171, 173–175, 180–181, 188, 196–197, 199–200, 213–215, 219–220, 222–223, 231, 239–240
Kleinian school *see* school, Kleinian
Kofman, S., xv, 240
Kohon, G., xiii, xxvi, 240
Kris, E., xiv, xvii–xxi, xxiii–xxiv, xxvii, xxix, 12–16, 19–25, 138–140, 142, 219, 226, 240
Kristeva, J., xxiv, 218, 232, 240
Kuhns, R., 184, 240

Lacan, J., xxii, xxiv–xxv, 212, 216, 232, 240
Langer, S., xvi, 17, 37, 230, 240
Laplanche, J., 232

Laurano, L., 87–88
Leonardo da Vinci, 4, 7–8, 67–68, 75, 81, 199, 207, 220–221
Lewin, B. D., 156, 240
Likierman, M., 224, 240
Little, M., 35, 164, 240
Lyotard, J.-F., 144, 240

Malatesta, S., 80
Marx, K., 188
Marxism, 77, 188, 215
Medley, R., 164
melancholy, 50, 75, 174, see also: depression
Mellis, M., 79, 84
Meltzer, D., x–xi, xiv, xxi, xxvii–xxix, 56, 61, 64, 71, 78, 86, 98, 103–105, 111, 120–122, 124–126, 130, 132–133, 184, 198, 215, 220, 222–223, 228–231, 241
Merleau-Ponty, M., 216
Michelangelo, 5, 79, 82, 88, 97, 220
Miller, L., 86
Milner, M., x–xi, xxi, xxvi–xxx, 14, 16, 20, 23, 36, 69, 78, 105, 119, 133, 137, 138, 141, 144, 146–147, 152–179, 182–183, 185, 191–192, 194–195, 198, 203, 209, 213, 217, 219, 222–224, 231–232, 241
Milton, J., xxviii, 104, 119, 130
Mitchell, W., 225, 241
modelling, 78, 86–87, 90–97, 197 see also: carving
Monet, C., 97
Money-Kyrle, R., 61, 64, 86, 198, 241
Moore, H., 134
Moses, xx, 5–6
mother see also: breast
    bad, 53–54
    body, 32–33, 37–38, 40, 53, 62, 66, 115, 119, 132, 203, 205, 208
    good, 53, 178
    -enough, 122, 181
    –infant relationship, 115, 131, 179, 188–189, 192, 231

reverie, xxv, 114–116, 133, 153, 173, 179 see also dream, day
mourning, 34, 42, 50, 55, 176, 181, 220, 222

narcissism, xxviii, 8, 133, 195, 216–217
Natkin, R., 105, 156, 187–195, 209, 212–213, 224
neurosis, xvii, xxx, 3–4, 21, 31, 77, 110, 159, 182
Nietzsche, F., 159, 185, 241
Northfield Military Hospital, 106

O'Shaughnessy, E., 110, 242
object, x, xiv, xviii–xix, xxiii, xxix, 8, 13, 22–23, 31, 33, 37–38, 40–49, 52–55, 58–61, 63, 68–70, 72–74, 76, 81–82, 90–91, 95–97, 107, 110–111, 115–119, 121–124, 141, 145, 160–161, 165–167, 170–174, 178, 180–184, 203, 206, 209, 211, 217–218, 220, 223, 230
    art, xi, xiv–xv, xxiii, 3, 20, 25, 61, 87, 125, 180, 219
    "bad", 46, 53–54, 56–58, 68, 73, 178
    external, xix, 31, 46, 48, 55, 57, 65, 139, 153, 171, 176–177
    "good", 46, 53–54, 56–60, 64, 73–74, 126, 133, 178
    internal, 31, 34, 46–47, 49, 54–55, 59, 62, 72, 115–116, 122, 133, 153
    part, 33, 56–57, 68, 73, 94, 96–97, 158, 171, 178
    primary, 32, 37, 66, 73, 77
    relations, xv, xxvi, 22, 31, 56–57, 73, 85, 87, 96–97, 107, 111, 158, 171, 174, 182–183, 216
    sexual, 13
    whole, 33, 68, 73–74, 78, 96, 98
objectivity, xxix, 4, 16, 18, 72, 74, 107, 135, 141, 144, 160, 173, 179, 182, 210–211, 213–214, 218
Olitski, J., 212–213

omnipotence, 4, 54, 58, 69, 71, 74, 78, 85, 88, 92, 97, 108, 110, 118, 121, 133, 154, 158, 171, 181, 223, 227
Othello, 59, 122
Oulten, J., 86

Paolozzi, E., 134
paranoid–schizoid, 30, 34, 39, 41, 52–58, 63, 67–68, 70, 73–74, 76, 78, 94, 96, 98, 107, 109, 111–112, 115, 121, 123, 132, 147, 151, 153–154, 166, 171, 174, 178, 197, 215
Pater, W., 48, 75, 78–80, 83, 85–86, 89, 144, 208, 214, 230, 242
pathography, xxvii, 3–4, 6, 11–12, 67, 220
Paton, H. J., 106
Payne, S., 31, 35, 164
Penny, N., 210–211, 242
phantasy, 8–10, 17, 21–22, 25, 31, 33, 35–47, 49, 51, 53–54, 56–57, 62–63, 68, 71–74, 78, 90, 92, 97, 108, 117, 119, 121, 126, 129, 139–142, 144, 155–156, 158, 161, 165–167, 171–172, 178, 181, 187, 199, 201–205, 208, 212, 223, 231
  destructive, 20, 33, 59, 73, 119
  inner, 48, 177
  primitive, 23, 45, 56, 144
  sadistic, 16, 33, 68, 119, 144, 174
  unconscious, xiv, xix, xxvii–xxviii, 10–11, 16, 20, 23–25, 31, 37, 43–48, 50, 53, 57, 62, 66–67, 78, 92, 108, 119, 127, 140–141, 152–153, 157, 165, 180, 197, 199, 201–202, 212, 220–222, 226–227, 229
Philipson, M., xxiv, 242
Phillips, A., xxv–xxvi, 216, 242
Picasso, P., 74, 94, 199, 206, 225
Piero della Francesca, 87, 93–94
Plato/Platonic beliefs, xxviii, 6, 63, 104, 106, 113, 119, 123, 127, 220–221, 223

Plaut, F., xxv, 242
Podro, M., xxi, 164, 217, 229, 242
Poincaré, J. H., 70, 106, 112, 116
Pollock, J., 149, 210
potential space, xiv, xxix, 118–119, 159–160, 170–171, 180–181, 188, 190–191, 193, 195, 197, 217–218, 224
process(es)
  primary, xvii, xxiii, xxx, 14–23, 25, 43, 47, 62, 138–142, 148, 162, 203, 224–227, 229
  secondary, xvii, xxiii, xxx, 3, 14, 16–17, 20, 47, 62, 138, 140, 149, 151, 157, 203, 224, 226, 229
projection, 6, 33, 39, 42, 44, 46, 48, 54, 57, 69, 74, 76, 83, 97, 106–107, 109–110, 114–115, 117, 121, 123, 141, 167, 173, 175, 192, 199, 207, 222
Proust, M., 69, 84

Quattro Cento, 79, 83, 87–91, 93, 204

Rank, O., xi, 8, 67, 146, 182–183, 242
Raphael, 207
Rayner, E., xiii, xxv–xxvi, 36, 242
Read, H., xv, 229, 242
Read, R., 80–81, 99, 242
regression, xvi, xix, 16, 19–20, 22–23, 42, 55, 69, 73, 76, 108, 139–142, 147–148, 171, 178, 209, 211, 223–224, 226–227
Rembrandt, 97
reparation, 34, 52–54, 60, 66, 72–73, 77–78, 89, 92, 98, 121, 154, 180, 190, 196–197, 199, 222–223
repression, xxiii, 4, 6, 10, 15, 17, 40, 42, 77, 117, 155, 181, 219, 222, 225
Rhode, E., 79, 82–84, 86, 98, 198, 242
Rhode, M., 86
Rickman, J., xxvi, 35, 66, 74, 106, 152, 242

Riley, B., 150–151, 227
Riviere, J., 231
Robson-Scott, W. D., 81
Rodin, A., 92
Rolland, R., 147
Romanticism, 6, 16, 176
Rosenfeld, H., xxviii, 109
Rothko, M., 106, 116, 120, 156, 187–188, 195–196, 209
Rudnytsky, P., 182, 242
Ruskin, J., 78, 80, 83, 85–86, 214–215, 242
Rustin, Margaret, 86
Rustin, Michael, 86
Rycroft, C., xxii, xxvi, 14, 16, 31, 36, 105, 141, 153, 156, 162, 190, 203, 222, 224–226, 242–243

Sachs, H., 8, 67, 75, 243
sadism, 38–39, 51–53, 57, 68, 71, 111, 119, 121, 165 *see also*: phantasy
  anal, 58, 152
  oral, 57–58, 152
  unconscious, xi, 70
Sandler, P. C., 103, 243
Sartre, J.-P., 216
Sarup, M., xxii, 243
Saussurean thought, 228
Sayers, J., xv, 232, 243
Scalia, J., 183, 243
schizophrenia, xxviii, 18, 30, 34, 39, 41, 54, 56, 58, 67, 103, 108–110, 116, 134–135, 141, 146, 153, 156–157, 160, 166 *see also* paranoid–schizoid
school
  Bionic, x–xi, xxix–xxx, 222–223, 227–228
  British, xiii, xv, xxi–xxvii, xxx, 9, 12, 14, 16–17, 20, 22–23, 30, 36, 64, 66, 95, 97, 105, 115, 133, 138, 152, 159, 162, 171, 180, 203, 213–216, 224, 227–231
  Freudian, x–xi, xvi, xx, xxvii, 8, 14, 16, 18, 21, 30, 32, 63, 66, 74, 80, 106, 133, 138–139, 171–172, 182, 198–199, 219–221, 227
  Kleinian, x–xi, xvi, xix, xxii, xxv–xxx, 16, 20, 22, 24–25, 29–30, 32–33, 35–37, 42, 46–48, 52–53, 58, 63–70, 72, 74–78, 82–84, 86–87, 92, 94–95, 98, 105–106, 108, 111, 115, 118–121, 133–134, 138, 140–141, 144, 150, 153–154, 156, 158–159, 165, 170–175, 178, 180–181, 184, 188, 195, 197–201, 204–205, 208, 211, 213–215, 219–224, 226–227, 231–232
  Winnicottian, x, xxx, 180, 190, 192–193, 216, 227–228
Segal, H., x, xxvii–xxviii, 29–30, 36, 41–43, 52, 54, 56–57, 62, 64–78, 98, 109, 111–112, 121, 132, 138, 152, 154, 157–158, 166, 197–200, 220–221, 223–224, 231, 243
sexual, 13, 71, 77, 121 *see also*: instinct, sexual
  development, xvi, 8, 143
  experience, 43
  fantasy, 43
  psycho-, xvi, 8, 33, 66
sexuality, 121
  infantile, xi, 8
Shakespeare, W., xxviii, 59, 104, 243
Sharpe, E., 66–67, 74, 231, 243
Shuttleworth, A., 86
Shuttleworth, J., 86
Silver, A., 37, 244
Smith, P., 80, 244
Sohn, L., 197
Sophocles, 104
Spector, J. J., xv, xxvii, 11, 244
Spitz, E. H., xiv, 8, 182, 244
splitting, 8, 54, 56, 58, 69, 74, 76, 85, 96, 110, 112, 114, 117, 135, 141, 153, 169, 175, 178, 215
Steiner, R., xxvi, 32, 45, 226, 239
Stokes, A., x, xx, xxvii, xxix–xxx, 11, 29, 43, 62, 64–66, 71, 75–76,

78–99, 112, 116, 125, 153, 158–159, 164, 168, 176, 187–188, 197–200, 202–207, 209, 211, 214, 219–221, 230–232, 244–245
Storr, A., 7, 225, 245
subjectivity, 5, 16, 90, 141, 160, 171, 173, 179, 182–183, 211, 213, 218
inter-, xx, 21, 24, 64, 231
superego *see* ego, super
Sylvester, D., 83, 150, 245
symbol(-ism), xv, xvii, xix, xxi, xxviii, 16–17, 21, 25, 30, 36–43, 46–47, 50, 53, 62, 66–68, 81, 83–84, 96, 110, 114, 119, 124–126, 140, 153–154, 156, 162–163, 166–169, 172–176, 178, 183, 196–197, 200–201, 216–217, 220, 228–229
equation, 38, 41, 154
formation, xxvii, 36–41, 62, 67, 69, 97, 122, 133, 154, 158, 167, 173, 175, 180
Symington, J., 103, 245
Symington, N., 103, 245

Tavistock
Clinic, 107
Press, 84, 96
Thanatos *see* instinct, death
Titian, 206–209
transference, 32, 134, 179, 197, 225
see also: countertransference
Trilling, L., 24, 245
Trotter, W., 106
Truth, 127–128, 131, 223
Turkle, S., xxv, 245
Turner, J. W. M., 97
Tustin, F., 124, 245

unconscious, xi, xiv, xvi, xix, xxiii, xxix, 8–11, 14–15, 18–21, 23–24, 32–33, 40–47, 59, 62, 72, 76, 81, 90, 98, 108, 128, 132, 137, 139–143, 145–149, 153–154, 156, 162, 171, 179, 202, 223–227, 229
see also: conscious(ness), phantasy, sadism
University College Hospital, 106

Vasari, G., 94, 202
Vermeer, J., 94, 217
Verrocchio, A., 88

Waddell, M., xxi, xxix, 105, 231
Winnicott, D. W., x, xiv, xxi, xxv–xxx, 9, 14, 16, 20, 31, 35, 69, 77, 92, 105, 115–119, 122, 131–132, 138, 141, 147, 152–153, 158–161, 170–175, 177–185, 188, 190–194, 197, 213, 215–216, 218–219, 221–223, 228, 231–232, 246
Winnicottian school *see* school, Winnicottian
Wisdom, J. O., 86, 119, 198
Wölfflin, H., 87, 246
Wollheim, R., x, xiv, xix–xxii, xxx, 6, 12, 61–62, 79–80, 82, 86, 90, 94–95, 98, 177, 187–188, 196–215, 218–221, 229–230, 246
Woolf, V., 164
Wordsworth, W., 176, 184, 230, 246
World War
First, 105
Second, 84, 106, 134, 213
Wörringer, W., 217, 246
Wright, E., xv, 11, 85, 190, 246
Wright, K., 190
www.artcyclopedia.com, 91, 94